Growing Up in Hitler's Shadow

Growing Up in Hitler's Shadow

Remembering Youth in Postwar Berlin

Kimberly A. Redding

Westport, Connecticut
London

Library of Congress Cataloging-in-Publication Data

Redding, Kimberly Ann.
   Growing up in Hitler's shadow : remembering youth in postwar Berlin / Kimberly A. Redding.
     p. cm.
   Includes bibliographical references and index.
   ISBN 0–275–97961–X (alk. paper)
    1. Youth—Germany—Berlin—Attitudes—Case studies. 2. Youth—Germany—Berlin—Social conditions—Case studies. 3. Socialization—Germany—Berlin—Case studies. I. Title.
HQ799.G32B467 2004
305.235′0943′155—dc22   2003068728

British Library Cataloguing in Publication Data is available.

Library of Congress Catalog Card Number: 2003068728
ISBN: 0–275–97961–X

First published in 2004

Praeger Publishers, 88 Post Road West, Westport, CT 06881
An imprint of Greenwood Publishing Group, Inc.
www.praeger.com

Printed in the United States of America

∞™

The paper used in this book complies with the
Permanent Paper Standard issued by the National
Information Standards Organization (Z39.48–1984).

10 9 8 7 6 5 4 3 2 1

Copyright Acknowledgments

The author and publisher gratefully acknowledge permission to quote from the following interviews (Note: per the author's agreement with interviewees, all but two have been rendered anonymous through the use of pseudonyms. The author also quoted from the preinterview surveys, which are in her possession.):

Barthe, 24 April 1998
Binkert, 11 and 19 December 1997
Bistop, 23 March 1998
Birkmann, 4 and 8 December 1997
Burkhardt, 21 January 1998
Dinkel, 2 and 6 February 1998
Distel, 12 March, 5 and 12 May 1998
Gottwald, 19 March 1998
Heinemann, 10 February 1998
Hirsch, 30 December 1997
Kanter, 2 April 1998
Kestler, 3 April 1998
King, 17 December 1997
Klinkert, 24 January 1998
Kösel, 6 March 1998
Middler, 13 January 1998
Miller, 24 March 1998
Mostel, 16 March 1998
Pastler, 5 March 1998
Pestopf, 15 May 1998
Pelsdorf, 9 March 1998
Quade, 19 February 1998
Rennebach, 27 February and 30 April 1998
Rippe, 7 May 1998
Schäfer, 26 March 1998
Schneider, 2 March 1998
Stumpf, 19 January 1998
Tinker, 25 March 1998
Völker (as a couple), 23 January 1998
Winkert, 17 February 1998
Zelle, 10 March 1998

Every reasonable effort has been made to trace the owners of copyright materials in this book, but in some instances this has proven impossible. The author and publisher will be glad to receive information leading to more complete acknowledgments in subsequent printings of the book, and in the meantime extend their apologies for any omissions.

Contents

Preface

This study has its roots in a year-long teaching assistantship at the Heinrich-Hertz Schule in Berlin-Friedrichshain.   As one of the first American assistants sent to the former German Democratic Republic (GDR) by the German Academic Exchange Service (DAAD), I was expected to invigorate English language instruction   at the *Gymnasium*, which was located just off the Frankfurter Allee. I lived only a few blocks away, subletting an unfurnished room from a young couple with a five-year-old daughter and a parakeet. The building was undeniably *Altbau*, dating from before World War II; my room had high ceilings, French doors leading to a dusty balcony, and a brown coal stove which the landlord informed me "was no trouble, just give it lots of air or we'll all die from the carbon monoxide."

My colleagues in the Hertz Schule teachers' lounge, of course, were well acquainted with the subtleties of brown coal heating. Yet some seemed to be slowly suffocating in the wake of German unification. They had grown up and found careers in the GDR, playing by the established rules; they knew where, within the confines of that authoritarian society, to find breathing space. After 1990, however, they faced new parameters, personified at the Hertz school by a new district superintendent (brought in from the West) and a young teaching assistant who, despite an obvious lack of pedagogical training, was instantly popular among students—she was, after all, a native speaker, an American.

On one level, students at the school confronted the same challenges. Like their teachers, they had developed expectations and goals—some of them quite explicit —which were anchored in basic assumptions about East German society and the future. They too were surprised by my pedagogical assumptions and methods. More significantly, they watched familiar authority figures—parents and teachers, for example—struggle with the consequences of unification. Yet the students had a fundamentally different perspective; they were young, twelve to nineteen years old.

Watching these young people adjust to abrupt sociopolitical change, I began to ponder other historical turning points, and was immediately drawn to 1945, when young Germans' expectations were similarly torn asunder.   At that time, members of the so-called Hitler Youth generation faced new opportunities and a very uncertain future, equipped with little but whatever lessons they could glean from wartime experiences. What had happened to these young people? How did they cope when the social parameters that had shaped (for better or worse) their daily lives not only ceased to exist, but were demonized by virtually the entire western world?   In what ways did Germany's defeat and sociopolitical transformation inform their passage from childhood to adulthood?

Over time, these broad questions about Berlin's postwar youth evolved into a study of the significance of youth experience in the early postwar era. I am grateful for the DAAD and Fulbright grants that took me to Berlin-Friedrichshain in 1991 and for later financial support from several institutions and organizations: the federal Foreign Languages and Area Studies program (FLAS), the DAAD, and the Social Science Research Council (SSRC). Additional fellowships and grants were provided by the University of North Carolina's History Department and Writing Center.

My analysis of youth experience relies on local archival research, as well as interviews conducted in Berlin during the1997–1998 academic year. Working with oral sources is simultaneously a rewarding and daunting task, and I was grateful to discover recorded and partially transcribed interviews in the archives of the *Heimatmuseum Charlottenburg* and *Geschichtswerkstatt Kreuzberg*. I reinterviewed some of these individuals, and used them (as well as the growing database of Berlin's *Zeitzeugenbörse* and advertisements in district newspapers) to locate other cohort members willing to share memories of youth with me. A total of nearly fifty contacts were sent introductory letters and short, preliminary surveys—the latter sometimes provided valuable insights into interviewees' past lives, and surveys used as direct sources are identified in footnotes.

About thirty-five Berliners participated in recorded conversations that lasted, on average, about three hours. Each interview began with a broad request to talk about experiences during and after the Nazi period, in response to which most cohort members spoke at length, interrupted only to clarify specific terms, names, and the like.   I then asked for their insights on a series of specific topics, including interpersonal relationships, school, work, church, family celebrations, political events, and leisure. Each individual was also asked to comment on the label "lost youth."   In numerous instances, interviewees offered additional insights when the recorder was off; most allowed me to quote notes from those conversations and unrecorded testimony is identified as such in notes. None of the Berliners with whom I spoke received monetary compensation. A few requested—and received—copies of the tapes and/or subsequent dissertation and some asked to have their anonymity preserved (consequently, all but two names have been changed).   Interviews were transcribed by native speakers, most notably Heidrun Brzenska; translations, however, are my own. Interviewees transferred all copyright and usage rights to me (through permission forms); tapes and transcripts are currently in my possession, pending other arrangements.

I found additional valuable sources, not to mention very patient staff members, in archival collections and museums throughout Berlin. Frau Miltenberger at the *Heimatmuseum Charlottenburg* (HMCB) and Frau Treziek at the *Kreuzberg Museum* were especially gracious, allowing me unfettered access to entire collections. I am also particularly thankful for the assistance of archivists at the *Bezirksarchiv Neukölln, Landesarchiv Berlin*, and the *Stiftung Archiv der Parteien und Massenorganisationen in der DDR im Bundesarchiv* (SAPMO). Mentors, support staff, and fellows at the Free University's Berlin Program for Advanced Studies shared research experience and insights, while the *Internationales Begegnungszentrum der Wissenschaft* in Wilmersdorf provided a home away from home.

On this side of the Atlantic, I have relied on mentors in Chapel Hill, including Dr. Konrad Jarausch, Dr. Gerhard Weinberg, and Dr. Kimberly Abels, and many others. Dr. Cora Granata, Dr. Elizabeth Peifer, and Katherine Ebel commented on specific chapters and topics, as did colleagues at Siena College's World War II Conference (June 2002) and the 2000 and 2002 meetings of the Oral History Association. Parts of this research were presented in each of those forums, as well as in the Fall 2002 issue of *Proteus—a Journal of Ideas*; many thanks to the peer reviewers who read those essays.

Final revisions would have been far more arduous without support from Carroll College, where particular thanks are due to student assistants Antje Eichler, Carolyn Hansen, Christine DeLashmutt, Erin Davis, Kimberly Fedder, Emily Koss, and Kirsten Matthis. All remaining mistakes are, of course, entirely my own responsibility.

Morgan, Thomas, and William endured my physical and mental absences with good humor and patience; I am especially grateful for the many ways they exemplify the energy and creativity of youth. Above all, thanks to my confidante and soulmate: Win.

Abbreviations

BBC	British Broadcasting Corporation
BDM	Bund deutscher Mädel (League of German Maidens)
CDU	Christian Democratic Union
DAAD	German Academic Exchange Service
DEFA	Deutsche Film-Aktien Gesellschaft (Berlin-based East German film company)
DM	Deutschmark (West German currency)
EKD	Evangelical Church in Deutschland (organization of Protestant churches)
FDGB	Freie Deutsche Gewerkschaftsbund
FDJ	Freie Deutsche Jugend (Free German Youth)
FDP	Free Democratic Party
FRG	Federal Republic of Germany
GDR	German Democratic Republic
GI	U.S. enlisted soldier
GYA	German Youth Activities
HJ	Hitler Jugend (Hitler Youth)
HJA	Hauptjugendamt
HMCH	Heimatmuseum Charlottenburg
KLV	Kinderlandverschickung
KMA	Kreuzberg Museum Archiv
KPD	Communist Party of Germany
LAB	Landesarchiv Berlin
LDP	Liberal Democratic Party
LJR	Landesjugendring

NAW	Nationales Aufbauwerk (National Reconstruction Project)
NSDAP	National Socialist German Workers Party
OMGUS	Office of the Military Government - United States
RAD	Reichsarbeitsdienst
RAF	Royal Air Force (British)
RIAS	Radio in the American Sector
RJF	Reichsjugendführung
RM	Reichsmark
SAPMO	Stiftung Archiv der Parteien und Massenorganisationen in der DDR im Bundesarchiv
SBZ	Soviet Occupation Zone
SCC	Sport Club of Charlottenburg
SED	Socialist Unity Party
SMAD	Soviet Military Administration in Germany
SPD	Social Democratic Party
SS	Nazi Schutzstaffel
US	United States
USSR	Union of Soviet Socialist Republics
WFS	World Festival Games

1

Being Young in Hitler's Germany

And we made music every evening. . . . I played in the quartet, second violin and in the orchestra. . . . I was [on the go] every evening, when there wasn't too much homework, that was all crammed on the weekend. . . . We talked about everything, and between classes with teachers or after school, it was one big community. . . . Truly, it was marked by hunger and want, but in my heart a very rich period; I wouldn't have missed it. And the friendships from those days, they've lasted a lifetime.[1]

We got together and did things, movies and the like. . . . And we wanted to dance, because in those days people were dancing on every street corner . . . in every larger pub . . . two or three guys made music, and there was dancing. . . . And we wanted to, but couldn't, so we went to dance school. . . . And it was everything to me, dancing was everything. And my apprenticeship, well, [it suffered] a bit. Thank God I had studied enough earlier and had it all [in my head] . . . . I was at this dance school almost every day. . . . My parents totally regretted that they'd let me go. . . . [But] it was fun and I did the decorations for the dances, or the advertisements and such. . . . Those were my best years; I've never regretted it.[2]

Such upbeat memories of youth in postwar Berlin may seem out of place. Between Anglo-American bombing raids and the Soviet ground assault, much of the city had been reduced to rubble. Calling themselves liberators, Soviet forces had terrorized many neighborhoods in the first weeks of occupation, and over the next few years, disagreements among the four occupation powers put Berliners in the middle of superpower rivalries.   Germany had been ostracized among nations, and the German people blamed for the deaths of more than six million Holocaust victims. Local officials, social workers, and scholars knew young Germans had been fully integrated into the war effort, serving as flak assistants, fire fighters, nurses' aides and even local militia fighters (*Volkssturm*).   Authorities also knew, from their own Nazi-era experiences, that the National Socialist German Workers' Party (NSDAP) emphasized the indoctrination of youth. Consequently, their postwar youth rehabilitation efforts were rooted in perceptions of young Berliners as apathetic, skeptical, exploited, and even maimed by Nazism. Looking back, however, the Berliners who were those postwar youth described themselves as busy, cheerful, and self-motivated, driven to achieve for themselves what society would or could not provide during the interregnum period.

This project uses interregnum-era Berlin as a window through which to reconsider these contradictory images of German youth after World War II. Drawing on both archival sources and oral testimony, it explores the expectations, daily lives, and personal initiatives of thirty-five Berliners as they matured through total war, capitulation, foreign occupation, and the establishment of two German successor states. The interviewees were born between 1926 and 1933, and except for periods of national service or evacuation, experienced World War II in the *Hauptstadt*, endured the city's postwar Hunger Years, and have spent their adult lives in the shadow of the Berlin Wall.   As young people, most lived in one of four districts of Berlin —Friedrichshain and Lichtenberg in the east, and Charlottenburg and Kreuzberg in the west.[3] The two eastern districts together comprise about one-seventh of Greater Berlin's land area, and in August 1945 had a combined youth population of roughly 17,350. Although smaller geographically, the two western districts had a similar youth population of around 17,500.[4] Friedrichshain and Kreuzberg were traditionally working class and were among the most devastated in the entire city by the end of World War II. They also shared a sector boundary after the war, a fact that informed interviewees' descriptions of the practical ramifications of conflict and compromise among occupation authorities. Lichtenberg and Charlottenburg also had working-class neighborhoods, as well as industrial sites, but these districts' residents were typically better off, living in more spacious flats or single-family homes.   Although also targeted by Allied air raids, Lichtenberg and Charlottenburg suffered less destruction than either of the two inner-city districts.[5]

While district boundaries became important under Allied occupation, eventually dividing this cohort of Berliners into *Ossis* (easterners) and *Wessis* (westerners), interviewees shared a common past shaped by the city's historical development and identity. Compared with other European capitals, Berlin has undergone numerous transformations in a relatively short period of time. The seat of nineteenth-century Prussian militarism, Berlin emerged as a major cultural center after World War I, with a music and theater scene that seemed to overshadow national and international financial crises. During the Weimar era,

Berlin's voters repeatedly rejected National Socialism; the Nazi party never won a legitimate election in Berlin, and only dominated local politics after arresting key leftist leaders. Beginning in 1933, the NSDAP aggressively nazified Berlin, trying to re-create the city as a model National Socialist *Hauptstadt*. Although the city escaped the firestorms that ravaged Hamburg and Dresden, it was devastated in the final months of World War II before being carved up, like Germany itself, among four occupation forces. The city epitomized superpower tensions during the Cold War, attracting international attention in 1948–1949, 1953, and 1961, while in recent years, building projects and political battles in Berlin have demonstrated both the opportunities and pitfalls associated with the unification of East and West. At the risk of overgeneralization, and for better or worse, the city's identity is one of dynamic adaptation to change, and cohort members personified that characteristic in their narratives; as youth, they adjusted behaviors and expectations to persevere through total war, unconditional surrender, postwar chaos, and Cold War division.

Yet this cohort's unique collective identity has been shaped more than by age-specific perceptions of local politics and historical events. Their memories also reveal the consequences of having been members of a generation first claimed by Hitler and then remobilized by other ideological forces after World War II. As a cohort, they share similar childhood memories, wartime experiences, and postwar attitudes. As individuals, their lives have also been shaped by efforts to negotiate history's predominately negative evaluation of their youth and to lead normal lives in a war-torn, illegitimated, and divided German capital.

SCHÖNE KINDERJAHRE IN NAZI BERLIN

I had "learned" the absurdity, danger and inhumanity of Nazi rule from a very young age, and had become used to it as a chronic reality.[6]

Explaining his indifference to the suffering of Jewish relatives, Heinrich Kupffer, born in 1924, also encapsulated the experience of an average youngster in prewar Nazi Berlin. While the rise of the National Socialists and the subsequent reorganization of German society has since been well documented, at the time, few Germans, let alone members of this cohort, acknowledged the potential "danger and inhumanity" of Hitler's plans. Like children everywhere, young Berliners internalized evolving cultural expectations, and usually adapted their behaviors accordingly. They were accustomed to seeing uniformed men in the streets of Berlin, and some even wore uniforms themselves, for example, while attending parades and other celebrations sponsored by the Nazi regime.

Not surprisingly, few offered any specific memories of the Nazi assumption of power—they were simply too young. Nonetheless, cohort members have since learned Berlin's prewar history, and this period certainly informs their memories and collective identity. First, recollections of the 1930s comprise a backdrop of comparatively normal peacetime against which interviewees compared the insecurity of the 1940s. Second, collective "pseudo memories" of the prewar Reich have shaped this cohort's narratives and self-perceptions.

As Berliners, interviewees seemed familiar with their city's political development in the 1930s. Recalling their childhoods, however, cohort members highlighted the daily routines that persisted in spite of social and political change. Only a block or two from Friedrichshain's *Frankfurter Allee*, for example, working-class families lived as they had for decades—in five-story tenement blocks, built around narrow, damp courtyards that extended three or four buildings deep from the street. Young children's lives took them through neighborhoods marked by home, school, local shops, and in some cases, church. While the children of more prosperous families lived in spacious apartments (or single-family homes) and enjoyed somewhat broader horizons, they too were at best only vaguely conscious of the Nazis' political transformation of Berlin.[7] For example, while most have since learned the details surrounding the Reichstag fire, few mentioned it in the context of their own experiences. Similarly, interviewees were generally aware of postwar analyses of the Hitler Youth (HJ), in which scholars have considered the organization as a mutation of earlier youth organizations and an exploitative extension of the Nazi party; the HJ was, for most, simply an unquestioned factor in childhood experience. Former participants—particularly in the *Deutsches Jungvolk* (the younger children's wing of the HJ)—typically described a welcome escape from the drudgery of schoolwork and daily chores and a chance to have fun with friends. Hitler Youth meetings, community service, and field trips constituted part of a normal, busy childhood.[8]

In addition to school and family activities, it was the service in the *Deutsches Jungvolk* that occupied our days. . . . Our meetings were held regularly on Wednesday and Saturday afternoons from three to five o'clock. Sometimes there were additional meetings in the evening and even on Sundays, an example of which was the youth film hour. On Sunday mornings at eleven o'clock we had to view a movie with an especially strong ideological message. . . . [Teachers] were ordered by governmental decree . . . to reduce considerably the rather heavy homework load on Wednesdays and Saturdays.[9]

Although most known for regulating HJ and educational policy, the *Reichsjugendführung* (RJF) also published a variety of inexpensive children's books and magazines, which cohort members read, emulated, and exchanged with friends. *Der Pimpf*, for example, a monthly publication for ten- to fourteen-year-old boys, offered twenty pages of fictional, biographical, scientific, and historical articles, as well as joke pages and letters from both active-duty soldiers and young HJlers who had overcome personal weaknesses. The magazine celebrated all military and technological achievements, both historical and contemporary, offering readers a vocabulary infused with military phraseology and symbolism, and suggesting that true German boys could overcome all physical and mental hardships to serve the *Führer*. In short, *Der Pimpf* reinforced what boys learned in the *Deutsches Jungvolk* while parallel publications for girls promoted the duties and rewards of domesticity and the ties between motherhood and *Vaterland*.[10]

Because the state oversaw virtually all educational and cultural opportunities for children and youth, even cohort members who never joined the Hitler Youth learned the predominant values—honor, loyalty, and a strong, racially based national identity. In some families, however, these ideological messages were mitigated by other influences, both before and during World War II. Young Catholics, for example, continued parish-level gatherings throughout Berlin, even after the central organizations were absorbed or dissolved.[11] Charlottenburger Frau Völker belonged to one such parish youth club.

Actually, the group was banned, but we met anyway, as protest against the HJ. They had brown vests; we wore—unofficially of course—dark blue. We were restricted to religious meetings, mass or confirmation classes, but we kept on meeting as we always had, just not so publicly. Through the church, we had a beautiful house on a large piece of property in Altbuchholz; we went out there—even during the war—and were free and could do as we pleased.[12]

Far from active opposition work, Völker's parish group nonetheless offered her an alternative to RJF social programs, as well as, over time, a distinctly different identity. Asserting the continuity of this influence throughout her childhood and youth, Völker also described her choices in terms of resistance.

Although unprotected by the papal agreements shielding Catholics, Protestant youth continued to gather throughout the Nazi era, as did socialist groups and others simply identified by the Nazis as "asocial cliques."[13] Interviewees Binkert and Dinkel counted themselves among these outsiders. Friends since childhood (and despite living on opposite sides of the Berlin Wall) they recalled dancing to banned music and discussing all manner of personal and political interests in cafes along the *Schönhauser Allee*—the "Broadway of Prenzlauer Berg."[14] Archival records and personal accounts suggest that the boys' activities were far from unique; young Germans avoided Hitler Youth activities for any number of reasons. While some were driven by particular religious beliefs or political convictions, many others, like Binkert and Dinkel, were simply being young, that is, challenging an authority that attempted to regulate or restrict their behavior. Sometimes, such rejection of prescribed norms was supported, even fostered, by young Berliners' parents. Cohort members recalled their mothers insisting—with various degrees of truthfulness—that a child was needed in the family shop, falling behind in their schoolwork, or ill. "My mother," noted Distel, "always tried to send me to BDM (League of German Maidens) as little as possible. To that end, she would play up the seriousness of a little cough if the leaders came to check on me."[15]

Cohort members rarely explained their parents' political leanings or responses to Nazi policies. Nonetheless, growing up in that regulated, highly politicized environment undoubtedly shaped familial relationships. The RJF's efforts to undermine parental authority and assume an ever-greater role in children's lives strained parent-child relationships, as did the fact that by the late1930s, many parents simply refused to answer questions about a growing list of taboo subjects.

One simply, that is, my parents, and the parents of many friends simply didn't talk about
the political situation . . . in those days, one couldn't speak with children . . . one never
knew how the children would answer questions—openly and truthfully—about what
went on at home.[16]

This fear-driven moratorium on discussion inadvertently supported Hitler's
plans to develop a youth groomed for instant action, not self-reflection and
independent thought.   Although quite understandable, an atmosphere of
intentional silence also shaped youths' postwar attitudes toward their parents
and the Nazi period, not to mention later relationships with their own offspring.
    Adults who did discuss political and social developments with children did so
at considerable risk, since youngsters were encouraged, not only in the HJ but
also in school, to doubt their parents and report inappropriate comments or
actions.   Even if parents effectively countered this message, they still had to
worry that a child might unintentionally pass along sensitive information.   Frau
Burkhardt, for example, recalled heated debates between her Social Democratic
parents and their friends.   Looking back, she wondered why her parents had
encouraged her attendance, since, as a self-described chatterbox, she could have
betrayed their political loyalties any number of times.[17]
    In general, and despite the post-1945 condemnation of Nazi-era values,
institutions, and traditions, social parameters of the prewar years formed a
template of normalcy for most cohort members.   The outbreak of World War II
did little to change that.   Young Berliners had seen war romanticized in films
and novels, learned about the alleged injustices of Versailles in school, heard
Hitler's promises of glory and honor, and internalized a militaristic vocabulary
in which every hardship was a battle and every success a victory.   Consequently,
while the German invasion of Poland constitutes a turning point in political
analyses and history textbooks, it figured insignificantly in interviewees'
personal recollections.   Even though most cohort members have since learned
the chronology leading into World War II, their memories of the late 1930s,
even some six decades later, were structured by more personal developments.
Friedrichshainer Frau Klinkert, raised by a widowed mother from the age of
five, epitomized interviewees' tendency to subjugate what they now recognize
as key political turning points to immediate familial circumstances and
developments.

We lived in very simple conditions. Our father had died already in 1938, when we [Frau
K and her twin sister] were five; that's when the struggle began for our mother. She had
given birth—to twins —in her thirty-eighth year, and that already had been a life-
threatening delivery. Then our father died when we were five, so that our mother at age
forty-three had to support us by herself. So, and then, in 1939 of all times, the war
started. . . . She was already sickly and then the exertion of birth and the poor living
conditions, our father had been a waiter and, like all Germans, frequently unemployed in
the thirties, and couldn't save much. Our mother was a seamstress; the pay for piecework
was very bad and so she watched after us and tried somehow at the same time to do her
sewing.[18]

Klinkert's portrayal of her childhood suggests that, at least in her mind, the outbreak of World War II constituted not a turning point, but rather yet another in a series of hardships. While her life was perhaps exceptionally difficult, other interviewees similarly blurred the boundary between peace and war. More than mere childlike naïveté, this tendency also reflects two historical facts. First, Nazi leaders had begun preparing Berliners for military conflict long before they issued any formal declarations of war. Some residents had participated in air raid drills almost four and a half years earlier, and massive air defense bunkers had been built at three points around the city.[19] Public air raid shelters had been established, and many residents had stocked their own provisional basement shelters with water, sand, and other necessities. Early rationing initiatives, begun already in August 1939, were quickly eased for the holiday season, while workers who lost their jobs when the state banned nonessential construction work soon found work in the booming defense industry. In 1940, the Hitler-Stalin Pact further stimulated the economy, and a successful *Wehrmacht* began sending home goods from both eastern and western Europe. After all the preparations, Berliners escaped significant air bombardment until August 1940, when British Royal Air Force (RAF) pilots hit Kreuzberg, and even then, regular air raids were still more than two years away.

Over time, of course, the war did creep into young Berliners' lives. The international conflict, for example, gave the RJF an excuse to expand state regulation of young people's lives, intensifying voluntary service programs and charitable campaigns. In Berlin, HJlers were recruited to patrol city streets and detain undesirable young people, who were often sentenced to psychological intimidation and heavy labor in designated youth reform centers.[20] The RJF also began consolidating paramilitary programs for school-aged boys and adjusted ideological messages to wartime themes.[21] More relevant to most young Berliners was the fact that fathers, uncles, cousins, and older brothers were drafted in ever-increasing numbers for various types of wartime service. Even this paternal absenteeism, however, was not necessarily new or abnormal; German society had traditionally defined fathers as breadwinners, decision-makers, and disciplined role models, and under Nazi rule, men were especially pressured to work long hours and support various state-sponsored organizations and initiatives. Such elements of continuity, combined with the relatively brief, successful campaigns in Poland and France, optimistic newsreels, the persistence of normal routines, intentional parental protectionism, and of course the ambiguous nature of childhood memories themselves, helped cohort members brush over the historical turning point of 1 September 1939. Their memories of *schöne Kinderjahre* (lovely childhood years), although peppered with propaganda posters, political rhetoric, and social pressures, focused primarily on people, routines, and values which were rarely altered by the outbreak of war.

This tendency to seemingly overlook significant historical developments can be further explained by psychological work on memory construction. On the most fundamental level, memories of early childhood (the youngest interviewees were only six when war broke out) are notoriously few, vague, and subject to suggestion. Thus, cohort members "remembered" celebrations and amusing anecdotes from their early years because older relatives recounted them again and again.   Although not truly autobiographical, these pseudo-memories nevertheless inform cohort members' self-perceptions and identities, and may be particularly significant for this cohort since they reinforce personal recollections, what psychologists call a pretraumatic stage of life. [22]   In other words, the undeniably difficult experiences of cohort members in the mid-1940s most likely strengthened typically nostalgic childhood memories, as youth clung to images of the peace-filled 1930s. After Germany's defeat, these same memories constituted the basis of youths' elusive quest to reestablish security.

Furthermore, these collective pseudo-memories of the prewar period have since been colored by both the postwar condemnation and subsequent close scrutiny of the Nazi era.   Memories of *schöne Kinderjahre*, for example, correspond beautifully with depictions of the mid-1930s as a time of economic recovery—a renewed prosperity for which many Germans thanked the National Socialists.   More concretely, defeat may have added new significance to Völker's youth club, encouraging her to describe the group's blue vests (most likely a long-standing tradition) as a symbol of opposition to the HJ.

Even Klinkert's childhood memories found substantiation in the accepted GDR historiography.   After struggling to overcome multiple hardships, the young proletarian found recognition and success in the nascent People's Republic (GDR). Lastly, narratives that downplay the beginning of World War II reflect Berlin's gradual evolution from Weimar metropolis to Nazi *Hauptstadt* and eventually, Hitler's final stand.

FROM HOME TO HOME FRONT

Although few young Berliners felt inconvenienced, let alone victimized, by war in mid-1940, virtually all had become intimately familiar with material hardship, fear and uncertainty by the end of 1943.   To some extent, this enhanced awareness reflects their maturation; most were between ten and seventeen years old and could no longer be shielded from the world around them. More concretely, the dramatic intensification of British air raids on Berlin in 1943 upset the daily routines of young and old alike, effectively ending what most cohort members considered a safe and happy childhood. [23] On the night of 1–2 March, for example, the most devastating RAF attack to date flattened buildings around *Prager Platz, Kaiserallee, Unter den Linden*, and *Friedrichsstraße,* and killed nearly 500 Berliners, among them six young antiaircraft assistants (*Flakhelfer*). [24] More than 250 Berliners were killed and 35,000 left homeless by British bombers on 23 August; equally destructive assaults came the next two nights and again from 31 August through 4 September. Another particularly harsh series of air assaults came in the second half of November, destroying cultural landmarks such as the National Library and the University. Attacks on Siemenstadt impaired industrial production, while explosions at the zoo and aquarium gave rise to rumors of famished tigers and crocodiles roaming city streets. Although repair crews worked around the clock, these persistent attacks began to cripple Berlin's economic and social infrastructure.[25]   By Christmas 1943, many young Berliners, including interviewee Herr Schneider, had lost almost everything.

The basement steps were still there, and in the shelter (formerly our laundry room), where we always sat, I saw the remnants of the suitcase my Mother always took with her. If I had been there . . . but she was alone on that particular night. The suitcase was covered in dust; it had held a ring or two and a sweater. It was awful . . . completely burnt out. I dug around and all of a sudden I had the ring in my hand, my father's wedding ring. I also found her watch; it had melted of course, but I was glad to have found it.[26]

News from the front, which young people heard on the radio and discussed in school, reminded Berliners that their suffering was far from unique. By 1943, Germans could no longer dismiss ever-longer casualty lists (framed in black) that filled local newspapers. Mourning families often dedicated a shelf, a table, or even an entire room to a fallen soldier's memory, an act that further reminded young people of the war's toll on individual families. Even children were urged to honor the dead by redoubling their own contributions to the war effort, and a whole series of governmental decrees underscored both the increasing urgency of the military situation and the critical responsibilities of German youth. The RJF declared 1943 the year of "German Youth in War Service," and intensified training and recruitment programs, while the Nazi government expanded draft registration laws. Beginning in 1943, sixteen-year-old boys and seventeen-year-old girls were required to register with wartime service officials, and most youths born in 1926–1927 were drafted almost immediately.[27]

Between 1943 and the end of the war, cohort members served in construction brigades, air defense units, armament factories, radio facilities, and special units of the military. In 1944 Frau Barthe, who had just turned eighteen, was drafted into the National Labor Service program (*Reichsarbeitsdienst*, hereafter RAD) and sent to work on a West Prussian farm.[28]   After helping with farm chores and childcare all day, Barthe returned each evening to quarters—often a requisitioned youth hostel or school—she shared with other RAD laborers. RAD regulations enforced a strictly regimented, quasi-military lifestyle that included six o'clock wakeup calls, cold water baths, daily inspections, and ideological lectures, and many participants recalled the experience as stressful and exhausting. Barthe, however, highlighted a welcome sense of belonging.

We were all so young, lying in bed each night I used to sing [to the other girls]. I'd have to say I enjoyed it. And the political side, well we were all used to it, from school. There was one girl, she was a *Mädelführerin* or something, from the BDM, and she went on about everything they did and all. . . . I never joined, and she told me once I should be ashamed to be a German girl. It never bothered me though. . . . In the evenings we all sat around, played games or patched up our things, we ate and sang [together], I can't remember but I think we had a radio too.[29]

Barthe's recollection is typical in several ways. First, it describes—even in the last months of the war—a relatively positive Nazi-era experience, not unlike that offered by former members of the Hitler Youth. Second, it demonstrates the persistence of *schöne Kinderjahre* images; Barthe recalled work-filled days, and what must have been fear-filled nights (particularly if the girls did have access to radio news broadcasts) as enjoyable and filled with innocent pleasures. Finally, Barthe's recollections of RAD service—like other childhood memories—have likely softened in comparison with subsequent wartime experiences. After eight weeks in bucolic rural Prussia, Barthe and her friends were ordered to evacuate, leaving behind their personal belongings. Barthe fled the advancing Red Army, at times on foot and in open rail cars, and when the girls joined another RAD unit, she learned that her mother had been killed in a British air assault on Berlin.

For other cohort members, wartime service marked the end of a protected childhood by revealing the increasingly obvious contradictions between National Socialist rhetoric and practice. Officials told Herr Schneider, for example, who was also drafted into the RAD, that he would spend the next year working on a farm in Poland. In reality, however, he spent only seventeen days at a RAD camp, learning to load and fire various weapons. Schneider recalled his initial confusion. "Labor Service was supposed to mean farm work, but I never caught a glimpse of a spade. Then I joined the army and was sent to Bavaria."[30]   Alfons Heck recalled similar contradictions in his description of daily routines at an exclusive HJ flight training camp. Even the youngest recruits noticed that commanding officers blatantly disregarded minimum weight requirements for glider pilots and, in an attempt to condense the course, reduced the prescribed one– to two–hour midday break to a mere twenty minutes. In addition, after having been encouraged to imagine themselves as elite *Luftwaffe* heroes, the young pilots felt deceived by recruiters; having volunteered to fly, they found themselves spending entire days in the kitchen (scrubbing pots or peeling potatoes) instead of the cockpit.[31]

Berliners too young to serve the war effort directly were similarly torn from their childhood routines in the final two years of the war, most often by the *erweiterte Kinderlandverschickung* (KLV). This school evacuation program had been established in 1940, but only began to enroll significant numbers of Berliners in August 1943, after *Reichsminister* Goebbels ordered all "unessential" residents to evacuate the capital and distributed a special memo to families with school-aged children.

To the Parents of Berlin's Schoolchildren:
The enemy's airborne terror pays no heed to the civilian population. The terror-bombers are engaged in a brutal war of annihilation against defenseless women and children. Concern for German youths, their health and their lives demand extraordinary measures. . . . Effective immediately, all Berlin schools, along with their teachers, will be evacuated. . . . . It is expected that parents will understand the necessity of these measures, taken in the interests of their children. Your cooperation will ensure that the evacuation takes place smoothly and that your children will be protected from the consequences of enemy terror.[32]

While the KLV program was not technically mandatory, Goebbels' warning, together with an accompanying announcement that public schools in Berlin would be closed indefinitely starting in September, drove thousands of Berliners to register their children for evacuation.[33] Frau Distel, thirteen at the time, was excited when her mother completed the application, since she and her friends anticipated a kind of extended holiday at a rural youth hostel or hotel. Instead, her school was sent to a rustic KLV camp in Deutscheneck, about 400 kilometers east of Berlin, where the city girls' dreams faded quickly as they encountered straw-filled mattresses, hand-pumped water, ticks, lice, and the hostile glares of the local Polish population.

Distel's account suggests the Deutscheneck camp was typical in terms of hygiene and social conditions, the latter of which were largely determined by relationships between the teachers and Hitler Youth leaders who regulated camp life. While most evacuees recalled their teachers as distanced but kind, the young HJ officials, who were charged with maintaining discipline, morale, and physical readiness, received less positive evaluations. These youth leaders, some of whom were only fifteen or sixteen years old, could override teachers' decisions, and sometimes used brutal tactics—such as midnight torture sessions—to keep younger children in line. Distel recounted no such actions in Deutscheneck, but Winkert, another KLV evacuee, described his camp as a "brutal community of children," which was more hierarchical, regulated, and intolerant than anything he'd previously experienced.

It was by no means all sweet and cozy; children can be really quite cruel and *very* [italics added] thoughtless. If anyone showed a weakness, he was in for it. Sometimes we tied schoolmates to the beds and whipped them. Some of the children just had it in them, were naturally aggressive or dominating, and no one stopped them.[34]

For Winkert, the KLV experience abruptly ended what had been a typically pleasant and protected childhood in Berlin. Distel had a somewhat easier time in the KLV, probably in part because she was better able to meet the physical and mental demands. In addition, she received frequent visits from her mother, whose conversations with camp officials and regular shipments of fruit and baked goods likely ameliorated physical hardship. Despite these mitigating circumstances, however, she too explained the eleven-month separation as beginning an extended period of uncertainty that forced her to grow up.

Berliners who avoided both national service and evacuation also saw their happy childhoods disappear in the second half of the war. Herr Rennebach was thirteen when he began serving twelve-hour shifts in the Kreuzberg fire patrol. His duties included reporting fires, recovering victims—or bodies—from collapsed buildings and administering first aid to survivors. Herr Völker described similar responsibilities in the Charlottenburg *Luftschutz*, which reinforced the overwhelmed and understaffed local fire department during air raids.

We were organized in little groups, regardless of HJ or Party status. We had little fire trucks, little carts actually, with a kind of hydrant and when it started burning, the fifteen of us 13–16 year olds would take off, go up into the buildings and put out [the fires] as best we could.[35]

The war, according to Völker, had rendered increasingly irrelevant the organized, heirarchical structure of Nazi society. Real life experience simply contradicted what he had been taught about Germany's military and technical superiority. Particularly after Berlin sent some of its fire fighting units to Hamburg after that city suffered devastating firestorms in mid-1943, local *Luftschutz* boys had to extinguish incendiary bombs and roof fires with almost no training and only the most rudimentary equipment.

The increasing chaos and danger of wartime Berlin, of course, paradoxically brought greater freedom for the youth who remained in the German capital. As public transportation broke down, parents could no longer expect children to meet familial curfews; a damaged streetcar or a sudden air raid could leave anyone stranded for hours. Everyone suffered from lack of sleep, and youths who had spent the night running a spotlight at a flak station could hardly be expected to finish chores or go to school.[36] In fact, *dienstverpflichtete Jugendliche*—which included virtually every youth twelve or older—had any number of excuses to skip school or even Hitler Youth obligations: a late air raid the night before, a bombed-out neighbor who needed assistance, or long lines at the ration card bureau.

Particularly savvy youths also found opportunities for greater self-determination in their interactions with the Nazi bureaucracy. By 1944, various service programs and branches of the military found themselves competing for a dwindling number of potential recruits. As a result, some young Berliners received draft notices from several offices almost simultaneously. While RJF officials had attempted to preclude recruitment controversies by signing agreements with both the SS (1938) and *Wehrmacht* (1940 and 1942), they could spare few officers to resolve the subsequent conflicts.[37] Creative, opportunistic young Berliners sometimes exploited this situation to delay or avoid mobilization.

Berliners' 1943 wartime experiences, of course, were eclipsed by the air assaults of 1944, especially after American pilots joined the RAF campaign and began staging daytime bombing runs. Each raid sent Berliners into air raid shelters for two to three hours at a time, and while interviewees made no mention of the additional daytime attacks, local information officers certainly noticed their effect on popular morale.

Accentuating what is already the most pessimistic atmosphere of the entire war, one can observe a mortal fear throughout the vulnerable regions of the Reich including Berlin. This is most apparent in the altered behavior of many citizens following daylight attacks. The public had endured nighttime raids with a certain bitter stoicism, [but] one can now observe a literal race for life in broad daylight. . . . At the moment, a majority of the population is just sick and tired of it.[38]

Berliners did enjoy a brief respite when Allied bombers were diverted to support the Normandy invasion of June 1944, but air raids resumed within a few weeks.[39] That same summer, an attempt on Hitler's life (led by General

Stauffenberg) sparked a fury of arrests in Berlin. Government leaders also canceled cultural events, mandated a sixty-hour workweek, and restricted train travel to and from the city. Later that fall, the approximately 60,000 member *Berliner Volkssturm* was called to active duty.

Young Berliners had largely escaped the immediate impact of Hitler's crusade to dominate Europe. This *Schonungszeit* not only protected them from physical harm, but also blurred the boundary between peace and war. Beginning in 1943, however, the war began shaking the pillars of childhood stability, and by the end of 1944, every member of this cohort had endured fear, loneliness, and personal loss. Having sacrificed—willingly or not—for *Führer und Vaterland*, they had also begun to see cracks in the Nazi regime's carefully nurtured façade of national unity and superiority. In short, experiences of 1943 and 1944 had reduced young Berliners' *schöne Kinderjahren* to idyllic memories.[40]

HITLER'S YOUTH?

As part of what researchers have called the Hitler Youth generation, this cohort has been the subject of scholarly analyses both during and after the Nazi era. One reason was that the NSDAP identified itself as a forward-looking youthful party, obviously coopting both the energy and idealism of the turn-of-the-century youth movement to celebrate young Germans' physical vitality, idealism, and loyalty. In addition, scholars—like Nazi leaders themselves—more clearly recognized youth as a unique stage of life. Prior to World War I, the study of youth had been left largely to psychologists and sociologists, who understood youth as an essentially ahistorical period of physical, psychological, and sexual maturation. Societal influences, most believed, might delay the timing or pace of maturation, but seldom altered generational experiences of youth in a significant way.[41]

World War I challenged many of these assumptions. Many Europeans—scholars and laypeople alike—believed the war had ruined virtually an entire generation of young men, and consequently began reexamining previous interpretations of the complex relationships between youth and modern, industrialized society. Siegfried Bernfeld, for example, challenged seemingly ahistorical patterns of development by studying how class and culture shaped youth experience. This dual nature of youth—informed by both innate features of human development and external, societal factors—became a key feature of academic research.[42] It was also embraced by emerging political figures—not only Hitler, but also Stalin, Mussolini, and Franco—who identified young people as the vanguard of a new Europe, and devoted considerable resources to winning the hearts and minds of youth.

The 1926–1933 cohort, which had been exposed to Nazi socialization and ideals since infancy, was considered equally crucial by researchers and political authorities after World War II. Both groups struggled with a fundamental question: to what extent had this cohort been brainwashed and/or exploited by the Nazi regime? Understanding the nature and malleability of youth became particularly important in Germany, since this generation—which had been claimed by Hitler—was now needed to rebuild German society. As historians and sociologists sought to understand young Germans' experience in the Third Reich, they turned to archival records from organizations like the Hitler Youth. Not surprisingly, these sources revealed much about proscribed behaviors and attitudes, resulting in studies that emphasized the structured, totalitarian goals of Nazi leaders but said little about regional, let alone individual, variations in youth experience.

Postwar officials—occupation officers, social workers, educators, and political activists—were more immediately concerned with Nazism's impact on German youth. However, while some had studied National Socialist institutions before the war, analyzed the tenets of the Hitler Youth, or observed educational practices, analyses of structures and ideology offered only minimal guidance to those charged with rehabilitating Germany's lost youth. Postwar leaders across the political spectrum faced a serious dilemma: they needed German youth to rebuild society, but wondered if the young veterans, former HJlers, homeless refugees, and half-orphans wandering Berlin's streets could be entrusted with such an important task. This was no mere intellectual quandary, but rather one that fundamentally shaped postwar officials' attitudes and policies. Rooting their perceptions of postwar youth primarily in the Nazis' proscriptive literature, postwar leaders assumed this cohort had been maimed; this assumption, which few young people shared, hindered efforts to remobilize youth for new responsibilities in postwar society.

For most of the 1950s and early 1960s, most historical studies were similarly structured by an archival record left from the Nazi era, subjugating wide variations in individual experience to analyses that emphasized the totalitarian nature of National Socialist society and the success of indoctrination and intimidation. While careful study of early postwar documents might have challenged these conclusions, several factors hindered efforts to challenge accepted generalizations about wartime and postwar youth.

First, the archival record of the Hunger Years (1945–1949), which might have offered clues to a more diversified understanding of youth experience and attitudes, was far from comprehensive. In Berlin, for example, a severe paper shortage after the war meant that the paper on which officials typed reports was often reused either by other civil servants or as kindling in the small ovens used for heating. Consequently, while the Berlin-Neukölln systematically collected memos, posters, and other documents, most other districts have only limited records from the period.

Cold War political tensions further stymied research efforts. Quite simply, it was far more important to win young people for current and future causes than to ponder their past experience. This was particularly true in Berlin, where the two ideologies stood face to face, competing for young people's loyalty. In the long term, Berlin's political and geographic division also thwarted efforts to develop a representative understanding of youth experience, since after 1961 few researchers could access both parts of a divided archival record. Furthermore, while the East German government encouraged documentation of youth activism, it was primarily interested in asserting the dominance and popularity of the state-sponsored Free German Youth (FDJ).

In the West, however, postwar researchers gradually embraced interdisciplinary approaches to the study of youth experience. In part, this acceptance was linked to the efforts of grassroots historians in the late 1960s and 1970s, who sought to overturn traditional master narratives by documenting individual lives and attitudes, particularly among representatives of the working classes.[43] Initially focused primarily on the Nazi era, oral history initiatives in Berlin, including the Kreuzberg-based *Geschichtswerkstatt*, the Technical University's *Erzählcafe*, and a relatively new *Zeitzeugenbörse* in Friedrichain, have since begun examining the postwar era as well. The Charlottenburg *Heimatmuseum*, for example, has long enlisted local residents in its efforts to collect oral testimony, archival materials and historical artifacts for museum exhibits. Within academia, oral history has gained increasing acceptance as a tool of what German historians call *Alltagsgeschichte* (lit. everyday history), which advocates a more qualitative, descriptive approach to social history. *Alltagshistoriker* have focused particular attention on the Third Reich and the GDR revealing the social complexity often obscured by totalitarian rhetoric and policies.[44]

Much like oral history and *Alltagsgeschichte*, this study reexamines generalizations applied to young Berliners after World War II. Archival records show that local authorities essentially divided youth into two groups: "activist" or "apathetic." The latter label (and its virtual synonym, "unorganized") reduced individuals with widely varying attitudes and behaviors into a single category that included not only the vast majority of Berlin's young people, but also most of the cohort members interviewed for this study. In this way, drinking, dancing, stealing, falling in love, selling on the black market, and challenging authorities were all seen as symptoms of the same affliction: asocial apathy. Oral history distances experience from the judgment of authorities to examine cohort members' self-perceptions. What did young Berliners expect—of postwar society, local and international officials, and themselves? How did they understand their own actions and attitudes during the early postwar era? How did this period shape their later lives?

Cohort members' answers to these and other questions point back to the issue of interdisciplinary research. On the one hand, oral narratives certainly bring the past alive in a very personal way, proving the existence of populations hidden in the written record and revealing the diversity of individual experience within common sociopolitical parameters. On the other hand, however, psychological research has shown memory's malleability; just as archival sources can be lost, altered, or simply wrong, so too can the human mind reshape the past in a variety of ways.[45] For example, interviewees often see themselves as storytellers. Seeking (not necessarily consciously) to please their audience, they may explain a series of occurrences as building to a climax, or highlight exciting moments to the exclusion of less eventful periods. Those who have recounted their stories multiple times may even organize their memories thematically, reshaping memories into a coming-of-age or rags-to-riches narrative.

Simultaneously, memories can be shaped to fit historical and/or contemporary societal expectations and/or individual needs. Klinkert's narrative of working-class struggle constitutes one example of this. More generally, cohort members explained *Endkampf* and postwar actions in ways that asserted pragmatism, confidence, and independence, while offering, as noted previously, nostalgic images of childhood. While this latter tendency is understandable, the notably optimistic accounts of the early postwar period, which was undeniably both physically and psychologically draining, are more problematic. On the one hand, individuals often paint their youth experiences in particularly glowing terms. On the other, however, the material and psychological circumstances of the 1940s challenged even the most optimistic young Berliners. While coping with the collapse of German society, cohort members struggled to find food, clothing, and shelter, as well as new foundations for postwar lives and identities. How, then, could they remember this period as "a very rich period" or "my best years?"

Underlying these issues lurk questions of historical accuracy and the constructed nature of all representations of the past. By focusing on experiential narratives, as opposed to political chronologies, oral history reminds us that even long-accepted temporal divides have been imposed on history; personal narratives may offer equally viable, experience-based periodizations.[46]

On a more concrete level, social psychologists have confirmed the relative accuracy of certain kinds of memories by examining the cognitive processes through which memories are constructed, retained, altered, and recalled.[47] Describing memories as constructed and stored in relation to other kinds of knowledge, psychologists such as Janice L. Howes and Albert N. Katz have shown that subjects display "useful" degrees of accuracy in recalling past events.

It is our impression that recall from remote memory need not be subject to the oft-heard criticism that it is invalid. If one asks for recall of specific events from specific time periods, both middle-aged and older-aged adults appear to do so with accuracy.[48]

Further scrutiny of this rather guarded conclusion has led to the discovery of a graphical memory "bump"—significantly more and better-quality recall of events from adolescence and young adulthood, stages of life crucial to maturation and identity development.[49]

The constructed nature of identity constitutes a third thematic pillar of this study. German unification has only invigorated a long-standing discussion on German identity in which scholars examined Germany's unique and delayed national political development and studied how Germans dealt with the stigma of Nazism. Since 1989, historians have reopened these and related debates, asking how decades of political and ideological opposition have shaped German national identity.[50]

This study asks how a specific cohort of Berliners has negotiated such questions on a personal level. It emphasizes mutually-informing links between self-perception and collective identity, suggesting that this cohort's identity has been shaped not only by common experiences during World War II, but also by similar ways of interpreting and contextualizing postwar opportunities and initiatives.

By late 1944, although the battle that destroyed their city had yet to be fought, young Berliners had learned to cope with hardship. The eldest (who turned nineteen in 1945) had spent years serving the doomed Reich, while even the youngest had sacrificed homes, loved ones, and daily routines. They had also internalized at least some aspects of Nazi socialization, learning, for example, not to ask questions or challenge authorities. Nazi society, however, had also, perhaps inadvertently, taught German youth at least four other important lessons, which would prove invaluable in the months to come.

Self-reliance. While the RJF claimed responsibility for educating youth and promoted camaraderie, physical prowess, and self-sacrifice, its programs often tore youth prematurely from their families. In the physical and psychological boot camps of the RAD, *Wehrmacht*, and KLV, young people learned to fend for themselves.

Luck. This cohort grew up with German legends, singing songs that predicted a glorious future and reading books that explained why Germany would soon dominate Europe. Watching bombs fall over Berlin, however, destroying entire city blocks while leaving other streets virtually unscathed, they saw another, harsher fate. Devotion to a cause might not be rewarded; anyone, regardless of political status, social standing, or race, could be killed by a shell fragment or buried alive in a bomb shelter.

Skepticism. The RJF rewarded action, not contemplation, and the best HJ, RAD, and KLV programs left little time for questions or self-reflection. As Nazi structures crumbled, however, youth saw wounded soldiers and desperate refugees filling Berlin's train stations, and gleaned information from news sources that directly contradicted the Nazi press. In other words, they began learning to believe only what they could see.

Caution. Since the advent of Hitler's regime, Nazi propaganda had promoted adolescent fearlessness. Increasingly obvious contradictions between ideology and practice, however, rewarded not blind leaps of courage, but wariness. Young Germans, like many adults, learned to better their chances of surviving the chaotic present—and an uncertain future—by delaying commitments and hedging their bets.

Interviewees rarely spoke of World War II in these terms. Asked how they survived bombings, evacuations, and life on the front lines, they pointed out that in such situations one does what's necessary and doesn't ask questions. Yet cohort members' Nazi-era experiences included not only indoctrination in a hierarchical, regulated, and mobilized society, but also the gradual disintegration of those very social parameters. The latter half of World War II taught young Berliners survival strategies and practical skills that would inform their later decisions and actions. Looking back, it seems that these lessons, not the stigma of belonging to a lost or skeptical generation, became the basis for interviewees' personal and collective identities.

NOTES

1. Burkhardt, 13,17.

2. King, 8–9.

3. Since archival sources made it impossible to attempt a close comparison of specific districts, I also included a few residents of Zehlendorf and Neukölln.

4. These numbers are approximate, including only legally registered 14- to 19-year-olds. *Berlin in Zahlen* (Berlin: Das Neue Berlin, 1947), 58, 61–63.

5. That said, Charlottenburg's main avenue (called the Otto-Suhr- Allee today) was heavily bombed.

6. Heinrich Kupffer, *Swingtime. Chronik einer Jugend in Deutschland 1937–1951* (Berlin: Verlag Frieling & Partner GmbH, 1987), 42–43. Also on German reactions to the persecution of Jews: Marion Kaplan, "Sisterhood under Siege: Feminism and Anti-Semitism in Germany, 1904–1938," in Renate Bridenthal, Atina Grossman, and Marion Kaplan, eds., *When Biology Became Destiny* (New York: Monthly Book Review Press, 1984), 174–96; Ian Kershaw, "The Persecution of the Jews and German Popular Opinion in the Third Reich," *Leo Baeck Institute Year Book*, 26 (1981), 261–89; Hans Mommsen, "Was haben die Deutschen vom Völkermord an den Juden gewußt?" in Walter H. Pehle, ed., *Der Judenpogrom 1938. Von der "Reichskristallnacht" zum Völkermord* (Frankfurt am Main: Fischer Taschenbuch Verlag, 1988), 176–200.

7. Surveys: Distel, Rippe, Pestopf, and Kösel.

8. Christine Schemmann, *Wie man kleine Nazis machte: Jahrgang 1925 im Krieg und danach* (Berlin: Frieling, 1996),16. On the Hitler Youth: Hans-Christian Brandenburg, *Die Geschichte der HJ. Wege und Irrwege einer Generation* (Cologne: Verlag Wissenschaft und Politik, 1982); Arno Klönne, *Jugend im Dritten Reich—die Hitler Jugend und ihre Gegner. Dokumente und Analysen* (Dusseldorf: Elgen Diderichs Verlag, 1982); Detlev Peukert, "Youth in the Third Reich," in Richard Bessel, ed., *Life in the Third Reich* (New York: Oxford University Press, 1987).

9. Walter Schumann, *Being Present: Growing Up in Hitler's Germany* (Kent, OH: Kent State University Press, 1991), 22.

10. *Der Pimpf* (Berlin: Zentralverlag der NSDAP), Duke University Special Collections e#10171. For other examples of stories and skits for children, see Calvin College's online Nazi Propaganda Archive http://www.calvin.edu/academic/cas/gpa/ (31 July 2003).

11. Lawrence D. Walker, *Hitler Youth and Catholic Youth 1933–1936* (Washington, D.C.: Catholic University of America Press, 1970). Although Walker's study shows that the largest central Catholic youth organization (*Katholischer Jungmännerverein*) was banned in 1939, it overlooks local parish initiatives. Also: Mattias von Hellfeld, *Bündische Jugend und Hitlerjugend. Zur Geschichte von Anpassung und Widerstand 1930–1939* (Cologne: Verlag Wissenschaft und Politik, 1987).

12. Herr and Frau Völker, taped interview. Also: Christel Beilmann, *Eine katholische Jugend in Gottes und dem Dritten Reich. Briefe, Berichte, Gedrucktes 1930–1945. Kommentare 1988/89* (Wuppertal: Peter Hammer Verlag, 1989); Werner Dolata, *Chronik einer Jugend. Katholische Jugend im Bistum Berlin 1936–49* (Hildesheim: Bernwar Verlag GmbH, 1988); Rainer Drews, *Zur Krise katholischer Jugendverbandsarbeit* (Frankfurt: Verlag Peter Lang, 1991); Felix Raabe, "Brücke zwischen Ost und West," in Bernd Börger and Michael Kröselberg, eds., *Die Kraft wuchs im Verborgenen.*

Katholische Jugend zwischen Elbe und Oder 1945–1990 (Düsseldorf: Verlag Haus Altenberg, 1993), 101–119.

13. The 700,000–member Protestant Youth League was officially integrated into the Hitler Youth in 1934. The rift between "German Christians" and the Confessing Church, however, extended deep into the field of youth mission work.

14. Dinkel was once arrested for allegedly corrupting his peers and listening to a foreign radio station. Surveys: Binkert, Dinkel. See also: Michael Burleigh and Wolfgang Wippermann, *The Racial State—Germany 1933–1945* (Cambridge: Cambridge University Press, 1993), 226; Alfons Kenkmann, *Wilde Jugend. Lebenswelt großstädtischer Jugendlicher zwischen Weltwirtschaftskrise, Nationalsozialismus und Währungsreform* (Essen: Klartext Verlag, 1996), 159.

15. Distel, 1. RJF officials lamented the detrimental impact of incompatible familial beliefs on youths' responsiveness and enthusiasm. See, for example, "Einfluß der HJ auf die Jugend," in Hitlerjugend memoranda, TS National Socialism Y67, Hoover Institute Archives. Also Claudia Koonz, *Mothers in the Fatherland. Women, the Family and Nazi Politics* (New York: St. Martin's Press, 1987), 286–287.

16. Distel, 1; Richie, 422; Schumann, 33.

17. Burkhardt, 1.

18. Klinkert, 1–2.

19. Howard Smith, *Last Train from Berlin* (London: Cresset Press, 1942), 38.

20. Hermann Langer, "Zur faschistischen Manipulierung der deutschen Jugend während des zweiten Weltkrieges," *Jahrbuch für Geschichte* 26 (1982): 338. On youth reform centers: Burleigh and Wippermann, 224–26; Langer, 344; Kenkmann, 146–48; 192–205; Klönne (1982), 260–68.

21. The consolidation of *Wehrertüchtigung* into three-week courses was one of Axmann's earliest initiatives as director of the RJF.

22. Gugleilmo Bellelli and Mirella Amatulli, "Nostalgia, Immigration and Collective Memory," in James W. Pennebaker, Dario Paez and Bernard Rime, eds., *Collective Memory of Political Events: Social Psychological Perspectives* (Mahwah, NJ: Lawrence Erlbaum Associates, 1997), Ch. 10; Martin Conway, "The Inventory of Experience: Memory and Identity" in ibid., Ch. 2; Jerome Bruner, "The Remembered Self," in Ulric Neisser and Robyn Fivush, eds., *The Remembering Self: Construction and Accuracy in the Self-Narrative* (New York: Cambridge University Press, 1994), Ch. 3.

23. Georg Holmsten, *Die Berlin Chronik. Daten, Personen, Dokumente* (Düsseldorf: Droste Verlag, 1984), 371.

24. Hans-Georg von Studnitz, *While Berlin Burns: The Diary of Hans-Georg von Studnitz 1943-1945* (Englewood Cliffs, NJ: Prentice-Hall, 1965), 37.

25. Studnitz,138–40. The intense bombing between 18 November and 3 December 1943 led some to call this period the first "Battle of Berlin." Ruth Andreas-Friedrich, *Battleground Berlin, Diaries 1945–1948* (New York: Paragon House, 1990),125–27; Holmsten, 378; Martin Middlebrook, *The Berlin Raids: R.A.F. Bomber Command Winter, 1943–44* (New York: Viking, 1988), 139–40; Studnitz, 140–44.

26. Schneider, 1.

27. Thereafter, officials repeatedly lowered minimum age requirements, until by early 1945 boys as young as twelve were welcomed as *Wehrmacht* volunteers. Hermann Langer, "Zur faschistischen Manipulierung der deutschen Jugend während des zweiten Weltkrieges," in *Jahrbuch für Geschichte* 26 (1982): 335–365. On young people's wartime duties: Karl-Heinz Huber, *Jugend unterm Hakenkreuz* (Berlin: Ullstein Verlag, 1982), 305–26.

28. Many of Barthe's RAD colleagues went on to serve as trolley conductors or flak assistants. On the RAD: Klaus-Jörg Ruhl, ed., *Unsere Verlorenen Jahre. Frauen in Kriegs und Nachkriegszeit 1939–1949 in Berichten, Dokumenten und Bildern* (Darmstadt: Luchterhand, 1985), 22–30; Christine Schemann, *Wie man kleine nazis machte* (Berlin: Freiling & Partner, 1995), 24–30.

29. Barthe, 1–4, 12–14.

30. Schneider, 3–6.

31. RJF, "Lagerordnung der Hitler Jugend" (1 June 1939), in *Vorschriftenhandbuch 2:486;* RJF, *Sportnachrichtendienst der Hitler-Jugend Sondernummer XXXI* (Berlin: 25 September 1942): 4; Alfons Heck, *A Child of Hitler—Germany in the Days When God Wore a Swastika* (Frederick, CO: Renaissance House, 1985), 60–62.

32. Copy in Distel, "KLV Lager in Deutscheneck" (undated, unpublished manuscript). See also: Klaus Grosinski and Mattias Schreyer, *Aus der Schule geplaudert. Schule und Schulalltag in Berlin in zweieinhalb Jahrhunderten* (Berlin: Moritzdruck, 1994), 83.

33. Interviews: Kestler, Klinkert, Pelsdorf, Rennebach, Winkert, Ziehlke. Distel described the situation as a "non-compulsory compulsion." Statistical estimates vary, in part because of often unclear distinctions between KLV and non-KLV evacuees, but more than five million German children (i.e., not including Dutch and Belgian participants) were evacuated at some point during the war. On the KLV: Gerhard Dabel, *KLV. Die erweiterte Kinder-Land-Verschickung. KLV Lager 1940–1945. Dokumentation über den größten soziologischen Versuch aller Zeiten* (Freiburg: Schillinger, 1981); Eva Gehrken, *Nationalsozialistische Erziehung in den Lagern der Erweiterten Kinderlandverschickung 1940 bis 1945,* Steinhorster Schriften und Materialien zur Schulgeschichte und Schulentwicklung, Bd. 8 (Braunschweig: TU Braunschweig, 1997); Jost Hermand, *Als Pimpf in Polen. Erweiterte KLV 1940–45* (Frankfurt: Fischer Taschenbuchverlag 1993); Bezirksamt Charlottenburg (Hrsg), *Kinderlandverschickung 1940–1945. Texte zur Ausstellung* (Berlin: Bezirksamt Charlottenburg, 1997); Claus Larass, *Der Zug der Kinder* (Munich: Meyster Verlag GmbH, 1983); Huber, 312–314; Schemann, 21–24.

34. Winkert, 2.

35. Völker, 1; Rennebach, 4.

36. On the *Flakhelfer*: Kösel, Miller, Stumpf. Also: Middlebrook, 154–55, 165; Hans-Dietrich Nicolaisen, *Die Flakhelfer. Luftwaffen- und Marinehelfer im zweiten Weltkrieg* (Berlin: Ullstein, 1981); ibid., *Gruppenfeuer und Sal ventakt*, vols. I and II (Büsum: Selbstverlag, 1993).

37. Oberkommando des Heeres (Berlin) to Stellvertretende General Kommandos X-XIII, XVI, XVIII, XX, XXI, 4 August 1941, *N.A.*, roll 349; Stammfuehrer Brandl (Augsburg) to Oberstleutnant Hartung (Munich), 13 April 1943, National Archives microfilm series T580, roll 349.

38. "Geheimer Lagerbericht des Sicherheitsdienst der SS," March 1944, quoted in Holmsten, 380–81. Also Bernd-a. Rusinek, "Desintegration und gesteigerter Zwang. Die Chaotisierung der Lebensverhältnisse in den Großstädten 1944/45 und der Mythos der Ehrenfelder Gruppe," in Wilfried Breyvogel, ed., *Piraten, Swings und Junge Garde. Jugendwiederstand im Nationalsozialismus* (Bonn: Dietz Verlag, 1991), 271–94.

39. Holmsten, 382.

40. Studnitz, 194–97.

41. Heinz Hermann Krüger, "Geschichte und Perspektive der Jugendforschung—historische Entwicklungslinien und Bezugspunkte für eine theoretische und methodische Neuorientierung," in Krüger, ed., *Handbuch der*

Jugendforschung (Opladen: Leske & Budrich, 1993), 17–30. See also: Eduard Spranger, *Psychologie des Jugendalters* (Heidelberg: Quelle & Meyer, 1924).

42. Krüger, 17–18; Siegfried Bernfeld, *Trieb und Tradition im Jugendalter: kulturpsychologische Studien an Tagebüchern* (Leipzig: J.A. Barth, 1931); Charlotte Bühler, *Das Seelenleben des Jugendlichen*, 6ᵗʰ ed. (Stuttgart: G. Fischer, 1967).

43. Throughout the nineteenth and early twentieth centuries, most German historians left analysis of oral accounts to anthropologists and folklorists.

44. Alf Lüdtke, *History of Everyday Life* (Princeton: Princeton University Press, 1995); Lutz Niethammer, ed., *"Die Jahre weiss man nicht, wo man die heute hinsetzen soll": Faschismuserfahrungen im Ruhrgebiet* (Bonn: Dietz Verlag, 1983); Lutz Niethammer, Alexander von Plato, and Dorothee Wierling, *Die Volkseigene Erfahrung: Eine Archäologie des Lebens in der Industrieprovinz der DDR* (Berlin: Rowohlt, 1991); Karl-Heinz Huber, *Jugend unterm Hakenkreuz* (Berlin: Verlag Ullstein, 1982).

45. Thompson (2000), 265. See also: John Bodnar, "Reworking Reality: Oral Histories and the Meaning of the Polish Immigrant Experience," in Ronald J. Grele, ed., *International Annual of Oral History, 1990* (New York: Greenwood Press, 1990), 57–68; Jenny Gregory, "Deconstructing Childhood Memories of Class," in ibid., 107–121; Erika Hoerning, "Memories of the Berlin Wall," *International Journal of Oral History* 8/2 (1987): 95–111; Gabriele Rosenthal, "May 6, 1945: The Biographical Meaning of an Historical Event," *International Journal of Oral History* 10/3 (November 1989), 183–93; Dorothee Wierling, "A German Generation of Reconstruction: The Children of the Weimar Republic in the GDR," in Luisa Passerini, ed., *Memory and Totalitarianism: International Yearbook of Oral History and Life Stories*, vol. 1 (New York: Oxford University Press, 1992), 71–88; Reinhard Sieder, "A Hitler Youth from a Respectable Family: The Narrative Composition and Deconstruction of a Life Story," *International Yearbook of Oral History and Life Stories*, vol. 2 (New York: Oxford University Press, 1993).

46. See Rosenthal (1989).

47. In psychology, these questions fall under the heading of "autobiographical memory," to distinguish from obviously overlapping studies of short-term memory and cognitive learning. Two good introductions to issues, methods, and theories: Martin A. Conway, *Autobiographical Memory: An Introduction* (Philadelphia: Open University Press, 1990); A.D. Baddeley, "What is Autobiographical Memory," in Conway, Rubin, Spinnler, and Wagenaar, eds., *Theoretical Perspectives on Autobiographical Memory* (Boston: Kluwer Academic Publishers, 1992), 13–29.

48. Janice L. Howes and Albert N. Katz, "Remote Memory: Recalling Autobiographical and Public Events from across the Lifespan," *Canadian Journal of Psychology* 1992 46(1): 92–116. Also: L.R. Berney and D.B. Blane, "Collecting Retrospective Data: Accuracy of Recall after 50 Years Judged Against Historical Records," in *Social Science Medicine* 1997 (10)1519–25; Jerome Bruner, "The Remembered Self," in Neisser and Fivush (1994), Ch. 3; Greg J. Neimeyer and April E. Metzler, "Personal Identity and Autobiographical Recall," in Neisser and Fivush, Ch. 6; Martin A. Conway, "A Structural Model of Autobiographical Memory," in *Theoretical Perspectives on Autobiographical Memory* (Boston: Kluwer Academic Publishers, 1992); Ulric Neisser, "Self Narratives: True and False," in Neisser and Fivush, Ch. 1; Michael Ross and Roger Buehler, "Creative Remembering," in ibid., Ch. 11.

49. Ashok Jansari and Alan J. Parkin, "Things That Go Bump in Your Life: Explaining the Reminiscence Bump in Autobiographical Memory," in *Psychology and Aging* 1996 11(31): 85–91; Howard Schuman and Jacqueline Scott, "Generations and Collective Memories," in *American Sociological Review* 1989 54(June): 359–81; Howard Schuman,

Cheryl Rieger, and Vladas Gaidys, "Collective Memories in the United States and Lithuania," in Norbert Schwarz and Seymour Sudman, eds., *Autobiographical memory and the validity of retrospective reports* (New York: Springer Verlag, 1994); Martin Conway, *Autobiographical Memory:: An Introduction* (1990), 39–41.

50. Peter Alter, "Das Nationalbewußtsein der Deutschen: Entwicklungslinien und Anfragen," in Werner Weidenfeld, *Geschichtsbewußtsein der Deutschen* (Cologne: Verlag Wissenschaft und Politik, 1987), 97–110; John Breuilly, *The State of Germany* (London: Longman, 1992); Mary Fulbrook, *German National Identity after the Holocaust* (Cambridge: Polity Press, 1999), Ch. 3; Jarausch, ed., *After Unity: Reconfiguring German Identities* (Providence: Berghahn, 1998). See also: *Restructuring Our Lives: National Unification and German Biographies, Oral History Review* 21/2 (Winter 1993). The issue includes contributions by Lutz Niethammer, Dorothee Wierling, Jurgen Lemke, Alexander von Plato, and John Bornemann.

2

From *wir* to *ich*:
Roots of Postwar Initiatives

Just as Berliners' memories of childhood and youth blurred the onset of wartime experience, so too did they obscure its conclusion. This doesn't mean that interviewees believed the end of World War II was unimportant. Far from it. Looking back with contemporary understanding of Hitler's goals and methods, they asserted the necessity of Nazism's defeat. However, while 8 May 1945 was, and is, celebrated as V-E Day, this date commemorates a *military* victory, but not necessarily an experiential turning point for individuals or cohorts. In fact, interviewees very rarely acknowledged a sudden, meteoric *Stunde Null* associated with 8 May or any other specific date. Rather, much as they recalled 1 September 1939 within the context of a long gradual descent from a "normal" childhood into a dangerous, fear-filled youth, cohort members included war's end in their memories of an extended *Tiefpunkt* defined by personal insecurity and social chaos.

"DAS ENDLOSE ENDE"

The collapse of what this cohort recalled as National Socialist "normalcy" began gradually with school closings, temporary relocation, and devastating air raids in 1943. By late 1944, however, few, if any, Berliners could deny the war's devastating effects on daily life. Most of the 3–3.5 million city residents (down from about 4.3 million before the war) had been bombed out of their homes at least once, some multiple times. Six of eight electrical power plants had been damaged, and a worsening coal shortage closed many businesses, depriving Berliners of both work and warmth.   By late January 1945, the *Reichsbahn* stopped delivering food and fuel to Berlin, and canceled local train service that linked residents to the farmers and villagers with whom they bartered for extra food. If Hitler's return on 16 January demonstrated his intent to hold Berlin at all costs, the throngs of refugees fleeing westward through the city suggested the probable outcome of any attempt to stop the advancing Red Army.

Among the thousands of Germans flooding Berlin's rail stations and feeding local rumor mills were young RAD conscripts and *Wehrmachthelfer*, as well as entire trainloads of school-aged KLV evacuees.   Herr Winkert, for example, spent fourteen days traveling from a KLV camp in Poland to Dresden.   Like other accounts of this time period, Winkert's memories of the trip westward highlighted his realization that Nazi society had essentially collapsed.

Our [flight from the Russians] began, in open freight cars in January. January 45 was very, very cold, and there we were heading west in these open trains. Each of us had a blanket, and we slept three or four together, all our blankets piled on top.   Otherwise we would've frozen to death. Along the way we got food from the Red Cross at train stations, but sometimes we just sucked on bread and margarine, frozen solid. I was badly frostbitten on my hands and feet [and] saw terrible things like mothers with frozen babies. [1]

On 3 February 1945, in the midst of this onslaught of frozen and hungry refugees, the USAF pummeled Berlin in the most devastating daytime raid to date. American bombers met almost no resistance and inflicted more than 2,600 casualties in less than an hour. Today, more than fifty years later, the attack stands out in many Berliners' minds for several reasons, most notably the particularly high death toll, which can be attributed to both the size of the raid (900 bombers and 600 fighter planes) and the throngs of refugees unable to find air raid shelters.[2]   Firefighters could no longer control blazes started by incendiary bombs, and the attack crippled public transportation in a city that had long prided itself on rapidly restoring service after earlier attacks. Finally, this raid is remembered as a turning point; although Soviet forces would not reach Berlin until April, the attacks of 3 February commenced a period of intense bombing meant to soften defenses for Soviet ground forces.   Between 21 February and 19 April 1945, the RAF directed thirty-six night attacks against Berlin, while the USAF continued the air assault during daylight hours, further straining the nerves of exhausted residents.[3]

Between air raids, local *Volkssturm* units reinforced military installations around Berlin. Neither Hitler nor the High Army Command had ever developed cohesive plans for Berlin's defense; two outer rings of protection, the furthest about thirty kilometers outside the city, consisted of little more than long trenches protected by occasional machine guns nests.[4] In the city itself, several enormous flak towers were meant to defend strategic points and provide shelter for local civilians.[5] In early 1945, *Volkssturm* troops, local residents and foreign laborers were ordered to reinforce both the outer rings and inner-city defenses. Lacking building supplies, trained engineers, and weapons, however, these conscripted laborers must have wondered if their efforts would slow, let alone stop, Soviet tanks.

Defying the obvious material deficiencies, Nazi officials offered increasingly fiery rhetoric and aggressive decrees, commanding Berliners to sacrifice themselves for *Führer und Vaterland*. Rather than lament the army's recent defeats, residents were told to use imagination and ingenuity to protect their homes from the barbarian invasion. The film *Kolberg* (depicting a battle between Pommerian volunteers and Napoleon's forces) opened in Berlin cinemas on 30 January and offered a similar message: fight to the death.[6] Reinforcing such attempts to assert German perseverance and superiority, radio and newspaper reports predicted the imminent deployment of victory-assuring secret weapons. At the same time, many Berliners found leaflets recruiting them for the new "German Freedom Movement Werewolf," whose members would continue the war even after formal capitulation.[7]

The regime's most successful propaganda campaigns underscored the supposed inhumanity of the Soviet military. Although the Red Army included not only under-supplied, ill-trained draftees but also well-disciplined professional soldiers, Nazi media depicted only one type: a bloodthirsty, uneducated beast.[8] Hitler's final war directive of 15 April 1945 warned Berliners to expect execution, deportation to hard labor camps, or sexual enslavement after the Russian arrival. Such statements only reinforced rumors of torture and rape spread by refugees from the eastern territories. Together with ingrained collective memories of past threats from the East, these stories terrified young and old alike.

We just sat there and waited to see what would happen. . . . Don't forget, we were all terribly afraid of the Russians. I remember as a child . . . there was an exhibit at the store, how the Russians murder their mothers and so forth. It was really bad, we were totally riled up and thought, they'll come, the Bolshevists with their knives and . . . well, everyone knows the story.[9]

Coming to terms with their fears, many cohort members also struggled to reconcile the tenets of Nazi socialization with recent experiences. This was particularly true for youths drafted for service in the *Reichwehr*, *Volkssturm*, or RAD. On the one hand, peer pressure, fear of local authorities, and the long-glorified image of a heroic death all worked to keep young draftees at their posts; Nazi socialization, after all, had only reinforced a natural adolescent desire to prove oneself, to fit in, and to shun those who didn't. On the other hand, young recruits also saw increasing evidence of the regime's imminent demise. The undefeatable *Reichwehr*, for example, suddenly seemed unable to stop the uncivilized Russian forces. In Berlin, even around-the-clock repair work could not overcome the damage wreaked by Allied bombers, while shortages increased, and the long-promised secret weapons failed to materialize.

Such irrefutable evidence must have raised questions about the regime's invincibility. However, although desertion rates rose during the last months of the war (despite the establishment of roaming trial and execution squads), few Germans acknowledged their doubts in public. Even looking back, cohort members rarely noted signs of societal collapse and seldom correlated personal memories with chronological accounts of the Battle of Berlin. Instead, interviewees described one or two vivid moments that exemplified their *Endkampf* experiences. To some extent, this narrative strategy simply reflects the chaotic nature of daily life in spring 1945. By the time Soviet troops reached Berlin's eastern suburbs on 22 April, most residents had turned inward, hoping to assure their own survival. Huddled in cellars or public shelters, they learned of Soviet advances from deserters, combatants, or perhaps an occasional BBC radio broadcast. The most reliable indicators of local conditions, however, were sounds coming from street level or the reports of neighbors who had ventured out to assuage thirst, curiosity, or claustrophobia.

They were shooting night and day, not the air raids, they had already destroyed everything, but the Russians, marching in from the East. We had no more water, one could dash out when it let up a bit, but even then people were hit by grenades. [The shooting] got so strong that we just stayed in the cellar; then suddenly it stopped, and we knew, now they're here, they've taken such and such street.[10]

After the war, such individualized, piecemeal knowledge of the *Endkampf* was reshaped in a variety of ways. Beginning already in May 1945, societal pressures, political developments, and evolving postwar identities transformed young Berliners' experiences of "the endless end" (*das endlose Ende*) into remarkably standardized key moments. These *Schlüßelerlebnise* rarely corresponded with the V-E Day noted in political histories of the war.

PERSONAL TURNING POINTS

In 1946, Prenzlauer Berg's schoolchildren were instructed to write essays responding to the theme "The Last Days of the War." Not surprisingly, most wrote about their own losses and/or their first encounters with Soviet soldiers. Many describe a sudden reorientation, a simultaneous realization that the war was lost and that the Nazi regime was evil. "It dawned on us," wrote Werner Richter. "We had been terribly betrayed. Now we saw that the Russians are people too."[11] Similar references to a sudden awareness of the Russians' humanity punctuated many of the pupils' compositions. In part, this reflects the circumstances in which they were written; Prenzlauer Berg fell into the Soviet sector, and local communists worked hard to convince Berliners they had been liberated by sympathetic forces. A year later, the pupils knew their audience, and most likely tried (intentionally or otherwise) to correlate their experiences with authorities' expectations. In addition, however, the essays suggest the significance of prior context; given the graphic anti-Russian propaganda of the Nazi era, any sign of civility from the conquerors would have left a lasting impression on young Germans.

The tone of these schoolchildren's 1946 essays finds partial resonance in the narratives offered by cohort members in the 1990s. Some East Berliners did echo the pupils' surprised and thankful reactions to Soviet occupation, remembering that their worst fears quickly subsided after receiving food or protection from a Russian soldier. However, interviewees only rarely described a precise moment when the guns stopped or the lights came back on. Frau Kanter, an East Berliner, did recall that in late April, her mother finally began burning the children's long-hoarded first communion candles. "Just as the last stub burned out," she noted, "the war was over."[12] Unlike the typical essayist, however, Kanter did not associate this key moment with an attitudinal reorientation on her part.   Instead, the chronological details of the *Endkampf* faded behind the theme of an ongoing struggle (before, during, and after the war) to live as a faithful Catholic.

This failure to associate the *Endkampf* with an ideological reorientation typified interviewees' accounts and set them apart from the Prenzlauer Berg essayists.   Instead, most highlighted similarly significant turning points from well *before* capitulation.   Contrary to what the essays and psychological theory suggest, interviewees did not reframe personal accounts to accord with generalized depictions of *Stunde Null.*[13]   Instead, they asserted distance from scholarly or media accounts of the war, pointing to *Schlüßelerlebnsße* that emphasize a sudden assertion of personal initiative weeks—or even months—*before* Germany's defeat.

Sisters Frau Pastler and Frau Barthe offered a dramatic example of this preemptive personal turning point as they recalled losing their mother, their home, and virtually all they owned on 3 February 1945.   Like many of her peers, Barthe had been drafted into the RAD some months before, and was working on a farm in western Prussia.   The younger Pastler had enrolled in technical training and lived with her parents in Berlin-Kreuzberg.   She described the day quite vividly.

[We] lived in the *Brandenburgstrasse* (today *Lübeckstraße*), and I went to school, studying technical drawing.   There had been a pretty large raid the evening, the night before, and so I had slept a bit late that morning.   I said to my mother—she was standing up on a chair taking down the black-out curtains—I said "Bye, I have to go." And she said, "go on, otherwise you'll be late."   And as I closed the door behind me, it was quite odd, a voice in my head said, *you forgot to kiss your mother*.   It was very strange, and I told a friend about it at school. . . . We were in school, and then all of a sudden air raid sirens.   There was a shelter in our school but we went to the big underground bunker at *Bahnhof Gesundbrunnen*.   It went on forever [lit: *Das war ein endlose Ende*]; we just wandered from room to room, people poured in, we just kept walking around, benches everywhere and then we found a place to sit. . . .   Afterwards, about 11 o'clock, our teacher said no [trains] were running and we should somehow get ourselves home. . . . So we walked towards *Alexanderplatz* and there was another alarm, and we went into a bunker. . . . I spent the night at my friend's house.   There was another alarm that night, back to the bunker, it was pretty heavy.   And then Sunday morning, we got up early and they offered me breakfast but I couldn't eat, I was worried.   I walked home, well, not home. . . . A policeman stood [at the corner], the whole street was just rubble, and I said, "I live here, I want to go home."   He [looked at me]: "There's nobody there, it's all destroyed."[14]

Pastler reacted to this news by frantically searching local shelters until she found a neighbor who had witnessed her mother's death.   Only later did she learn that her father had survived the attack, having spent the night on *Luftschutz* duty at work.   Barthe's RAD group, meanwhile, had just evacuated their workcamp. Following orders, Barthe had left all her belongings behind (pending shipment on a later transport), and fled the advancing Red Army, first on foot and later by train.   Along the way, she heard rumors—presumably from soldiers and other refugees—of a heavy raid in her neighborhood, but had little access to reliable information.   Substantiated news of the raid eventually reached her in an overcrowded RAD barracks in Mecklenberg.

We heard that everything had been destroyed in Kreuzberg, around the *Moritzplatz*, and I said, "*Mensch*, then I've been bombed out! I live there!" And all my things left in Prussia, they were never picked up; the Russians were already there—must have been happy to find all we'd packed up for them! . . . And then I just waited and finally the telegram came, the mail took forever, of course, and I got the news [that] Mother died in the rubble. I just couldn't believe it. The others wanted to comfort me and told me to lie down. . . . I said, "I can't do that, can't be alone, tell me something funny. I need to be distracted, I can't dwell on it or I'll go crazy." It took about a week [for the paperwork to go through] and then I was discharged from the *Arbeitsdienst*, and came home. . . . And then we cried.[15]

Through their mother's death, the two girls were reunited. Barthe recalled refusing to grieve until she returned to Berlin. Over the next several years, the sisters were virtually inseparable, relying on one another for advice and support. Neither Barthe nor Pastler offered details about their relationship with their widowed father, noting only that he slept at work after being bombed out and that they made most important decisions independently.

After struggling to find a room in war-torn Berlin, Barthe and Pastler left the city, seeking temporary refuge with an aunt in Mecklenberg. During the last weeks of the war, the aunt's family fed and clothed the homeless girls, and also hid them from several bands of drunken Red Army troops. Barthe and Pastler recognized their relatives' sacrifices, but both women highlighted their country cousins' inability to empathize with their losses. Describing their arrival, Pastler remembered their aunt's less-than-heartwarming greeting, "Well, so there you are with your *Pappkarton*." These words seemed to set the tone for the remainder of the young Berliners' extended visit; interviewed separately, both women noted the lack of warmth and graciousness in their relatives' hospitality. Pastler was particularly annoyed when the comparatively well-off Mecklenburgers began stealing from the Soviet occupation forces, who ordered the village women to alter cast-off German uniforms for their own ill-equipped soldiers.

We sat in a circle, those who didn't have sewing machines, and had to cut and finish buttonholes and sew on buttons. The way we did it, phh, it was good enough for *them*, crooked, and then set the buttonhole with a few stitches, that was good enough, three stitches for a button, the main thing was to get lots done. . . . And then we started, we noticed that some women took a pair of pants with them sometimes. . . . My sister said, "they're all stealing and haven't lost a thing and we have nothing; we'll take a pair of pants for our father. . . . And what happens? *We* get caught." I thought we'd go crazy because the translator, he, well, it was said they'd do house searches all over and such. We were so scared, couldn't tell my aunt and uncle, because we were scared of them too. We couldn't eat and couldn't sleep, we were at our wits end, my goodness, it's us they catch and everyone else, who haven't lost a thing, and so on and so forth. . . . And [the neighbors] all said, "let them conduct their searches, I have nothing," even though we knew they actually had taken things. Everyone did. And after the Russians left, we saw, they were all running around in khaki and things made from parachutes, parachute silk. Suddenly everyone had white blouses from parachute silk. And out of the supply parachutes—they were red—suddenly everyone was wearing red skirts. We said, "it's nuts, they look at us like we're thieves, and they themselves took things!" Once, my cousin came home with a huge packet of thick packing string, and his wife knit sweaters from it. And my aunt said "you girls, you're so stupid. You don't have sweaters either, you could get some too, go down there tomorrow morning around five, to the train station. There's a car of it." And there were lots of these packets, wrapped up in paper . . . and down at the end a little fire where the Russians were sitting. We hid behind a tree and I said, "Come on, I can't do it." And my sister, "Wait, wait til he's gone, I'll get it. And as [the patrol] reached the other end, she grabbed a packet and we ran up the street. . . . At any rate, we got home, now we had a packet too, now we could knit ourselves sweaters. So we unwrapped it, took off the paper, and we had cording. Besides the twine, there were these simple thick cords. We got the wrong package. And we said, we'll just make pullovers out of cording. And they just about laughed themselves sick, my aunt said "you're even too stupid to steal!" But it wasn't funny to us. And I said, that's it, "I won't take it any more." And anyway, we were homesick, we really were.[16]

Looking back, Pastler did see the humor in the incident. Nonetheless, it reemphasized the Mecklenburgers' selfishness and unsympathetic hospitality. Such encounters fueled Pastler's decision to return to Berlin in August 1945. This step apparently shocked the aunt and uncle into waiting all night with her at the train station, but otherwise didn't change their frugal habits. Pastler recalls that her stingy aunt "packed just a bit of oatmeal and bacon in my backpack, so that 'when you find your father he has a bit to eat.' I mean, she could've given me, they were always slaughtering, and really could've spared me a lot more. But they were very miserly in that respect."[17]

The Berliners' depiction of their aunt's indifference stood in sharp contrast to what Pastler suggested was a close relationship with their mother. After the 3 Febuary air raid, the sisters' family—even their own father, who couldn't even find them a place to live—seemed to leave them to their own devices. This sudden, very concrete sense of being left alone typifies interviewees' wartime turning points. Prior to the air raid, the girls looked to authority figures—parents, teachers, and RAD leaders—who both regulated daily life and provided basic necessities. After this episode, however, both sisters highlighted their joint independence. Barthe resigned from the RAD, Pastler quit school, and, having been disappointed by their relatives, the girls took personal responsibility for their own lives.

The theme of self-sufficiency and independence persisted through the women's accounts of later developments. Ignoring their aunt's advice, both women returned to Berlin in late summer 1945, finding material conditions decidedly worse than on the farm. New postwar regulations meant that although the younger Pastler (legally a dependant minor of her father) could reclaim her Berlin domicile, Barthe was no longer considered a legal resident. She was eligible for neither employment nor ration coupons, so with nothing to barter, the sisters lived on a single ration card for some months until they managed to secure Barthe's legal status. In short, the air raid compelled the sisters to make an abrupt shift from dependence on the guidance of trusted adults and authoritarian regulations to active autonomy.

Clearly, the unexpected, violent death of a parent marks a particularly momentous turning point. That said, other cohort members attributed similar long-term significance to less serious events. Already by early 1945, well before capitulation, young Berliners had begun shedding Nazi-era identities and beliefs.

Herr Rennebach, drafted into the *Wehrmacht* in 1944, offered another example of such precapitulation turning points. Rennebach served for about ten weeks before using personal charisma—and luck—to secure a discharge. Although RJF regulations prohibited such fraternization, Rennebach described chatting and flirting with older girls who worked as military nursing aids. This pleasant pastime, he soon discovered, could have practical repercussions. While plotting how to leave his unit, he found himself unexpectedly dismissed, and only later noticed that his travel documents and discharge papers had been signed not by an officer, but by one of his former heartthrobs in the *Kriegshilfsdienst*.

At face value, Rennebach's dismissal shares little in common with Barthe and Pastler's tragic loss. Both episodes, however, were recalled as significant turning points. Like the sisters, Rennebach described himself as a member (willing or not) of Nazi society, a youth who essentially played by the rules. The circumstances of his discharge, however, taught him the value of personal connections. Through the rest of the interview, Rennebach highlighted his charismatic abilities, repeatedly noting how he mitigated punishment and won favors by charming influential women and public authorities.[18]

Although Rennebach's young admirer may have forged discharge papers for many soldiers, Rennebach himself had not taken any active steps toward desertion. He had contemplated going home, and when the opportunity arose, he made the most of it. This too is typical of cohort members' precapitulation turning points; interviewees rarely, if ever, described consciously seeking ways to assert independence. Wartime experiences, however, had taught them to seize windows of opportunity; finding themselves isolated, literally or figuratively, they distanced themselves from the past, asserted personal autonomy, and took responsibility for their future.

In the spring of 1945, Herr Winkert seemed to leap at the unexpected chance to shape his own destiny. He described himself as a rather unsuccessful HJler, physically weaker than other boys and emotionally immature. Nonetheless, he was drafted into an HJ *Panzervernichtungseinheit*, and spent several weeks on patrol duty. One afternoon, a lookout spotted Soviet troops marching down a nearby road. Following orders, Winkert and the other boys scrambled into the bushes to change from their military uniforms into the less incriminating HJ shorts. Winkert smiled as he recalled what happened next.

I came back out of the bushes onto the path and *none* of my buddies were anywhere to be seen. Not one! I was completely alone. So I walked along, all by myself . . . and came to a Russian putting up signposts. He showed me a sign, with the Cyrillic letters [spelling out Berlin] and I followed those signs. . . . I joined up with *Wehrmacht* soldiers at first, but that was no good, they were all taken prisoner. So I went on by myself, mostly at night. And there were so many women and children with wheelbarrows and such, they saw me as their protector, in a way, although I was just a child. I stole a bicycle and then another, it had no tires and broke.[19]

At first, Winkert was shocked—for the first time in months, he was suddenly "completely alone" in what appeared to be hostile territory. After getting directions from the enemy, he set out for home, traveling alone to avoid being associated with the *Wehrmacht*. En route to Berlin, Winkert was surprised to discover a group of officers and nurses quietly waiting out the war in a rural castle, but decided to focus on his own survival; after accepting food and medical care, he stole one of their bicycles. Later, Winkert even disproved the Nazis' anti-Russian rhetoric. Having fallen asleep in what he thought was an empty barn, he woke to discover an exhausted Soviet soldier snoring peacefully nearby.

Like Barthe, Pastler, and Rennebach, Winkert recounted his final encounters with Nazi structures as a personal turning point, distanced from the broader historical context. Winkert's three-week odyssey through contested countryside helped him shed the *Hammerkind* role he had played in the Hitler Youth. Despite prior failures, he had proven his resourcefulness and self-sufficiency. Like his peers, Winkert highlighted this autonomy in later portions of his narrative. Thanks to his newly acquired self-confidence, for example, he once staunchly strode into a Soviet officer's headquarters to demand (albeit unsuccessfully) the return of a stolen suitcase.

KLV evacuees also described similar personal turning points, as demonstrated by Herr Zelle's memories of 1944–1945. Zelle, along with some 500 other young Berliners, had been evacuated to a KLV camp near the Polish town of Kalisch. As advancing Soviet tanks and artillery approached in January 1945, all five hundred children were crowded onto the last train headed westward. According to Zelle, neither Hitler Youth leaders nor their adult chaperones knew where they were going, and the young evacuees found themselves being shuttled around from one crowded town to the next. Finally, he recalled,

We were unloaded in Chemnitz on 21 January and taken first to a local inn. . . And then I was taken to a private home, and we were ordered to report to school every day. But that didn't last long, and the air attacks started, in the night of 14–15 February on Chemnitz. . . . And conditions kept getting worse in Chemnitz, due to the continuous air raids, and so the Berlin children from these four schools were rounded up again . . . and were shipped on further towards Plauen. Then they were split up and our bunch—125 or 130 kids—was broken off and housed . . . in a village by Hölßnitz.[20]

In the confusion of this second relocation, Zelle had been left behind. Unwilling to take responsibility for his care, officials in Chemnitz put him on yet another train. After following "assorted adventuresome paths," he rejoined his schoolmates in yet another makeshift evacuation camp.

That didn't last long, until the beginning or middle of March . . . we heard the front coming closer and closer, the German troops kept retreating further. . . . I got together with a classmate, who lived on the same street in [Berlin]-Friedrichshain, and we said we have to get home. . . . We did get some support, not from the teachers, of course . . . but our nurse who had accompanied us from the camp in Kalisch and was also responsible for things like ration cards and so forth . . . she let a few so-called *Reisemarken* [travel ration cards] fall into our hands. And so we took off. So, and in this way, with all kinds of adventures, along the destroyed train tracks and using all kinds of tricks, I made it back to Berlin.[21]

Zelle's memories of his two-day trek through the contested countryside paralleled Winkert's recollections in many ways. After months of accepting others' authority, each boy abruptly abandoned the regulated lifestyle and collective mentality fostered by the Hitler Youth and other National Socialist programs. Like Barthe and Pastler, they downplayed any adult assistance; in this case, the camp nurse didn't "give" Zelle the ration coupons, but, as he said, "let them fall into our hands."

Beyond suggesting a pattern of precapitulation turning points, the narrative styles of these stories raised interesting questions about gender patterning in memory construction. Was it only coincidence that both Zelle and Winkert highlighted excitement and adventure, revealing no sense of fear, doubt, or loneliness? Had all those stories of HJlers overcoming danger and self-doubt inadvertently prepared these boys to cope with Germany's defeat? Although a similar emphasis on personal responsibility punctuates Barthe and Pastler's narratives as well, the women, trained to serve the Reich in a protected domestic sphere, had different expectations. They sought a substitute family in Mecklenburg, and recalled considerable surprise and dismay at their relatives' callousness. That said, both men and women recalled rising to the occasion, successfully meeting immediate personal needs with minimal outside assistance. In the process, they seemed to forge new perceptions of themselves and their capabilities.

In grammatical terms, many personal turning point stories were characterized by an accompanying narrative voice shift. Interviewees typically spoke in the collective "we" or anonymous "one" (lit. *wir* or *man*) when describing earlier experiences. Most switched to the first person singular "I" (*ich*), however, when recalling the postwar period, and the shift seemed to correspond with this particular key moment. In some cases, of course, young people (such as Winkert) did find themselves literally alone, abruptly torn from what one former participant called the *brutale Kindergesellschaft* of the HJ, RAD, or KLV. Pastler and Barthe had perhaps even more reason to emphasize their loneliness and isolation after their mother died.

As part of a retrospective narrative, however, the coordination of a personal turning point story and a narrative voice shift may also be a strategy to downplay associations with the Nazi regime. While highlighting—and quite inaccurately, in most cases—their childlike passivity and lack of culpability under Hitler, they used this key moment to demonstrate a sudden appropriation of agency before the regime actually fell. As will be seen in the next chapter, this new "*ich*" took calculated risks, made difficult decisions, and accepted personal responsibility. Furthermore, such assertion of personal agency proved to be a central theme of interviewees' postwar narratives.[22]

The same assertion of agency suggested by a narrative voice shift is substantiated by a less pervasive but still observable change in how cohort members speak about their parents. As social historians have frequently observed, German fathers (and fathers in other western cultures as well) were typically less involved in their children's daily lives before the sexual revolution of the 1960s, while mothers figure quite predominantly in recollections of childhood. These distant fathers often became even more isolated during World War II, through military service, longer working hours, or simply the emotional toll of trying to provide for and protect a family in a war zone.

Following this model, interviewees often credited their mothers with great fortitude during the war. This changes, however, after capitulation. Despite the pervasive image of the *Trümmerfrau* (a woman who cleared rubble and salvaged reusable bricks) in historical accounts of postwar life, interviewees often depicted their mothers as suddenly physically and psychologically drained. In reality, of course, the end of the war did not free mothers from any of their earlier responsibilities, and Berlin's food and housing crisis actually worsened after capitulation. Mothers often remained both sole breadwinner and head of household for months, if not permanently. Still, the assertion of youthful autonomy seems to push these women into the background, contradicting the popular imagery. Winkert, for example, insisted that "I did everything myself," only reluctantly recognizing that his mother had in fact done much to ensure his postwar education.

Both the voice shift and memories of a suddenly less influential mother figure reflect in part simply the maturation process of a cohort moving through adolescence, rejecting values previously taken for granted, and distancing oneself from parental authority. However, the voice shift also challenged postwar scholars and social workers, who believed a blind group mentality was one of the longer-surviving tenets of Nazism. Cohort members' narratives suggest that this enforced cohesion was one of the first aspects of Nazism to be abandoned.

Seen in this light, the voice shift may also constitute an attempt, conscious or unconscious, to come to terms with the Nazi past. Individual responsibility, and even the possibility of personal initiative under Nazi rule, is ameliorated by the use of "*man.*" Shifting to the "*ich,*" particularly if linked to a personal experience that occurred before 8 May 1945, allows cohort members to distance themselves from the regime, implying that even if they had been socialized by Nazism, they came to their senses before defeat had actually occurred. Using these personal turning point stories to mark the end of parental authority in their lives may even help some interviewees avoid discussing a parent's implication in the Nazi system. More generally, it suggests an attempt, experienced or remembered, to distance themselves from a generation that brought Hitler to power. Cohort members' recollections of personal turning points support a collective identity built on a relatively passive *reception*, but active *transcendence*, of the Nazi legacy.

Less apparent were strategies through which cohort members came to terms with a theme found in virtually all descriptions—personal, popular or scholarly—of Berlin in 1945: rape. The sexual abuse of German women by Soviet soldiers has become part of the collective memory of World War II for both male and female Berliners, and while I never directly raised the issue, nearly all interviewees alluded to rape. Some described hiding places and schemes to protect young women. Others detailed their own experiences at the hands of Russian soldiers. Frau Miller and her younger sister, for example, were living in their family's small garden house when Russian troops arrived.

My father had built boxes for the china, but on March 18, the day we were bombed out, my mother had unpacked it all because company was coming. So it was all destroyed and we had these boxes and [my sister and I] were laid in them, with the mattresses on top, and there we were. . . . [The Russians] came and said "You hiding soldiers," and wanted to shoot into the boxes. My mother screamed and they pulled out my sister, looking awful of course. . . she let out such awful sounds and went and sat in the outhouse making grotesque faces. . . my father said [to the soldiers] she had gone crazy in the war. And then they pulled me out, I had just gotten the cast off my arm, it was thin and hairy and wrinkled. . . they took one look and got scared. . . . They didn't do anything to *us*, but my mother.[23]

Experiencing or witnessing violent sexual assault obviously reinforced collective images and rumors. However, even cohort members who neither saw nor were threatened with physical abuse talked about rape. Their recollections suggested that this theme, like the turning point stories, served several functions in personal narratives. First, accounts of rape graphically illustrate the fear and insecurity felt by cohort members at the time, emotions that were otherwise brushed over, particularly by men.

Second, memories of rape, whether rumored, feared, or experienced, blurred the experiential boundary between war and occupation. Fear of marauding Russians—and to a lesser extent, black Americans—had been promoted by the Nazi propaganda machine. Formal capitulation, however, did not immediately reduce the danger. On the contrary, most assaults occurred in the four to six weeks *after* Berlin fell to Soviet forces.[24]

Third, some cohort members used the rape theme to introduce a very different image of the Red Army. On the one hand, Soviet soldiers raped women and girls, deported men and boys, and stole radios, jewelry, and bicycles. On the other hand, they were also characterized as *kinderlieb*. If young Berliners could disguise themselves as children, they had nothing to fear from the Russians. In this context, Winkert, again noting his physical immaturity, explained, "They never did anything to me. They really love children, they're not monsters."

This image of the kindly, liberating Russian was later cultivated by the East German state, as German communists sought to win support for their close ties to Moscow.[25] It also turned up, however, in West Berliners' narratives. Herr Bistop, for example, believed the Russians' infatuation with children protected him during a series of "awkward encounters" with officials. The fifteen-year-old had received a legitimate medical discharge from the local *Volkssturm*, but was compelled by his mother to don an old pair of *Lederhosen* when Russian soldiers entered the neighborhood. Bistop found the clothes childish, but believed his appearance, accentuated by malnutrition, saved him from deportation to the Soviet Union.[26]

Despite the similarities, cohort members' memories of rape also demonstrated the impact of forty years of divided experience. Most notably, East Berliners more often sought to explain or empathize with the soldiers' actions. Beyond offering examples of good Russians, some, such as Birkmann, envisioned themselves in similar scenarios.

It's clear that if I, a Soviet soldier, had just fought my way through [eastern Europe] I saw what the Germans had done. And the officers of course had to encourage their men crossing the border—besides the fact that they had Mongols among them, from villages and these tribes where a man shows his hospitality by offering his wife to his guests. Well, and then you attack, your buddy is dead, you've not had a woman for months, and well, men do have sexual urges.[27]

While certainly not implying that East Berliners tolerated sexual aggression, Birkmann's statement suggests how collective and official depictions of *Stunde Null* may have influenced personal recollections of defeat and occupation. East German officials strove to depict Soviet soldiers as benevolent liberators, not vengeful conquerors. Forty years of state-sponsored German-Soviet friendship leagues and cultural exchanges may also have informed individual and collective narratives of the war's end. In contrast, West Berliners' images of barbaric Russians found confirmation in Cold War-era rhetoric, which only reinforced preexisting anti-Soviet stereotypes.[28]

Not all interviewees followed these typical narrative strategies. Some, such as Burkhardt (the future socialist party activist) and Kanter (the Catholic who devoted her life to mission work), highlighted an antifascist mentality that persisted unchanged—or even validated—by their experiences of the mid-1940s. A few distanced themselves from historical developments by stressing elements of continuity—routines that persisted through and beyond the *Endkampf*. Auto mechanic's apprentice Birkmann, for example, recalled missing a few days of work in early May, after which he and his colleagues began repairing Soviet vehicles. Similarly, Frau Völker, who had worked long hours processing insurance claims throughout the war, resumed her work within the first days of capitulation.

Finally, there were also exceptions to the precapitulation narrative voice shift. Klinkert, for example, the twin raised by a single mother, retained the plural voice throughout her narrative. In part, this probably reflected a close relationship with her twin sister; even more than half-orphans Barthe and Pastler, the Klinkert girls shared clothes, food, schoolbooks, and hobbies. As will be seen, however, Klinkert's memories of the postwar period were anything but passive. She described a virtual blur of activity as she and her twin asserted their capacity for work and ingenuity—supporting their mother, pursuing educational opportunities, and fulfilling a variety of FDJ obligations.

"DEN KRIEG AUSSPUKEN": SUMMER 1945

Just as cohort recollections of the final months of World War II focused on highly personalized episodes, so did memories of early occupation lack references to the military, political, or administrative transformations of Berlin. The SMAD's (Soviet Military Administration in Germany) early efforts to restore civic order, encourage cultural performances, and promote a new political order faded behind images of persistent chaos. In personal narratives, individual efforts to secure food or income took priority over the public health crises or the inter-Allied disputes that dominate authorities' memoirs and social histories.[29]

That said, cohort members recalled the *herrlichen Sommer* of 1945 in particularly vivid terms, often offering more detailed imagery than of either the war itself or the years that followed. By all accounts, it was an unusually early, long, and warm summer, characterized by a somewhat surreal sense of personal freedom. A photo of girls relaxing by a lake in the Grunewald exemplifies this atmosphere; laughing and sunning themselves, they seem oblivious to the makeshift grave, a cross hung with three helmets, in the foreground.[30]

Scenes of such careless youthful abandon amid postwar devastation were part of everyday life in 1945 Berlin, and many interviewees described similar scenarios. Charlottenburg resident Herr Heinemann, for example, recalled meeting two HJlers who had just abandoned their plan to continue fighting, per Hitler's orders, as undercover Werewolves. It was a warm day, and the three boys "peacefully [lounged] there in the sunshine, along the canal . . . [all the while] defusing their stash of stockpiled personnel mines." No adults seemed to notice, let alone question, what the boys were doing; it was just another example of oddly juxtaposed images of war and peace.   Herr Stumpf also described the casualness with which he and his friends approached potentially life-threatening pastimes.

We found these flare-like shells; they're like fireworks. We'd found a whole bunch of [them] made of aluminum, about this long and it shoots up a shell and it falls back slowly, red, or white or green or yellow. . . . And then we built magnesium torches . . . . we lit them [in the dark] and it was like broad daylight . . . I'd light the things and roll them along the street. One time [a] policeman had just turned the corner on his bicycle and the thing came rolling down towards him . . . luckily he had a sense of humor![31]

Looking back, both Heinemann and Stumpf were struck by their risky behaviors. Nonetheless, the men presented them as typical of that first postwar summer. As their peer Herr Kupfer said, "wir wollten den Krieg ausspuken." [32] Having survived the war, they tried to put it behind them as quickly as possible.

A second similarity among cohort members' memories from the summer of 1945 was a fervent desire to dance. Banned during the war as frivolous and disrespectful to the valiant German soldiers, dancing would become the most-cited leisure activity for young Berliners, and the image still persists in popular collective memory.   Young dancers conveyed optimism as they sought to celebrate life and make up for lost time, yet the dance craze quickly became a problem for municipal officials, as bars and dance clubs of widely varying repute sprang up throughout the city. Although few offered much in the way of liquid refreshment or atmosphere, a live band—even three or four musicians—offered distraction enough for young Berliners. Most youth sought out music from America, often nursing a single glass of punch for hours or smuggling their own beverages into nightclubs; with swing music and jazz, young Berliners relished an interlude of post-apocalyptic escapism.

Swing music had a certain drive, you can't compare it to today's beat . . . but this drive fit somehow to the whole atmosphere of having survived the war. When I hear the Glenn Miller Band, the St. Louis Blues March especially, that was a music that just did something for us (lit. *hat uns was gegeben*).[33]

Youth authorities blamed all kinds of immoral and semilegal activities on this postwar dance frenzy. Considered inevitable by many, as a reaction to wartime prohibitions, the dance craze seemed to confirm officials' paranoia about the effects of Nazism on the young generation. Administrative records from the early postwar years document endless discussions about this particular aspect of the broader "youth problem." Admittedly, many young people did flout civilian law and occupation regulations in pursuit of dancing and related disreputable behaviors. Bistop, for example, explained that music had become a top priority by mid-May. Together with two friends, he invited acquaintances to an evening of dance, borrowing a wind-up gramophone and a stack of records. Unfortunately, the youths could find no refreshments suitable for the anticipated female guests.

We had this idea to host a party, and for a party you need something special. Next to the Russian headquarters was a bombed-out house where [we] knew there was wine buried, right next to the Russians, four or five bottles of wine . . . of course there was a curfew, from ten in the evening until six I think . . . but we got the wine.[34]

Smiling, Bistop noted that "not only the flowers bloom in May," thereby confirming authorities' argument that the postwar *Drang nach Tanz* led to other inappropriate activities. Having stolen wine and encouraged flirtatious behavior, he also broke curfew a second time to escort a guest home.

Bistop's activities constituted the most common—and mildest—examples of the link between young people, dance, alcohol, and crime. Observing and fearing more violent behavior, municipal officials attempted, albeit ineffectively, to regulate dancing. Attempts to offer alternative, healthy music rarely proved successful, while frequent police raids only taught youth to be vigilant and move from club to club. Nonetheless, some 300 thirteen- to twenty-one-year-olds were arrested in a carefully planned crackdown in Friedrichshain on 29 September 1945. Officers justified their focus on youth (as opposed to older patrons) by identifying them as "suspects in a growing number of break-ins [who] constitute furthermore the majority of clientele in the district's coffeehouses and dance bars. They likely fund these outings through illegal acts." Unfortunately, the arrests had no noticeable impact on either dancing or the district's crime rate.[35]

Images of the western Allies, most notably the Americans, also dominated cohort memories of summer 1945. While some cohort members recalled British soldiers as polite and reserved, and one noted his father's work with French forces, virtually all interviewees offered vivid description of the American influence on their immediate postwar experiences. To young Germans struggling with psychological stress and material deprivation, the GIs—who raced their jeeps through rubble-lined streets and tossed candy to local children—epitomized freedom and prosperity.[36] The "American way of life," as portrayed in books and Hollywood films, was particularly attractive, and the smartly–dressed young soldiers brought these fictionalized portrayals to life.

Virtually all interviewees recalled a specific, personal encounter with American GIs. Beyond the soldiers' well-groomed (and well-fed!) appearance, cohort members noted that African American soldiers, much like the *kinderliebe* Russians, immediately negated earlier stereotypes. Interviewees also highlighted the American values of entrepreneurship and individuality. Less naïve than their Soviet counterparts, the GIs quickly developed a reputation as knowledgeable and well-paying customers who rewarded the practical skills honed by many youths in previous months.[37]

Most cohort members depicted the summer of 1945 in predominately positive terms, a virtual Nirvana, according to one woman. At first glance, this may seem odd, even historically inaccurate, to those familiar with the extent of physical destruction and material hardship. To a cohort that had endured the war, however, other characteristics of this first postwar summer stand out just as clearly. Capitulation coincided with the beginning of what virtually all eyewitnesses described as a particularly long and beautiful summer. Faced with dark, damp winters, Berliners have traditionally relished summertime, taking full advantage of the city's many parks and lakes. After a winter of war, the warm, dry weather was particularly welcome.

Summertime also made daily life somewhat easier. While living conditions were still cramped and often quite primitive, at least Berliners could expect to get a full night's sleep. If curfews limited social activities, at least the long summer evenings alleviated the problem of lighting homes and streets. Rickety temporary bridges, unstable piles of rubble, and hidden *Blindgänger* made travel dangerous and time-consuming, but at least a trip to the communal water pump was no longer life-threatening. In other words, material hardship was recalled primarily as an element of continuity bridging wartime and postwar experience; these young Berliners had endured the *Endkampf*, and found its aftermath, at least during the summer months, relatively tolerable.

Second, wartime experience and propaganda had prepared youth for a harsh Allied occupation. Cohort members recall wondering, for example, if Berlin's entire male population would in fact be shot, imprisoned, or deported. Others feared their nation would be eliminated and that Germans would become slaves of the Allied powers. Haunted by such dire predictions, even relatively neutral experiences were cause for relief, while small gestures of generosity became cause for celebration.

In addition, the political conflicts that had already begun dividing the Allied Kommandatura were still largely beyond the experiential space of most young Berliners. The occupation forces did license and distribute newspapers, sometimes allowing the German staff considerable editorial freedom. During that first summer, however, occupation officials tried to present a relatively unified face to the local population, and kept their most heated disagreements behind closed doors.

Finally, even youths who read the papers or seriously contemplated Germany's future had more pressing concerns in mid–1945. Most helped to secure food, housing, and fuel for their families. Virtually all sought to overcome gaps in their education or employment history. Finally, these young Berliners wanted, at long last, to simply have fun, and the chance to finally relax with friends was often enough to color memories in particularly rosy terms.

All in all, the summer of 1945 was a somewhat surreal, condensed opportunity for cohort members to "catch their breath." Between extended periods of mobilization, first for the war effort and later for physical and societal reconstruction, they seized this opportunity, amid the confusion-filled early occupation period, to just be young.

This is not to say that interviewees denied the hardships that characterized daily life in postwar Berlin. Pastler, for example, described living with her sister on a single *Hungerkarte* (the lowest ration card level) in a stranger's flat while her father fought off a lung infection in the hospital. Looking back, however, she nonetheless concluded, "it was a quite pleasant time, actually."

More typically, cohort members related postwar difficulties in conjunction with memories of the winter months (1945–1946 and 1946–47), as well as the Blockade winter of 1948–1949. In other words, summer 1945 was remembered as an essentially positive interlude, between longer eras that tested their resilience and self-sufficiency.

THE YOUTH PROBLEM

The exaggerated sense of euphoria described by interviewees complicated the work of officials charged with rehabilitating Berlin's youth, and the *Drang nach Tanz* was only the tip of the iceberg. Social workers, foreign observers, and leaders across the political spectrum decried what they saw as young people's moral decline. Many had in fact anticipated the crisis and were eager to explain the apparent social collapse. American military researchers, for example, distributed predeployment informational pamphlets, warning GIs to be particularly wary of German youth, who they believed had become reckless, brainwashed Nazis.[38] Even to native German officials, young people's desire to laze about, their predilection to sneak off into the ruins with friends, and the rising juvenile crime rate seemed to prove youth had been unable to resist Hitler.[39] Above all, postwar officials denounced young Berliners' poor work ethic and underdeveloped sense of responsibility. One KPD (communist party) official in Friedrichshain summarized his observations of that first postwar summer.

It is clear that German youth, left largely to themselves, without orderly lives, without occupational training, robbed of all developmental and educational options by Hitler's war . . . possesses none, or scarcely any, of the necessary prerequisites for antifascist youth work.[40]

Having been forced into wartime service, German youths were considered both intellectually and emotionally underdeveloped. Not surprisingly, officials found evidence to support these conclusions in the very locales with which cohort members associated their brief postwar utopia. The several blocks around the *Schlesische Bahnhof*, where so-called street gangs fought over squatters' rights to former air raid shelters, were considered particularly dangerous. In such unsupervised settings, argued researchers, an already disadvantaged generation could only suffer further decline. Concerns about Nazism's legacy and a dangerous physical environment were further heightened when authorities turned their attention to social conditions. How could they hope to remedy the youth problem without addressing the deplorable home relations?

A lack of space and light pushes children out of their homes. Parents have nothing with which to amuse them and have little . . . authority over children who perpetually roam the streets. It is very difficult for parents to keep their children from falling into bad company.[41]

While officials hoped to remedy the social and material problems, the issue of parental authority was particularly troublesome. An estimated one–third of young Berliners had only one living parent, and an even greater number were considered temporary half-orphans, as their fathers had not returned from prisoner of war camps.   Mothers, meanwhile, were described as being too overextended or exhausted to question their children's whereabouts or doings.[42]

To some extent, of course, older generations typically blame youth for challenging social norms, and postwar officials were well aware of this.   Many of them had in fact witnessed or participated in pre–1933 youth organizations and believed they understood young Germans' desire for an independent youth culture.   At the same time, the image of these Imperial and Weimar-era youth movements had been heavily tarnished by memories of the Hitler Youth, and given Nazi-era experiences, intergenerational mistrust ran in both directions. While authorities feared that German youth had been irreparably maimed, young people observed that the National Socialists had met little resistance from most adults.

The American influence further complicated generational relations, particularly in Berlin and the American zone. To German youth, American culture represented new ideas, personal freedom, and an escape from the hardship of postwar life.   To many German adults, however, the sudden influx of American films, music, and consumer products constituted a new cultural threat; they saw Germany's own rich musical and literary traditions being overwhelmed by the Anglo-American assault.

Authorities and activists had little time to come to terms with these complex issues. The most pressing question was not if German youth had been or were being corrupted, but whether or not they could be taught to contribute to Germany's future development.   Clearly, Berlin's "*nationalsozialistisch verseuchte Jugend*' needed a good dose of culture, structure, and political guidance, and in summer 1945, appeals like this one from the Neukölln *Jugendausschuß* were posted throughout the city.

German youths will one day be the bearers of the German nation.   It is their responsibility to erase the enormous stain that Hitler has imprinted on the German people; to make up for the wrongs of their elders; [and] . . . through tireless work on themselves, through intense participation in reconstruction, to earn back the trust of other nations.[43]

The *Jugendleiter* who drafted this statement hoped to attract youths to participate in the Youth Committee's social, educational, and volunteer programs.   He mitigated allusions to pride, guilt, and generational identity with a salute to youths' presumably inexhaustible energy.   Yet the response to this multipronged approach seems to have been minimal at best.   Certainly some young Berliners recognized an opportunity to help shape a new society.   These idealists, however, comprised only a small minority.   More pragmatic youths may have hoped participation in *Ausschuß* activities would lead to a job, while others attended just one or two programs, taking a wait-and-see attitude toward the new bureaucracy. To many young Berliners, however, the language of such appeals from youth officials was only too familiar. They no longer wanted to be described as the bearers of the German nation.   The idea of personal or national sacrifice sounded too much like Nazi rhetoric.

The adults were right, of course. Berlin—and Germany—desperately needed its youth. Yet as this *Aufruf* suggests, Berlin officials were not sure how to recruit or train youth for this work. Were young soldiers, *Luftwaffenhelfer*, and HJlers victims or perpetrators? If this generation was indeed emotionally retarded, could even *volljährige Jugendliche* be held to adult legal standards?[44] How could authorities define, let alone reeducate, a cohort that had grown up too soon yet remained psychologically immature? How could one hope to guide this particularly needy generation that was itself lacking in leadership (i.e., males)? By what means could activists encourage youths to move beyond expected immorality and political apathy?

Again, conditions in 1945 Berlin left local authorities little time to dwell on these questions. Recognizing a window of opportunity, the SMAD had included directives for youth in its earliest plans for occupation. Repatriated German communists, some of whom had spent months discussing how to incorporate youth into reconstruction, rehabilitation, and reparation efforts, led initial recruitment campaigns. With this head start, the KPD would dominate communal rehabilitation efforts in Berlin throughout the first year of occupation.[45]

KPD activists promoted a united, nonpartisan, antifascist youth movement. As a first step, they established antifascist youth committees in all twenty administrative districts of Berlin. Although critics—contemporary and later historians among them—saw the committees as little more than poorly disguised communist youth groups, organizers did recruit representatives from across the political spectrum. Many politically minded youths, often the children of Weimar-era activists, also saw potential in these early committees. Socialist Heinz Westphal, for example (who would become a cofounder of Berlin's Falcon organization), observed that in Tempelhof, the antifascist committee did facilitate productive discussions between social democratic and communist factions.[46] After only a few weeks of work, however, the *Jugendausschüsse* lost much of their original spontaneity and independence when they were absorbed into the municipal bureaucracy under the auspices of the district *Volksbildungsämter*. Key subcommittees were soon dominated by representatives of the KPD, and in mid June, twenty-five year-old Heinz Kessler, who had proven his willingness to work with the Soviet leadership on the *National Kommittee Freies Deutschland*, was appointed chair of Greater Berlin's *Hauptjugendausschuß*.[47]

Youth officials at all levels faced public health crises, a lack of trained personnel, and severe material shortages as they sought to mobilize Berlin's dance-crazed youth in mid-1945. Seeking facilities for their new antifascist youth centers, for example, district *Ausschüsse* competed with private entrepreneurs who envisioned cafés in the same buildings—often former HJ clubrooms, garages, or storefronts. Once they found space, activists confronted equally difficult problems converting the rooms into appropriate youth centers. Such logistical hurdles were particularly difficult to surmount in the most devastated inner-city districts, where intervention was most urgently needed. The Kreuzberg *Jugendauschuß*, for example, quickly found rooms for five of six planned youth centers, but as fall approached inspectors determined that the majority could not be used in cold or wet weather. Similarly, a Lichtenberg activist reported that thirteen of twenty-one local centers were "functional" by mid-September, but noted that at least five of these were only "short-term solutions," unsuitable for use during the upcoming winter months.[48]   In neighboring Friedrichshain, officials optimistically announced the establishment of a district lending library, youth orchestra, and physical education program, only to discover that the necessary books, instruments, and sports equipment had disappeared in the early weeks of occupation.[49]

Despite these difficulties, the communal *Jugendausschüsse*, in conjunction with district and central *Kunstämter* and *Sportämter*, offered young Berliners a surprisingly varied program by midsummer 1945. Reports indicated particular interest in theatrical and musical groups, as well as swimming, sports, and of course, dancing.[50] However, while participants recalled these activities in the context of a carefree postwar summer, organizers hoped to lure youth into the more serious tasks of political and material reconstruction. Thus, in addition to sponsoring leisure programs, the *Jugendausschüsse* cosponsored youth work programs throughout Berlin. By the end of July, for example, Neukölln's committee had, despite a lamented lack of skilled leaders and resources, recruited about 170 youths to clear parks, rebuild playing fields, and organize a children's field day.[51] Later that summer, Frau Pastler was hired to pick vegetables for the Kreuzberg *Jugendausschuß*.

We got forty-eight *Pfenning* an hour, and well, anywhere there was a bit of dirt, they'd grown vegetables. . . . We harvested kohlrabi, and there was always a supervisor from the *Gartenamt* to see that we didn't mess around or hide [some] in our pockets or anything.[52]

Although both young workers and their supervisors understood the necessity of such work, neither side appreciated the other's performance or attitude. Participants, for example, frequently complained that the work was more or less compulsory, drawing obvious comparisons to National Socialist work initiatives and public service programs. Public officials, on the other hand, lamented young workers' tendency to pocket harvested vegetables, and insisted that, unlike Nazi work programs, these antifascist initiatives promoted a healthy work ethic rooted in genuine volunteerism. Such optimism notwithstanding, organizers quickly discovered that "political work among Berlin youth is one of the most complicated problems of all," and admitted that the youth work programs had failed to foster the desired civic spirit. By October 1945, a new *Jugendnoteinsatz* program required participants to also participate in vocational training and ideological seminars.[53]

Solving the "youth problem" in 1945 also entailed reopening public schools as soon as possible. Like the work programs, school was supposed to get young people off the streets, provide much-needed discipline, and teach them to be responsible citizens in postwar society. Once again, however, material conditions thwarted efforts to reach out to young Berliners. In one report, for example, the Friedrichshain *Schulamt* announced that classes had reconvened already in May 1945. A second memo, however, explained that school officials were repeatedly compelled to find new facilities as occupation forces requisitioned buildings for other purposes. As a result, pupils usually cleared rubble for a few hours each morning before gathering in "interest groups" for instruction in foreign languages, math, and other subjects. The district had no suitable textbooks, and teachers were unable to group the ever-fluctuating number of pupils into age- or ability-based classes.[54]

Conditions varied somewhat from district to district, but overall, of the nearly 23,000 classrooms available in Berlin before the war, only about 3,050 were safe enough to be used in 1945. Not surprisingly, overcrowding, together with textbook and teacher shortages, severely compromised educational quality. Magistrate officials readily admitted that school was meant primarily to keep young Berliners off the streets, but even this goal proved elusive, since two institutions often shared one facility, each using the building for a few hours each day.

For many potential pupils, the value of formal education, particularly under such mediocre conditions, faded in light of more pragmatic goals. Young people often found themselves responsible for other family members, and very few were able to resume previously held positions. Opportunities for undereducated youths were scarce, since in Berlin's postwar economic climate, employers could afford to be choosy. The most available jobs were also the least desirable; clearing rubble, for example, was not only exhausting, but also took a heavy toll on shoes and clothing. Serving the occupation forces was among the best jobs, although even this option was not risk free. Herr Stumpf, for example, found work at a British fueling station, but was fired for allegedly cooperating with soldiers who skimmed gasoline to sell on the black market.[55]

Even those who wanted to go to school could rarely afford to attend on a daily basis; other concerns simply took priority. Herr Zelle, for example, had enrolled in school, but regularly skipped class to barter with relatives who lived about a hundred kilometers from Berlin.

We took butter from the black market, because you couldn't get it in the countryside . . . butter, yarn and whatever they needed there—that with the butter was crazy, taking butter to the farmers, but we took the stuff and [traded for] tobacco wares. . . . And then we sold the cigars and such here in Berlin. . . . Sometimes I went with my father, and sometimes by myself. It kept the family above water, we could buy extra bread, for example. . . . And well, yes, my school work suffered, I can't deny that, but I never noticed a long term deficit. On the contrary, it fostered a capitalist spirit![56]

Zelle's retrospective self-evaluation was typical. On the one hand, he acknowledged that skipping school might have appeared short-sighted, and pointed out that priorities change under difficult circumstances. On the other hand, he described his illegal activities enthusiastically; sitting in a classroom with seventy-odd other pupils paled in comparison to successfully completing a financial transaction in the Soviet Zone. Yet Zelle's preferred extracurricular activity did more than provide food and a chance for adventure. First, it reinforced the youth's sense of independence. Equally important, it helped him adapt survival strategies into useful skills; while admitting that his education suffered, Zelle suggested that haggling with relatives better prepared him for adult life.[57]

Cohort members who did pursue education in the first months after capitulation similarly highlighted their own initiative and perseverance.

Charlottenburger Herr Heinemann, for example, explained that dedicated pupils helped repair local schools.

> In the midst of all the destruction, the Schiller Gymnasium hadn't been badly hit. We started school again in August [1945]. The roof was damaged and we were told, no classes the next two days, because we have to fix the roof. And then the whole student body built a chain from street to rooftop and passed the shingles along. . . . In terms of school, the collapse [of the Reich] didn't mean much. Dr. Sange rounded up all the teachers who weren't somehow [deemed politically] corrupt, [so] we had some of our former teachers. . . . Our director kept us from chaos . . . through all the bad times, when others had to go to school in the afternoons, we *never* had two shifts.[58]

Not particularly interested in formal youth work programs, Heinemann willingly committed several days to reroofing his school because he himself, not some anonymous organization, would directly benefit from the effort. The work paid off, he noted proudly, emphasizing that his school director never resorted to the half-day shift system adopted by most school administrators.

The material conditions Heinemann described hindered the efforts of educators, municipal officials, and antifascist (often abbreviated to "antifa") youth committees. Looking back, however, it seems that the material factors contributing to the youth problem may have distracted organizers from a number of less tangible problems. First, the communist activists who dominated early rehabilitation efforts shared perceptions of German youth that were rooted in National Socialist propaganda. In other words, they had studied *prescriptive* literature—RJF publications that depicted model HJlers and explained how German youth should behave. Not knowing exactly how those ideals had translated into practice, most assumed the worst—that the Nazis had effectively brainwashed the vast majority of young people. Returning exiles in particular had little way of knowing how the parameters of daily life had changed for Berlin's youth in the last months of the war. Consequently, they could not determine if and to what extent such practical experience may have ameliorated or contracted Nazi ideals.[59]

The antifa committees' reliance on these perceptions of the recent past alienated many young Berliners. Youths with demonstrated leadership abilities, primarily former HJ and BDM *FührerInnen*, were denied positions of responsibility. Many of those who had participated in Nazi organizations felt that antifascist leaders, drawn from the resistance or exile community, had no sympathy for their prior experiences. Youths who recalled other traditions, such as religious groups or athletic clubs, often preferred reestablishing these earlier ties. While those groups faced similar material circumstances, they offered young people a less politically charged leisure option.[60] Some members of the Prenzlauer Berg youth committee came to recognize that activists' inability to connect with young Berliners was partly a result of the persistence of stereotypes.

> It's apparent that some leaders go about reeducation . . . in a completely inappropriate fashion. It is wrong, pedagogically, to identify members of the HJ and BDM as "Nazi bandits". . . . We cannot work from the point of view of an adult

authority. [Rather] we must win youths' trust through painstaking *Kleinarbeit* and comradely cooperation.[61]

Even when local leaders assumed that young Berliners had accepted the tenets of National Socialism and willingly participated in Hitler Youth rallies and demonstrations, they often failed to recognize how their own initiatives, in form at least, emulated Nazi-era programs. This was most apparent at large, central gatherings. According to one astute observer, for example, a city-wide commemoration of the Victims of Fascism backfired not because young people had become oblivious to human suffering, but rather because it reminded them of compulsory ceremonies they had attended during the war.[62] In a similar vein, Lichtenberg officials seemed surprised that young people overwhelmingly rejected their proposal to develop a special youth committee greeting or emblem. While the officials hoped to thus foster a sense of unity and cooperation, young Berliners immediately recalled the *Hitler-Gruß* and HJ proficiency badges.

Throughout Berlin, former HJlers frequently disrupted antifa committee meetings, accusing organizers of perpetuating practices they claimed to oppose. According to one Prenzlauer Berg official, such attacks only confirmed the thoroughness of Nazi indoctrination; young Berliners were no longer able to distinguish between a "youth movement" and a "state youth organization." Such attitudes, as well as the antifa activists' insistence that youth should immediately (and once again) shoulder the nation's burdens, led young people to either reject the youth committees outright or delay committing themselves to any kind of formal membership.[63]

A second problem lay in the fact that the *Jugendausschüsse* were expected to simultaneously regulate youth and represent their presumably spontaneous antifascist interests. According to reports from June 1945, the youth committees' responsibilities included caring for refugees and needy minors, overseeing group homes, and preventing youth crime, as well as promoting "appropriate" leisure activities and community service.[64] In other words, while encouraging local youth committees to attract young Berliners through cultural programs, municipal authorities simultaneously expected the committees to register, police, and essentially conscript them. In some districts, officials even considered requiring written evaluations of young volunteers. A Prenzlauer Berg authority, for example, suggested issuing report cards for each youth in the district, evaluating their work performance and attitude. Similarly a member of the Friedrichshain Jugendausschuß proposed calibrating ration coupons to individuals' work habits.[65]

Given the circumstances, some of these proposals were understandable. The mandatory daily registration of unemployed youths, district-wide curfews, and even job counseling programs, for example, were clearly intended to curb crime and help young Berliners find jobs, and the antifa youth committees fulfilled these tasks with support from the *Sozialämter* and other municipal authorities. Nonetheless, the *Jugendausschüsse* were among the most visible representatives of municipal authority at the local level, and thus bore a large share of criticism. Seeing the words *Jugendausschuß Charlottenburg* or *Zentraler Jugendausschuß* on handbills announcing new regulations and policies, youths were apt to perceive the youth committees as an arm of the state, not an opportunity to express their own ideas.

Third, the youth committees and the KPD initially underestimated the significance of postwar demographics. Specifically, the population of fourteen- to eighteen-year-old males had shrunk from 108,000 in 1939 to an estimated 26,000 in 1945.[66] Beyond the obvious social problems caused by the so-called *Frauenüberschuß*, the shortage of young males was problematic because the committees had counted on this cohort to play a particularly active role in reconstruction efforts. Furthermore, antifa activists frequently dismissed the leadership potential of young women, assuming that *Berlinerinnen* were too susceptible to the corruptive power of the dance halls, which "lure countless young girls down the path of lust . . . [where] they frequently fall victim to prostitution."[67]

Recruitment problems only worsened after political parties—first the KPD, then the SPD and CDU—received permission to recommence work in Berlin, and began essentially competing with the theoretically neutral *Jugendausschusse* for politically engaged young people. Relatively few in number, members of this small but necessary subcohort found that their ideas were neglected in favor of programs for both younger and older residents.[68] Even events intended for youth frequently evolved into *Kinderfeste*, simply overrun by younger children. Youthful activists also resented what they saw as an over reliance on older antifascists, criticizing their inability to distinguish between Weimar-era attitudes and the goals of this new, unifying youth movement. After hearing one too many nostalgic stories, "activist" and "apathetic" youths at one gathering interrupted organizers, demanding, "No politics in the youth committees!"[69]

A fourth obstacle dividing young Berliners and the youth committees was that the very characteristics of summer 1945 welcomed by the former were considered problematic by the latter. For example, youth committee leaders blamed the beautiful weather of that first postwar summer for lowering attendance at lectures and other events. Cohort members' interest in swing dancing was considered even more detrimental. Although some officials were reluctant to ban dancing outright, they promoted "healthy alternatives"—folk dancing, lay theatre productions, and reduced-priced film screenings—to lure young Berliners away from "pubs of questionable character."[70] Both archival and eyewitness accounts suggest, however, that while these opportunities were more popular than academic discussions of political theory, they couldn't begin to compete with the *Drang nach Tanz*. The mere suggestion that this might be possible only confirmed to many youth that the committees were simply out of touch.[71]

Finally, organizers' ideas about what it meant—or should mean—to be young in a post-Nazi world conflicted with young Berliners' own notions. Most officials, including *Ausschußleiter* and work program leaders cited earlier, understood their task in terms of rehabilitating youth for future endeavors. That is, they tried to foster the traits they believed young people would need to build a new Germany: a strong work ethic driven by a sense of collective responsibility and political consciousness.   Recruitment flyers frequently emphasized young people's responsibility to clean away the "stain of Nazism, carry the burden of reconstruction, and earn the trust of peace-loving nations, which we through our own guilt have lost." Although reports repeatedly confirmed that young Berliners preferred cultural and athletic opportunities, the *Jugendausschüsse* insisted on offering lectures entitled "The Free Democratic Struggle," or "Introduction to Historical and Dialectical Materialism," and blamed local leaders or youths themselves when crowds failed to materialize.[72]

In short, Berlin's youth committees underestimated young Berliners' overwhelming desire to simply be young in the weeks after capitulation. With few exceptions, youths weren't ready to again submit personal desires in pursuit of societal goals. Recent experience had taught them to focus on their own immediate needs, and they yearned to recreate long-harbored images, rooted in vague memories of *schöne Kinderjahre*. As they recounted their memories of 1945, interviewees depicted that first postwar summer as an opportunity to recover previously denied experience.

This is not to say that cohort members denied the enormous task of material and societal reconstruction that lay ahead. That would have been virtually impossible, given the conditions in which they lived. Furthermore, most did in fact quickly turn their attention to establishing routines, careers, and personal relationships. However, individual accounts of the summer of 1945 do suggest a temporary suspension of reality, and this interpretation is indirectly confirmed by reports describing youth apathy. As Frau Völker explained, young Berliners needed a chance to catch their breaths. Having learned to take care of themselves during the demise of the Nazi dictatorship, they did so after capitulation, using the warm summer months to reenergize themselves for future efforts.[73]

Further evidence of this can be found in archival reports about youth committee and municipal initiatives that were well received by young people. Although by November 1945 only about 8,000 young Berliners were regularly attending youth committee functions, one-time events such as folk festivals, *Bunte Abende* (amateur variety shows), and sporting events had attracted some 80,000 youths. One Friedrichshain official eventually concluded that district youth could perhaps only be reached through *Sportfeste*.[74] Such events, free of politics and requiring no long-term commitment, catered to young Berliners' desire for a chance to be young and carefree. Officials' attempts to respond to legitimate concerns about illegality and immorality, however, only reinforced young people's equally understandable suspicions that the youth committees were just another regulatory arm of the state. Consequently, and increasingly as the summer of 1945 faded into fall and winter, Berlin became home to a variety of independent initiatives pursued by youths who had learned to serve their own needs.

Cohort members' narratives illustrate the combined impact of the practical lessons of total war, the personal turning points identified previously, and the problematic relationship between youth and youth committees. The gradual disintegration of National Socialist society had taught young Berliners self-reliance, and this would become a leitmotiv of individuals' postwar narratives. If German youth initially refused to shoulder what the antifascist youth committees defined as their generational responsibility, in other words, the burden of the past and of reconstruction, they did not shirk day-to-day responsibilities. Having learned in recent months how quickly circumstances can change, they focused on satisfying immediate material, familial, and social needs.

Unemployment, crime, disease, and divorce statistics from Berlin do, of course, point to a social crisis in the months following German capitulation, and such conditions transformed some youths into hardcore thieves, prostitutes, or even gruesome serial killers. Such individuals, however, like those who threw themselves into the work of the antifascist youth committees, constituted a minority. Many more laid the foundations for individual postwar identities in less radical ways. They cleared rubble, patched roofs, and rebuilt homes. They worked long hours for low wages, often in primitive working conditions. They mastered the unspoken rules of a black market both regulated and patronized by foreigners. They provided food for their families. All the while, they also made time to assert their youthfulness, forming dance bands, celebrating birthdays, and organizing potlucks. Even the groups considered most ruined (*verdorben*) and lost by city officials, namely, the black marketeers and the *Amiliebchen*, pursued opportunities that displayed an acute awareness of the realities of occupation.

In the last months of World War II, this cohort had learned, among other things, to depend on their own creativity—and luck. Young Germans were prepared to apply these lessons while waiting to see what the postwar world would bring. Whether or not they had actively supported Hitler, most took from the Nazi era an ability to hedge their bets, take one day at a time, seize opportunities without flinching, and rely on their own skills. Expressing individuality once restricted by Nazi policies and Allied air raids, young people also took advantage of the chance to find their own space and express their own tastes.

NOTES

1. Winkert, 1; Zelle, 1–3. Also: Claus Larass, *Der Zug der Kinder* (Munich: Meyster Verlag, 1983); Doris Fürstenberg, "Sicher wieder nach Hause? Das Ende der Kinderlandverschickung," in Bezirksamt Charlottenburg, *Kinderlandverschickung 1940–1945 Texte zur Ausstellung* (Berlin: Bezirksamt Charlottenburg, 1997); "Bericht einer Mädchenklasse über die Rückführung aus der KLV," in ibid.

2. Georg Holmsten, *Die Berlin Chronik, Daten, Personen, Dokumente* (Düsseldorf: Droste Verlag, 1984), 384–5. American casualty estimates are usually higher. Erik Smit, Evthalia Staikos, and Dirk Thormann, *3 Februar 1945. Die Zerstörung Kreuzbergs aus der Luft.* Exhibit catalog (Berlin: Verlag Gericke, 1995).

3. Holmsten, 385.

4. Wilhelm Willemar, Oberst d.A., ed., *The German Defense of Berlin*, Foreign Military Studies series (Historical Division Headquarters, U.S. Army Europe, 1954), 1, 10–11, 64.

5. Holmsten, 388. Structurally, the flak towers were the strongest elements of "fortress Berlin," although the soldiers who occupied them frequently lacked both weapons and ammunition. Troops in both the Friedrichshain and Zoo towers continued to resist attack after being completely surrounded, and casualties inside resulted from overcrowding more than enemy fire. Willemar, 25–39.

6. Kolberg premiered simultaneously in besieged La Rochelle. Anthony Read and David Fischer, *The Fall of Berlin* (New York: W.W. Norton, 1993), 233–234.

7. Ruth Andreas-Friedrich, *Battleground Berlin, Diaries 1945–1948* (New York: Paragon House, 1990), 242.

8. John Strawson, *The Battle for Berlin* (London: Batsford, Ltd., 1974), 159.

9. Schäfer, 4.

10. Tinker, 1; Völker, 1. Also: Detlef Mittag and Detlef Schade, *Geschichte vom überleben in der Nachkriegszeit* (Berlin: Das Arsenal, 1983). On a slightly younger cohort, see: Detlef Mittag, *Kriegskinder, 10 Überlebensgeschichten* (Berlin: Internationale Liga für Menschenrechte, 1995); Wulf Köhn, "eine Neuköllner Nachkriegskindheit 1945–50," in Klaus Wiese and Ilona Zeuch, eds., *Berliner Schuljahre. Vier Errinerungen und Berichte* (Berlin: Overall Verlag, 1995). On an older cohort: *Berlin nach dem Krieg, wie ich es erlebte. 28 Erlebnisberichte von älteren Berlinern aus dem Wettbewerb des Senators für Arbeit und Soziales*, Schriftenreihe Berliner Forum 9/77 (Berlin: Presse und Informationsamt des Landes Berlin, 1977).

11. Werner Richter, "Kampf um den Senefelderplatz," quoted in Günter Wehner, "Die Schlacht um Berlin April/Mai 1945—Aus der Sicht von Schüleraufsätzen des Jahres 1946," in *Deutsche Jugend zwischen Krieg und Frieden 1944–1946*, ed. Ingo Koch (Rostock: Verlag Jugend und Geschichte, 1993), 65–68. The quoted essay is also available in the Bezirksarchiv Prenzlauer Berg.

12. Kanter, 2–3.

13. Psychologists and sociologists suggest that older adults in particular rely heavily on collective stories to structure retrospective accounts of public events, and because it dramatically altered German society, the end of World War II would be especially susceptible to collective reconstruction. James W. Pennebaker and Becky L. Banasik, "On the Creation and Maintenance of Collective Memories: History as Social Psychology," in James W. Pennebaker, Dario Paez, and Bernard Rime, eds., *Collective Memory of Political Events: Social Psychological Perspectives* (Mahwah, NJ: Lawrence Erlbaum Associates, 1997), 3–20.

14. Pastler, 1–3.

15. Barthe, 3, 5.

16. Pastler 9–10, 12–14.

17. Barthe, 14, 17–18.

18. Rennebach, 1–2.

19. Winkert, 3–5. For similar turning point stories, see: King, 1–2, 5; Schneider, 4–6; Miller, 1–2; Schumann, 152–63.

20. Zelle, 1–2.

21. Ibid., 2–3.

22. Rolf Schörken has also observed both these mentality-changing incidents (*Schlüsselerlebnisse*) and the *ich* motive, but does not directly associate the two. Schörken's interpretation is a bit confusing. On the one hand, he noted his interviewees' tendency to describe Nazi-era lives in a more passive manner, suggesting the use of a more active voice to describe postwar experiences (using evidence from essays written in 1946–1948). Yet he later suggested young Germans continued to explain themselves through the passive, plural voice in the postwar period. Rolf Schörken, *Luftwaffenhelfer und Drittes Reich. Die Entstehung eines politischen Bewußtseins* (Stuttgart: Klett-Cotta, 1984), 45–47, 107, 113, 125–28, 147.

23. Miller, 5. Also Barthe, 4; Pastler, 6–7; Pelsdorf, 3; Rippe 3, 11.

24. Heinemann, 6; Klinkert, 21–22; Rennebach, 12; Schäfer, 4; Stumpf, 9. For more context, see the archival collection of the "Frauen und Soldaten" Project, Heimatmuseum Charlottenburg.

25. Winkert, 5. See also: Alan L. Nothnagel, *Building the East German Myth: Historical Mythology and Youth Propaganda in the German Democratic Republic 1945–1989* (Ann Arbor: University of Michigan Press, 1999), ch. 4.

26. Bistop, 2. Although not mentioned in this context, Bistop was likely also protected by the fact that his father was a well-known (and much-needed) surgeon. Also: Miller, 12; Pestopf, 3–4.

27. Birkmann, 10.

28. "Fremde Männer als Eroberer und Befreier," in Ulla Roberts, *Starke Mütter-ferne Väter. Töchter reflektieren ihre Kindheit im Nationalsozialismus und in der Nachkriegszeit* (Frankfurt: Fischer Taschenbuch Verlag, 1994), 120–132. On divided memories of easterners and westerners, see Alexander von Plato and Almut Leh, *"Ein unglaublicher Frühling" Erfahrene Geschichte im Nachkriegsdeutschland 1945–1948* (Bonn: Bundeszentrale für politische Bildung, 1997), 139–147.

29. On early disputes among occupation forces, see: Hans Herzfeld, *Berlin in der Weltpolitik 1945–70* (New York: de Gruyter, 1973); Udo Wetzlaugk, *Die Allierten in Berlin* (Berlin: Verlag Arno Spitz, 1988), 25–28, 31–38.

30. See Roland Gröschel and Michael Schmidt. *Trümmerkids und Gruppenstunde* (Berlin: Elefanten Press, 1990).

31. Heinemann, part II, 2–3; Stumpf, 9–10. Also Esters; Kanter, 3; Tinker, 4–5.

32. Lit. "spitting out the war." Kupffer, 81. The summer is also described as a *Denkpause*. Also, Kanter, 3; Tinker, 4–5; Lydia Esters, undated recorded testimony, Geschichtswerkstatt Kreuzberg.

33. Zelle, 17–18; King, 8.

34. Bistop, 4–5.

35. Tinker, 6; Kriminal Kommission Friedrichshain, "Bericht," 1 October 1945, LAB STA Rep 135/1 415; Polizei Präsidium Berlin, Kriminal Kommissariat Friedrichshain, "Betr. Schutz der Jugend," 5 October 1945, LAB STA Rep 135/1 415.

36. Schneider, 16–17; Bistop, 5; Richie, 639.

37. Schörken, *Jugend 1945*, 110; Recorded interview with Lydia Esters, undated, Geschichtswerkstatt Kreuzberg.

38. "Pocket Guide to Germany" (Washington: U.S. Government Printing Office, 1948), 7–8.

39. Report, KPD Berlin, September 1945, LAB I/20/040, 11; H.W. Maw, "Jugendgefährdung und Jugendkriminalität in Berlin," undated, ADW Allg Slg C 65.3, 1–3; Berliner Inneren Mission Bericht, "Jugendliche in Gefahr. Jugendliche Verbrechen in Berlin," July 1946, ADW GV 14; Hilda Thurnwald, *Gegenwartsprobleme Berliner Familien* (Berlin: Weidmannsche Verlagsbuchhandlung, 1948). Also Bruchner, 20.

40. "Bericht über die bezirkliche Jugendarbeit von Anfang Mai bis August" (Friedrichshain 9 August 1945), BArch SAPMO DY 30/IV 2/16/211, 39–40.

41. Maw, "Bericht über Studienergebnisse August-Dezember 1946," Friends Relief Section, ADW Allg. Stg. C 65.3 (The report draws its statistical evidence primarily from 1946, but notes that little has changed since the collapse of the Third Reich); Podewin, 121; HJA Jahresbericht 1947, LAB C Rep 118 Nr 757 B1 6-16 (This report compares statistics from 1945, 1946, and 1947).

42. On mothers' work: Ruhl, 127–30, 195–212; Thurnwald 25–37.

43. Leiter des Jugendausschuß Neukölln, "Aufruf," Summer 1945, SAPMO DY 30/IV 2/16 211, 81.

44. Not until 1947 would a youth amnesty law officially clarify the issue of youth culpability, and even this official determination could not really solve the question of young people's roles in Germany's past, present, or future. Magistrat Groß Berlin,

Abt. Sozialwesen, letter to Allied Kommandatur, 20 March 1947, LAB STA Rep 118-1 159.

45. SMAD officials first accepted licensure petitions on 10 June. The KPD's petition was granted on 11 June, and those of the SPD, CDU, and LPD on 15 June, 26 June, and 5 July, respectively. Although all four parties, as well as both the Catholic and Protestant Churches, immediately articulated goals for youth, this chapter focuses on the antifa committees because they dominated early efforts and since youth organizations (including the Berlin FDJ) were not authorized until 1946.

46. Interview with Heinz Westphal, quoted in Gröschel and Schmidt (1990), 29. Also: Senat von Berlin, Hrsg., *Berlin Kampf um Freiheit und Selbstverwaltung* (Berlin: Heinz Spitzung Verlag 1961), Schriftenreihe zur Berliner Zeitgeschichte, Band 1, 82.

47. Podewin, 121; Walter Ulbricht, Speech to KPD conference, 25 June 1945, in Gröschel and Schmidt (1990), 24.   Each *Ausschuß* included representatives for culture, sports, unions, work programs, schools, and the somewhat ambiguous subcommittee for "girls' questions." While some sections of the central magistrate began work on 20 May 1945, the *Hauptjugendausschuß* (established on 14 June) first convened on 20 June. The new magistrate included both this committee, under the auspices of the *Volksbildungsamt*, and a separate *Jugendamt*, which was a subsection of the *Amt für Sozialwesen* and consequently concerned itself with social work in the narrow sense (caring for orphans, etc.).   As time passed, organizational structures changed, particularly in the western districts, as noncommunist majorities gained more authority. In 1947, for example, the BVV Charlottenburg voted to dissolve the local *Jugendausschuß*, although many officials were simply transferred to the *Rat für Volksbildung's Abteilung Jugend*.   Hirsch, lecture transcript, 3 June 1989, Charlottenburg Heimat Museum Archive; Ulrich Mahlert and Gerd-Rüdiger Stephan, *Blaue Hemden Rote Fahnen. Die Geschichte der Freien Deutschen Jugend* (Opladen: Leske & Budrich, 1996), 20–22; Gröschel and Schmidt, 24–26; KPD Berlin, Report, September 1945, LAB I/20/040 16–17.

48. Lichtenberg Jugendausschuß, mid-September Report 1945, SAPMO DY 30/IV 2/16 211, 63; Kreuzberg Jugendausschuß, Report, Fall 1945, SAPMO DY 30/IV 2/16 211, 53.

49. Podewin, 116–17; Zentrale Jugendausschuß Groß Berlin, "Bericht über Jugendkulturarbeit," 11 October 1945, SAPMO DY 24/87.

50. Neukölln Jugendausschuß, "Tätigkeitsberichte," 1945, SAPMO DY 30/iv 2/16 211, 88–92, 108–10.

51. Ibid. The youth work programs were unrelated to the Soviet practice of drafting able-bodied Berliners off the streets to move supplies, clear rubble, or dismantle industrial machinery.

52. Pastler, 18.

53. Bezirksleitung der KPD Berlin, "Tätigkeitsbericht," 31 October 1945, SAPMO ZPA NM 182.852, 11–23, section Ie; *Berlin im Neuaufbau*, 111; Gröschel and Schmidt (1990), 12.

54. Schulamt Friedrichshain, "Berichte," 10 June and 12 June 1945, LAB STA Rep 135/1 #328; Heinemann, 1; Mostel, 3–4.

55. Stumpf, 1.

56. Zelle, 14–15. On 14 June 1945, Berlin's police commenced their first widespread crackdown on the black market, arresting more than 400 individuals. Holmsten, 397. Also on the black market: Pelsdorf, 16–17; Tinker, 6.

57. Zelle, 14–15. Local officials did recognize that hunger kept young Berliners from school, and soon addressed the problem by offering free hot lunches at school.

However, they had little sympathy for what Zelle described as his efforts to gain practical sales experience. Already by mid-June, city police had arrested as many as 400 "entrepreneurs" in a single raid. Holmsten, 397.

58. Heinemann, 1; 9bid., BA Charlottenburg interview text, 2;   Schulamt Charlottenburg, "Bericht," 31 August 1945, LAB Rep 07 Acc 3075 #5063/I. Also: Bistop, 5; Klinkert, 3; Pelsdorf, 3–4; Pestopf, 5; Winkert, 5–6; Zelle, 10.

59. KPD Berlin, "Bericht," September 1945, LAB I/20/040.

60. BA Prenzlauer Berg, "Verwaltungsbericht," 1 October 1945, SAPMO DY 30/iv 2/16/211; 11. Heinemann, 2.

61.   SAPMO   DY   30/IV   2/16/211,   204–206;   "Bericht   des   Zentralen Jugendausschußes Berlin," 9 August 1945, SAPMO DY 30/IV 2/16 212, 210–215.

62. Jugendausschuß Friedrichshain, "Bericht," 14.9.45, SAPMO DY 30/IV 2/16/211, 38; Jugendausschuß Charlottenburg, "Bericht," undated, LAB Rep 207 Acc 3075 #5063/I.

63. Jugendausschuß Lichtenberg, survey report, undated, SAPMO DY 30/IV 2/16 211, 63–64; BA Prenzlauer Berg, "Bericht," 1 October 1945, SAPMO DY 30/iv 2/16/211.

64. Jugendämter Friedrichshain und Prenzlauer Berg, Reports, 26 June 1945, LAB STA Rep 118 145.

65. Memo, undated, LAB C Rep 900 Nr i/3/9/096; Friedrichshain Jugend Ausschuß, "Bericht," 9.10.45, BArch BY 30/IV 2/16 211.

66. Gerhard Keiderling, Die Berliner Krise 1948/49 Zur imperialistischen Strategie des kalten Krieges gegen den Sozialismus und der Spaltung Deutschlands (Berlin: Akademie Verlag, 1982), 55.

67. Polizei Präsidium Berlin, Kriminal Kommissariate Friedrichain, "Betr. Schutz der Jugend," 5 October 1945.

68. SAPMO DY 30/IV 2/16/211, 204-6; BArch DY 30/IV 2/16 211, 149–51.

69. "Bericht" 1 October 1945, SAPMO DY 30/iv 2/16/211; KPD Berlin, "Bericht," September 1945, LAB I/20/040, 14–19.

70. KPD Berlin, ibid.; Zentrale Jugendausschuß Gross Berlin, "Bericht über Jugendkulturarbeit," 11 October 1945, SAPMO DY 24/87; Jugendausschuß Prenzlauer Berg, "Bericht," fall 1945 (undated), LAB Rep 118, Nr 117.

71. Of course, young Berliners' love of swing and jazz was only the tip of an iceberg; their fascination with American music, film, fashion, and lifestyle would be blamed for impeded rehabilitation efforts for years to come.

72. Undated flyer, SAPMO 30/IV 2/16 211, 8; Bezirksamt Charlottenburg, lecture schedule, undated, SAPMO DY 30/IV 2/16/211, 6–7; KPD Berlin Report, September 1945, LAB I/20/40, 18; "Bericht des Zentralen Jugendausschußes Berlin," 9 August 1945, DY 30/IV 2/16 212, 210–15 (Noting the ineffectiveness of discussions, this report criticizes both youth and their leaders); "Bericht 6. Magistratsitzung 11.6.45," in Dieter Hanauske, Sitzungsprotokolle des Magistrat der Stadt Berlin 1945–46, Part I, 1945 (Berlin: Berlin Verlag 1995), 123; Bezirksleitung der KPD Berlin, "Tätigkeitsbericht," 31 October 1945, SAPMO ZPA NM 182/852, 11–23.

73. Völker, 2.

74. "Ein halbes Jahr Berliner Magistrat. Der Magistrat gibt Rechenschaft" (Berlin, undated), 127; "Volksfest Bericht," LAB C Rep 900 Nr i/3/9/096; SAPMO DY 30/IV 2/16 211 s53; Report, 14 September 1945, SAPMO DY 30/IV 2/16/211, 138; "Bericht des Zentralen Jugendausschußes Berlin, 9 August 1945, SAPMO DY 30/IV 2/16 212, 210–15.

INTERLUDE I

Depraved Girls

Not surprisingly, girls and young women constituted a problematic group for postwar social and municipal authorities. Perceptions of unmarried women had troubled European society for centuries as potential instigators of social turmoil and immorality, particularly in periods of rapid change and upheaval. [1] Single women threatened a social order that firmly tied reproduction to marriage. National Socialism addressed widespread concerns about women by exulting motherhood as a patriotic duty and offering maternal incentives for marriage and childbirth. Specifically, the Nazi state encouraged German girls to see themselves as "brave and strong women, who will be the comrades of [male] political soldiers—and who will go on to live in their families as women and mothers, and help shape our National Socialist worldview . . . girls and women who know about the necessities of life in the German nation and act accordingly."[2]

Marriage and motherhood were glorified and rewarded to the point that, even when industrial capacity was hurt by labor shortages after 1939, relatively few German women worked outside the home. Not until 1943 were women (ages 18–45) required to register for war-related work, and even then, pregnant women, as well as those with either one child under age six or two children younger than fourteen, were exempted from conscription, suggesting little change in beliefs about woman's primary functions in society.[3]

Of course, the domestic ideal did not always reflect reality. That said, most of my interviewees described their mothers as apolitical housewives. Supplemental paid work was considered temporary and thus not central to perceptions of their mothers. After the war, however, it became clear that women would remain long-term, if not permanent, single heads-of-households. Cohort members saw their own mothers overstepping traditional gender boundaries, and realized that, given wartime casualties, they themselves could not count on marriage and motherhood.[4] This very problem, the misnamed *Frauenüberschnuß*, worried authorities.

Even though the problem—the particularly uneven male/female ratio in postwar Berlin—would have been more accurately described as a "male shortage," officials discussed it as a surplus of women, implying that even this numerical imbalance was somehow women's own fault.[5] Early postwar reports suggest that this numerical imbalance was particularly worrisome for youth officials. For one, most girls had been taught, both by tradition and by RJF programming, to expect and to prepare themselves for marriage and motherhood, and Nazi society had offered mothers both symbolic and material rewards. This intensive emphasis on motherhood worried postwar youth officials. One communist activist summed up the concerns of numerous colleagues, observing that "[Girls] have few chances of getting a man, so that for them, life no longer really has any meaning."[6] A life stripped of meaning, of course, is in itself a lamentable fate. What worried officials most, however, was the collective social effect of Berlin's *Frauenüberschuss*. The prospect of marriage, they believed, had a moralizing effect on society, as girls "saved themselves" for the wedding night. Without this kind of self-policing, young *Berlinerinnen* put not only themselves, but all youth, and perhaps even the future of German society, at serious risk. A stroll through Berlin's dance clubs confirmed one Friedrichshain official's worst fears.

[Dance halls] lead countless young girls down the path of vice. Defiled so young, they often fall victim to prostitution. [These girls] also drive boys to play cavalier, thus spending sums of [stolen] money on them. Wild dancing, depraved *Zeckereien*, and in the end, sexually transmitted diseases, destroy their health. We must attack pornography and trashy literature and films. Our youths must be led back to simplicity. The ban on admittance to peep show establishments should be raised to as high an age as possible. Young people's natural, and in itself surely not reprehensible love of dance must be steered in the right direction."[7]

Young women and girls, argued the commissioner, should be held responsible for a surge in immoral behavior in postwar Berlin. If girls weren't competing with one another for attention and sexual favors, honorable German youths and young war veterans would not be led into lives of crime. Girls might "fall" into prostitution as young innocents, but they quickly evolve into active agents of immorality, without whom peep shows could not exist.[8]

The police commissioner viewed nightclubs and dance halls within a context of health and crime crises; rising crime rates seem directly related to the greater opportunities for socializing available to Berliners after the war. Like many of the older generation, he pointed back to an earlier era, when German youths were content with simpler pleasures, such as folk dancing, waltzes, and polkas. This era of innocence had ended with two dramatic events that corrupted Berlin's girls through a sudden unnatural sexual awakening.

First and most famously, the early weeks of Soviet occupation included the rape of countless *Berlinerinnen* by Red Army soldiers. It was impossible to calculate exactly how many women had been violated, let alone how many cohort members (most of whom were in their teens at the time) had lost their virginity in this way. Nonetheless, virtually everyone in Berlin—public officials, military officers, refugees, and permanent residents—knew women who had been raped, some multiple times, and this knowledge certainly colored youth authorities' expectations of youth behavior in the years to come. Furthermore, although there have been few public references to this period of widespread and typically unpunished rapes, it has become a part of Berliners' narratives of the 1940s. Rippe's account is typical, in that it links stereotypes about the Red Army—a topic rarely addressed by postwar youth authorities—with one of these same officials' key concerns: relationships between German girls and American men.

And slowly the Russians advanced, middle, end of April [1945]. Things got harder, we heard different rumors, and always hoped that the Americans would get here quicker. We couldn't understand in the least, why the Americans had stopped somewhere there along the Elbe, and didn't keep marching. We couldn't imagine that the Americans wouldn't want the glory of taking Berlin, that they'd just leave it for the Russians. . . . At any rate, [on 25 April] the first Russians banged on the door. There were about eight of us, all women, no men, [just] women and two children. My mother and I opened the door, they were very friendly, must have been officers, and searched the house. . . . I had a big spyglass, which I used to watch the airplanes. . . . And anyway one Russian took my spyglass, looked through it, smiled and gave it back. And also said to my mother, "*Mutter, Tochter*," quite friendly, and they left again. We said, "Wow, the Russians are really nice. The propaganda's not true, it was all nonsense."

And then came the next Russians, Mongolian, that's what they looked like, with slightly slanted eyes. And he, one took me away, my mother tried to stop him but was thrown aside. He took me first into the coal cellar, I thought he was going to shoot me. I had no idea. Rape, well, I didn't really know exactly what that was. And then he took me into a flat and raped me. And when I resisted he reached for his pistol, to say he'd shoot me. So of course I didn't resist after that, and it was over quickly and I was somehow just glad a bit later to land back by my mother. Alive, but raped. And the other women were next, thank God not my mother, and then we thought about what to do, it can't go on like this. Either we run to the woods, or hide, and then I dressed up like a little child, so with pigtails. And in front, I had a tooth I took out, a fake tooth, from after an accident, and I laid in bed and my mother dressed up like an old woman, and when the Russians came, they came all the time, I always said "iezkuchol," it means something like "child sick," we'd picked that up someplace . . . and the Russians were really friendly, gave me a piece of bread sometimes. They had sympathy for a sick child. . . .

On 28 May school started again, we were all very thin and starving, and for the most part raped, but we didn't talk about it. . . . We all must have wanted to forget, everyone wanted to forget, and no one wanted to tell about it again, I couldn't talk about it either. Now I can, but for years I couldn't talk about it, the rape. . . . In school, I didn't learn much, I quit in July, the end of July. It was really hard for me, and I was really bad in school, just couldn't grasp it anymore. . . . I didn't understand math, and Latin, it was just too hard. And a half-hour walk to get there, and hungry, and I just didn't care about school anymore . . . had so many other worries. I hardly learned anything at school, have no real diploma. It was about three months and I dropped out. . . . Everyone had worries, problems too, but you just had to cope with them. . . . I couldn't go to my mother, she had enough other worries. I mean, I got along well with my mother, but sexually, there was no explanation, that didn't exist.

I had an American boyfriend once. Well, no, I had a crush on an American, an officer, when I was sixteen, very handsome, blond, from Florida, and I always went to him in his flat. That was a given, he had a flat, and we just had two rooms; my mother never said anything. It was clear nothing happened. And so I went there in the evenings. There was nice wine and we talked and he kissed me, yes, and then well, one day he led me into the bedroom. Then I understood, "God no, you don't want that!. And maybe a child, no, then you'd be an *Amiliebchen*," and I got up and went home. He was shocked and I never saw him again. . . . And I was shocked at him, how he somehow, it was understood then that if you had sex, you didn't love [the girl], love meant wanting to get engaged and then married. But so, quick sex. You knew right away, the man only wanted sex and didn't love you. So I stood up and besides, one worried about getting pregnant. Got up and left and . . . it lasted a few weeks and I saw him often and we talked, kissed sometimes, but nothing more. And one day he wanted the ultimate, all the way. And I was shocked. And it was over. And I never got anything else from him, I'd sometimes gotten chocolate and so forth, that was the end of it. And then he left; he was transferred. I can't say anything more about the Americans.[9]

While losing her virginity at the hands of a pistol-wielding "Mongol" traumatized Rippe, and she now associates her inability to process the experiences with subsequent problems at school, she did not view being raped as either unexpected or atypical—such were the Russian barbarians. What shocked her was the way *American* men treated German women.

In general, this *Amiliebchen* phenomenon comprises the second stage of young Berliners' fall into immorality. Rippe was quite clear on this point. Like so many of her peers, she had long yearned for a taste of the American way of life. In the months after the war, she sought out American movies and music, and was thrilled to learn that U.S. forces had finally come to Berlin. Having put America on such a pedestal, however, her hopes were dashed, and she learned that Russian Mongols and American GIs were in some ways quite similar.

Frau Tinker also described affairs between western soldiers and German girls. Although she herself never succumbed to American advances, she highlighted the social stigma attached to such voluntary relationships.

It was the *Fräuleinwunder*. I didn't go out with them. . . . My husband [had been] in the navy, came into the navy very young and was a submarine wheelman, and had a girlfriend here in Berlin, a pretty blond who was quite gay, or at least in the pictures she always looked lively. And later my husband was in a POW camp, in England and then in Canada, and they had an absentee marriage [*Ferntrauung*], even though they hardly knew each other; they were young and she was only sixteen or seventeen. Then, when he came back, he didn't return from Canada until 1947 or '48, [and] then he discovered. . . . Of course, as a prisoner, he had nothing, and she just had a tiny flat, and then he heard from everyone that his wife went out with the Americans a lot and was gone and was, well, one of those *Amiliebchen*, as we said. Well, and then he, he was totally distraught but she reassured him somehow, it'll never happen again or something, and at any rate they stayed together a little while and then he went *Hamstern*, that was normal, they had to . . . you'd go to some village and take everything you could trade so that you got something. . . I never went *Hamstern* but my husband went, we didn't know each other yet, he was still married. And then he figured out that while he was gone, she went back [to the Americans] when he wasn't there because she got nice things. And that was the end of it and he got a divorce.

He left, moved in with his parents and studied at the university and became a teacher, and that's when we met, when he was divorced, and she went with an *Ami* to America. What's that automobile town . . . with huge slaughterhouses? Yes, Chicago, she moved there and apparently had a child and then wrote him too, that she wanted to see Germany again and wanted to get together with him. I heard about it and thought, "well, do what you want.' But I was furious that he met with her and [she showed him] she was staying in a pension on the *Ku'damm*, and had smart clothes and everything, as he told me. I got a bit mad, she tried to so, well it seemed she wasn't so happy, and she wanted to have him back. But for him it was over, you know? At any rate, she went back and then we got married. Later, it was years before we married. And, yes, well, that's why they broke up, that was the starting point, wasn't it? That she was so interested in the *Amis*, because of the money.[10]

Tinker depicted her husband as a victim of his first wife's immoral and disloyal behavior. He was a war veteran, for whom the young German woman should have saved herself, instead of yielding to the lure of western materialism.[11] She paid for her greed and indiscretion, first as the guilty party in their divorce case and then through what Tinker assumed was a less-than-successful marriage in the United States. Both Rippe and Tinker's descriptions of failed relationships with GIs would have been welcome additions to *Jugendämter* reports on the "girl problem" in the early years of occupation. Not surprisingly, criticism of Americans' seductive power was especially vehement in communist-dominated districts, where youth authorities had a vested interest in pointing at the misguided and doomed nature of fraternization with those they dubbed the "self appointed colonial rulers."[12] Policing such relationships was more problematic in the American sector, where authorities were not only dependent on U.S. aid, but also subject to the occupiers' own regulatory efforts.

The combination of the *Frauenüberschuß* and women's dangerously sexual nature also perplexed adult activists trying to recruit young Berliners into reconstruction efforts and nascent political organizations. On the one hand, the lack of young men meant that activists needed to include and nurture women as future leaders. On the other hand, however, enhancing young women's public roles reawakened concerns about immorality that had haunted earlier coed youth groups.

In postwar Berlin, where both the authority and the public were already sensitized to girls' problematic sexuality, few organizations could afford to risk allegations of sexual impropriety. The SPD-sponsored Falcons, the largest political youth movement in West Berlin, found itself in this dilemma in the early 1950s. One incident garnered enough attention that Herr Böhme, a Falcon organizer, was called to task by the mayor's office. Böhme's response to the mayoral inquiry tried to both quell fears and assert the SPD's belief that coeducational activities were key to the party's future.

After the Falcon camp closed on 13 August 1953, six girls (ages 14–17) and two boys (14–15) and one leader (male 18) had planned to sleep together for a night in one tent. After a warning from police, they did use two tents. The Falcons' response to this incident is that the organization has a coed policy for its children's camps, but not for camps for [youths] ages fifteen and over. The Falcons will reiterate this policy to its group leaders. Should more be done in this particular case? We are calling a meeting with representatives from the relevant officials and the *Landesjugendring*.

signed Böhme[13]

Böhme had no need to explain why the above situation was problematic; the image of six girls and three boys in a single tent - even the large military-issue tents often used by the Falcons—speaks for itself. He was relieved that in this particular incident, police stepped in before the youths actually commenced any immoral behavior, but wonders out loud if it is enough that Falcons leaders reassert their official position. Rhetoric alone, as both Böhme and the mayor realized, could not regulate youthful sexuality.

Frau Burkhardt, who joined the Falcons at thirteen and quickly rose through the ranks of local leadership, recalled an awareness of authorities' concern about the coeducational camping trips. However, whereas Tinker acknowledged the legitimacy of such fears, Burkhardt dismissed them as essentially unfounded.

I was thirteen in 1945. Perhaps we were intellectually more mature then and shaped by our wartime experiences . . . and my parents belonged to the founders—the re-founders—of the social democratic party here in Charlottenburg, and I was interested and so on exactly 4 November 1945 went for the first time to a Young Socialists gathering. . . . And I was right there from the beginning, and we got the information that there'd be twenty zones, or rather sectors, and from each district a representative would be nominated, and they'd meet in the SPD bureau . . . and we met then with Heinz Westphal I can't recall exactly, but mid 1946 at the latest we met in the SPD Berlin central office. . . I as the representative from Charlottenburg, I was fourteen then, nominated at thirteen, one of the youngest there . . . we had twenty representatives, at least one from each district, and had discussions, what shall we do. Young people were surrounded by rubble, they were hungry and half-frozen, nothing to wear, and we wanted to motivate them. . . .

[In] 1947, when we hardly had a tent or anything, we went camping along the Havel. And we froze. Let me tell you, about 3 A.M., or three thirty, when it got really cold, we all crawled out of the tents and made a campfire to warm up . . . about thirty-five, forty of us. . . . 1948 in the spring, we had a camp on the Little Wannsee, and cooked so, dried vegetables over an open fire. It was terrible. . . . But we had a lot of fun and always had a ball and played games and somebody else had a chess board, and the next had [such and such], and above all singing, always music and dancing, and it was a happy group of young people. . . .

And then 1949, yes, the *Falken* continued of course, but my personal engagement, I started working in 1949 and was still studying in the evenings, and so [couldn't] always be there. I still played the violin with the Singing and Music Group, I was needed there. And I went occasionally, but it's just that with eighteen or nineteen . . . people pair off and that doesn't fit so much in the group. So, for us, coupling-off was looked down upon. We were very prudish back then. And one just couldn't talk about a lot of things. And then if a couple kissed somewhere, they'd be teased and called names for months, we say . . . there's a phrase, it's probably not in the Duden [dictionary—KAR]. *"Der kleinen Hans, den man ein bißchen neckt,"* it must come from "necken." It's just a phrase we used, and they'd be, as Berliners say *"auf die Schippe genommen"* [raked over the coals], and we didn't like that, although even then girls and boys were always together [in the *Falken*]. The evangelical youth, weren't many Catholics in Berlin, but they too, the evangelical groups were split by gender. . . . And we, we were however, always boys and girls together, we found it normal, and coeducation in the schools came then later. . . . Some said it was immoral, that we were together, and but, well I can say, we had the highest morals; nobody there, when we slept in tents, there was no contact. We were, very, very, well, today one would say old-fashioned. . . . Look what we wrote then:

> In Germany's worst days together we came,
> Though above us the sky was still red from flame.
> The strife was finally over, our camaraderie was still strong
> Together towards the future in a joyful Falcon throng.

> United in friendship, with singing and games,
> We set out on the path towards our great aims.
> Escaping from the ruins, into the meadows and woods
> No regrets, out into the world like the falcons we soar.

> We Falcons will not falter, should one give up the fight
> Rather, we are comrades, and so restore his inner light.
> Ever ready for new friendships, we work, travel, give aid.
> We Falcons gladly fight for Germany's future and new fate.[14]

Burkhardt defied postwar authorities' assumptions about girls and their seemingly problematic nature. Wartime experiences had not, in her view, stripped German youth of their morality and sense of social responsibility. Rather, war and defeat had left young people, male and female alike, more mature, so that a fourteen-year-old girl was capable of engaging SPD leaders in heated debates. Far from being depressed, skeptical, apathetic, or prepared to sell their bodies, she and her peers demonstrated optimism, creativity, and a willingness to work hard. Finally, Burkhardt was proud of her peers' moral self-policing strategies, noting that even "pairing off," let alone flirting or physical contact, was considered taboo and scorned by the youths themselves.

The girl problem in postwar Berlin reveals a clash between old and young, and between authorities' perceptions and youths' attitudes. Reflecting long-standing social norms and fears, as well as their understanding of National Socialist ideology, officials remained pessimistic, and in the early 1950s, both successor states considered the reestablishment of behavioral norms and marriage—albeit on different terms—an important part of their national social agendas.[15]

Reminiscing cohort members expressed three kinds of responses to such documented societal concerns about postwar girls. First, they admitted and defended their desire to "be young" by engaging in what they considered carefree activities—dancing, dating, and camping. Second, they frequently dismissed broad condemnation of their activities and peer group as based on evidence of a small minority of girls. Finally, looking back, and comparing their memories to contemporary youths' public displays of affection or violence, they often asserted their own sexual naïveté and the innocence of their own social experiences. Frau Pestopf, for example, tied memories of Berlin's postwar nightlife not to social ills, but rather to healthy and natural leisure pursuits.

Sometimes we took boat excursions. In those days, you [would] take a steamship to Köpenick across the Müggelsee, and that was beautiful. Wannsee was less interesting and the other was also less expensive, somehow. . . . And a school chum, Karin, her parents had a pub, a little hut, out in Köpenick, you had to go through the woods a bit, and you could stay over the weekend. Saturday-Sunday and then back [to the city] because we had to work, and we also went dancing. . . . No disco music, but live bands, accordion, drums. . . . We just went wherever there was music. There was one dance club, I think it was called The Palms or something, it was quite famous. I also went dancing at the Resi, with telephones on the tables. One time I remember, with a friend. It was Christmas day 1950 or 51, she came over to coffee and we fixed ourselves up and went to the Resi. . . . Table telephones and also a pneumatic mail system (*Rohrpost*). And so [men could ask] from their table, "Would you like to dance?"

It was interesting and that's how I met my first husband. . . . He sent mail or called, and then he came to the table, and I was away. It took three tries, he told me, and then I was finally happy. And we, I married in 1955, I was twenty-one. . . . Of course we were in love, a crush, you're seen and the man makes a compliment, that's really nice. Then there was also getting out of the house, if possible [into] our own flat, but that didn't work at first, so we sublet from colleagues. We lived there two years and then my daughter came. While I was in the hospital a flat became available, in the building I'd always lived in, above my parents. But it was our own place. So I got out of subletting, [only to go] from one dependency straight into the next. I had rough years with my parents. Mother worked at home, she sat at the sewing machine from morning 'til night, Father lost his job. That's when the drinking started. Got into the wrong crowd, and there was always financial troubles and fighting, and [I] the oldest was the glimmer of light, and they crept down here. Whenever my parents fought or there were sibling fights, they always came to me. My mother and father too, and that was too much for me, so that I hardly noticed that I had my own family. . . . It was hard as a young woman, I was always so serious and tense. . . . All because I moved back there. I was glad, but I would never do it again. And won't, my parents both died more than twenty years ago.[16]

Pestopf's account contrasts markedly with the negative context in which police authorities observed Berlin's nightlife. The Köpenick pub was to her a safe haven, seemingly far from the destruction so evident in Berlin proper. Under the chaperonage of a friend's parents, she enjoyed not wild modern dancing, but rather the music of small neighborhood bands, formed wherever a few instruments could be rounded up. The bands likely played the swing music about which the police commissioner complained, but Pestopf, like other cohort members, emphasized the improvised, enthusiastic yet innocent style of the performances.

Even in the city itself, at nightclubs like the Palms or "the Resi," Pestopf's nightlife experiences were nothing like that noted by patrolling police officers. Had Pestopf been better off financially, we might presume she frequented high-class establishments at which "wild depravity" was not tolerated. However, given Pestopf's financial and familial circumstances, it seems unlikely that either club was particularly exclusive. In contrast to the police commissioner's description of smoke-filled dance halls filled with drunken and lust-crazed youths, Pestopf's account is reminiscent of a Fred Astaire–style movie, in which nicely dressed girls sit at tables, demurely waiting for invitations to dance and then losing their hearts to handsome and honorable gentlemen.

Within this romanticized depiction of postwar social life, Pestopf acknowledged a key theme of cohort members' life narratives—the theoretical opportunity for independence was indeed, she acknowledged, an ulterior motive of many would-be brides. In her case, and many others, the yearned-for marital freedom was very long in coming. However, whereas officials blamed demographics and youthful promiscuity, Pestopf pointed to the persistence of intergenerational familial problems. Frau Barthe offered another example of such interfamilial disagreement regarding the "girl problem."

I met my husband in 1948, through my brother-in-law. My sister and he had written each other when he was in [Allied] captivity. And then he came back . . . and they went out a lot, and I said, "Why do I always sit alone at home," and he, my brother-in-law said, "Well, I have a buddy who was in the camp with me; he lives in East Berlin, but we could all four go dancing together." So we made a date and that's how I met my husband. . . . My stepmother, she thought, "[I can't] let anything happen," and you know, she always sat there right beside us. And my husband, he never could kiss me in front of people, he was too embarrassed. So she sat there, my father would go to bed, and she'd yawn, and I'd say, "Don't you want to go to bed?" "I'm not tired," and she sat there until he left.
But then weekends, they went out to the country, they had a little piece of land, and my fiance stayed with me. . . . And later she was so surprised that I was suddenly pregnant! She'd say, "I just can't figure out how that could happen!" And then I had trouble with her when we got married because the baby was born in November and we got married in May. "It'll be a six-month child," she told me every day. And I said, "Well, you don't need to look at it if it embarrasses you." One time she just pushed me so far, it was too much, and I bawled, and didn't speak to her for a long time. And my father didn't like that, he always said, "Can't you just get along?" I said, "She has to apologize, not I. She's provoked me every day, and for a long time I didn't say anything, but it's too much if she's going to reproach me every day." Yes she was rather unmodern, she just couldn't understand.[17]

Like Pestopf, Barthe saw nothing unusual or problematic in the way she met her husband; writing letters to soldiers had been encouraged during the war, and a blind date was certainly preferable to sitting at home with a depressed widower. As if addressing authorities' fears about youthful immorality, Barthe observed that her date wouldn't even kiss her in public. In fact, the only problem in the relationship was Barthe's stepmother, who made no effort to understand or "mother" either of the two sisters. In other words, while youth officials considered *verwahrloste Mädchen* primarily as a cause of moral decay, Barthe and her peers understood their plight in a broader social context that included wartime experiences, familial crises and shattered dreams. They saw their personal relationships not as opportunities for immorality or escapism, but rather as avenues through which they could simultaneously assert their youthfulness and pursue personal goals.

NOTES

1. The German phrase *verwahrloste Mädchen* referred to female youths who had broken the law as well as those who, due to broken families, unemployment, or other circumstances, were considered at risk for engaging in immoral behavior. It translates as both "neglected" and "depraved."

2. Jutta Rudiger, "On the Self-image of the League of German Maidens" (1939) quoted in Michael Burleigh and Wolfgang Wippermann, *The Racial State Germany 1933–1945* (Cambridge: Cambridge University Press, 1992), 235–36.

3. Jost Hermand, "All Power to the Women: Nazi Concepts of Matriarchy," *Journal of Contemporary History* 19:4 (1984): 649–67; Leila Rupp, "Mother of the Volk: The Image of Women in Nazi Society," *Signs* 3 (1977), 362–79. Also: Renate Bridenthal, Atina Grossmann and Marion Kaplan, eds., *When Biology became Destiny - Women in Weimar and Nazi Germany* (New York: Monthly Review Press, 1984); Karin Hausen, ed., *Frauen suchen ihre Geschichte: Historische Studien* (Munich: Beck, 1983); Claudia Koonz, *Mothers in the Fatherland: Women, the Family and Nazi Politics* (New York: St. Martin's Press, 1987); Jill Stephenson, *Women in Nazi Society* (London: Croom Helm, 1975); ibid., *The Nazi Organization of Women* (London: Croom Helm, 1981). Pointing to more relaxed divorce laws, Stephenson points out that motherhood took precedence over marriage.

4. Ulla Roberts, *Starke Mütter, ferne Väter. Töchter reflektieren ihre Kindheit im Nationalsozialismus und in der Nachkriegszeit* (Frankfurt: Fischer Taschenbuch Verlag, 1994), 41–45. Also: Lerke Gravenhorst and Carmen Tatschmurat, eds., *Töchter-Fragen NS Frauen Geschichte* (Freiburg: Kore, Verlag Traute Hensch, 1990); Atina Grossmann, "Feminist Debates about Women and National Socialism, "*Gender and History*, 3:3 (Autumn 1991), 350–58.

5. Katherine Leota Dollard, "A Tool of Social Reform: The *Frauenüberschuß* of Late Imperial Gemany" (Ph.D. diss., University of North Carolina at Chapel Hill, 1992).

6. KPD Berlin Report for September 1945, pp. 13, 16. LAB I/20/040.

7. Friedrichshain Criminal Commissioner, "Report on Youth Protection" 5 October 1945 LAB STA Rep 135/1 415.

8. Thomas Grotum, *Die Halbstarken. Zur Geschichte einer Jugendkultur der 50er Jahre* (New York: Campus Verlag 1994).

9. Rippe,. 3, 11, 14–15.

10. Tinker, 21–22.

11. Protokoll, Jugendkommission Sitzung 12 October 1949, LAB C Rep 900 IV 1–2/16 481.

12. Protokoll, Jugendkommission Sitzung 12 October 1949, LAB C Rep 900 IV 1–2/16 481.

13. Böhme, Note for the governing mayor, 10 October 1953 (regarding an incident on 22 August 1953) LAB Rep 12 Acc 1327 Nr 111.

14. Burkhardt, 1, 2, 4–6, 17, 18, and song manuscript: "Wir haben uns gefunden als Deutschland schwer in Not und über uns der Himmel war von dem großen Brennen noch ganz rot. Der Zwietracht nun ein Ende, Kameradschaft immerdar in einer kleinen Gruppe als zukünftige freudige, lustige Falkenschar. In Freundschaft stets beisammen, beim Singen und beim Spiel, so haben wir begonnen, das ist der Weg zu unserem großen Ziel. Heraus jetzt aus den Mauern, hinaus in Wald und Feld und keiner wird's bedauern, wir ziehen wie die Falken in die Welt. Will einer mal versagen, wir Falken kennen's nicht. Dann sind wir Kameraden und geben seiner Zukunft wieder Licht. Wandern und helfen zur Freundschaft stets bereit, wir Falken streiten freudig für Deutschlands Zukunft und die neue Zeit."

15. Gisela Helwig and Hildegard Maria Nickel, eds., *Frauen in Deutschland 1945–1992* (Bonn: Bundeszentrale für politische Bildung, 1993); Peter Kuhnert and Ute Ackermann "Jenseits von Lust und Liebe?—Jugendsexualität in den 50er Jahren," in Heinz-Hermann Krüger, ed., *"Die Elvis-Tolle, die hatte ich mir unauffällig wachsen lassen." Lebensgeschichte und jugendliche Alltagskultur in den fünfziger Jahren*

(Opladen: Leske & Budrich, 1985), 43–83; Robert G. Moeller, *Protecting Motherhood: Women and the Family in the Politics of Postwar West Germany* (Berkeley: University of California Press, 1993).

16. Pestopf, 1–2.
17. Barthe, 19–20.

3

The Hunger Years

After describing key moments of the *Endkampf* and first postwar summer in vivid detail, Berliners initially had little to say about the early years of occupation. Instead, they often painted "the Hunger Years" in broad strokes, summed up by a few key phrases that—at least to cultural insiders—conveyed far more about postwar Berlin than their literal meaning. These phrases reveal not only how local and international political tensions shaped East and West Berliners' experiences and memories, but also that these often overlooked years constituted a crucial period of identity construction for Berliners born in 1926–1935.

As they moved from childhood to adulthood during the uncertain 1940s, cohort members found themselves intensely scrutinized by activists, bureaucrats, and researchers from across the political spectrum. Many described Berlin's postwar youth as politically apathetic, morally self-serving, and psychologically maimed. At the same time, however, German and Allied officials alike competed for youths' loyalty, promoting new ideals and attempting to mold young Berliners into particular societal roles.

Such competition exposed a numerically small cohort to what was initially a variety of viewpoints, offered them unprecedented leadership opportunities, and permitted selective participation, a strategy already practiced in the first postwar summer. Many were understandably reluctant to commit to any one ideological camp, but explored the new cultural and political diversity as they sought foundations for postwar lives and identities. Building on the lessons of self-preservation learned in the last years of the Nazi regime, young Berliners took their time, testing the new ideas and seeking individual paths to postwar normalcy in both private and public life.

Unfortunately, the uneasy wartime alliance between the USSR and the western Allies that had produced this window of opportunity for youth dissolved far too quickly. The 1948–1949 Blockade and airlift compelled many Berliners—young and old alike—to pick sides in an increasingly polarized political atmosphere. Personal experiences and anecdotes about the Blockade fit into distinctive eastern and western versions of a collective postwar narrative.

More than the political context in which they moved, however, interviewees described their individual initiatives during this early postwar period, focusing particularly on leisure activities. Hobbies and personal pursuits stood out in cohort members' narratives for several reasons. First, pursuing even simple hobbies often entailed considerable sacrifice and commitment, which, together with the typically intangible rewards, cemented leisure activities in interviewees' minds. Second, hobbies provided a particularly necessary distance from home lives that were often wrought with tensions—about past identities, present responsibilities, and future prospects. Finally, unsure of their city's future role, let alone their nation's place in the international community, young Berliners found a necessary anchor in their hobbies. In short, leisure activities not only filled material and psychological needs, but also helped cohort members compensate for familial, social, and political instability. Over time, these hobbies became a pillar of adult identities rooted in perseverance and independence.

KEY WORDS

"Das waren eben die Hungerjahre" (Those were the Hunger Years, afterall).

Sugar beets growing in the city parks, dresses cut from prewar curtains, *Malzkaffee* as ersatz coffee, and toast spread with roasted flour and oil. Long barefoot walks through rubble-strewn streets, endless lines for everything from milk to newspapers, cold nights in unheated flats. Compared to the air raids, frozen treks across the eastern Reich, and encounters with Red Army soldiers that characterized wartime memories, postwar experiences offered little potential for dramatic storytelling. Rather, *Hungerjahre* evokes drudgery and scarcity, both endured with the hope that life had to get better.

Following on the heels of a rather surreal summer of peace, winter 1945–1946 brought the first of annual health, food, and medical crises that plagued Berlin for the rest of the decade. The first postwar winter was actually milder than expected, but a continuing onslaught of refugees (legal and illegal) ravished Berlin's limited food supplies. Supplementary shipments from the western occupation zones were often delayed when Soviet authorities restricted railway usage through the Soviet Zone.

The second postwar winter was even worse. Despite record-setting temperatures, an ongoing coal shortage compelled city officials to limit households to two and a half hours of electricity per day. Local businesses, unable to power equipment or heat offices, laid off nearly 100,000 workers.[1] Similarly short on fuel, school officials closed buildings for weeks, and even when classes were offered, pupils were kept home by a lack of shoes or winter clothes.[2] Sociologist Hilda Thurnwald found that these school closings had a particularly demoralizing effect on secondary students. Youths of this cohort had typically lost a year or more of education during the war, and returning to the classroom entailed overcoming considerable psychological and material hurdles. Like all pupils, these youths had trouble acquiring even the most basic school supplies. In addition, however, many had taken on significant responsibilities in the war effort; joining younger peers seemed like a step backward on the road to maturity and independence.

Thurnwald's study is particularly interesting because she brought together statistical summaries and qualitative analyses of nearly 500 case studies collected in 1946 and 1947. In this way, Thurnwald painted a vivid picture of the combined effects of wartime destruction and seasonal conditions on everyday life.

The long-lasting and extreme cold of winter 1946/47, and the resulting severe wood and coal shortages forced many families to accustom themselves to colder temperatures in their homes. In 1945–46, most described as "warm enough" room temperatures of 13–15 degrees. These families now [early 1947] consider room temperatures of 10–12 Degrees Celsius adequate. Nine of 154 households had no heat in January 1947, and another forty-eight could heat only one room, and that to a temperature of less than ten C. . . . The food situation for most families is [also] worse than the previous year, despite the elimination of ration level V, and although an increase in [foreign donations] to schools and daycare centers have provided some relief. . . . Thirty of 154 families lost their potatoes due to freezing, many other families were unable to bring earned or begged potatoes and vegetables [into Berlin] from the countryside, and promised packages could not be sent [due to the cold and increased police patrols].[3]

The magistrate responded to the crisis by opening public warming rooms and eliminating the lowest ration level (the *Sterbe-* or *Hungerkarte*), but could offer little further relief. Of 350 student teachers surveyed by Thurnwald in early 1947, 253 lacked winter shoes and 98 were without winter coats; less than half had eaten a warm dinner, and a quarter had skipped breakfast. In February alone, more than 180,000 cases of tuberculosis were identified among Berliners ages fifteen to twenty, while nearly a third of surveyed youths suffered from chronic conditions including malnutrition, frostbite, diphtheria, and circulatory ailments; some 60 percent of school-age Berliners were infected with worms. The cumulative effect of physical deprivation further manifested itself in high absentee rates, an inability to concentrate, and increased susceptibility to depression.[4]

The international community was well aware of Berliners' hardships, and numerous charitable organizations offered assistance. Most relief efforts, however, such as the British "Stork" program, which evacuated at-risk individuals to the western zones, focused on younger children.[5] Among the older 1926–1933 cohort, foreign relief agencies officially targeted youths who held physically demanding jobs, came from tuberculosis-infected families, or faced difficult social or familial conditions. Virtually every youth in Berlin met at least one of these conditions, but no interviewees described receiving either foreign aid or the special Christmas packages distributed to "needy" youths in both 1946 and 1947. Some did recall receiving hot meals through a city-wide school lunch program, but again, most nutritional subsidies were directed at pre-adolescents.[6] Consequently, cohort members were usually underweight and overtaxed both physically and psychologically, leaving them vulnerable even during the warm summers. In 1947, for example, polio swept through Berlin; beyond permanently disabling many survivors, the epidemic closed schools, youth centers, and sports facilities yet again.[7]

In short, both the degree and persistence of physical deprivation during the *Hungerjahre* were worse than many youths had known during the war itself. As a result, cohort members' narratives often blurred the boundary between war and peace. Instead, daily experience imprinted memories of an era of hardship beginning in the early 1940s, ending after the Blockade, and punctuated not by political change as much as by personal turning points. "Those were simply the Hunger Years," and cohort members seemed to find little reason to dwell on the difficult—and for the most part irresolvable—conditions of daily life.

That said, these difficulties certainly informed interviewees' values and self-perceptions. They learned, as young people, to get along with very little, to make do. Looking back, they often contrasted their own material modesty with the expectations of their children and grandchildren. On a deeper level, memories of scavenging and improvising nourished interviewees' sense of themselves as unusually self-reliant and independent. Whether or not a particular wartime *Schlüßelerlebnis* had altered their self-perception, interviewees persistently highlighted their own autonomy and self-sufficiency during the *Hungerjahre*.

"Die Soldaten waren eben da" (The soldiers were simply there).

Already noted as significant in memories of summer 1945, occupation troops and policies shaped Berliners' lives and opinions throughout the postwar period. The military presence would be normalized in later years, but seemed especially invasive in the mid- to late 1940s. Beyond imposing curfews and other regulations, all four military administrations hired local civilians as wait staff, kitchen help, drivers, translators, and secretaries. Young Berliners found these jobs quite desirable, since potential fringe benefits—such as a warm workplace or access to food, and coal—outweighed drawbacks that included long hours and a lack of job security.

Like native officials, the occupation powers sought to rehabilitate what they believed to be Berlin's maimed youth. Cohort members' memories of such efforts were often limited, and clearly influenced by both prior expectations and subsequent experiences. Thus, West Berliners highlighted encounters with GIs, who were famous for engaging youths in conversation on the street, joining in games of streetball, and attempting to share a love of baseball. Recognizing both their city's special relationship with the United States and my own U.S. citizenship, most West Berliners noted the Americans' friendliness and apparent wealth. Zehlendorfer Herr Birkmann, however, who eventually moved to East Berlin, pointed out the immoral excesses of capitalism. Birkmann recalled, for example, being paid only a bowl of soup after cleaning officers' pistols and learning that at least one Berlin family had sold their car for a carton of cigarettes. In short, American soldiers often took advantage of hard-off Berliners, and in this imported culture, anything could be had for a price.

[The Americans] were all businessmen. We repaired their (private) cars. And once a guy came in a jeep and offered to sell my boss gasoline, which we needed. [He] lifted the seat, opened the cap. Twenty minutes later he was back with another full tank! He must have either cut a deal with the filling station [or something]. . . . That would've been impossible in the German army, they would've counted and recounted all the canisters. But for the Americans, anything is possible![8]

To westerners—and probably to most U.S. citizens—Birkmann's last comment might suggest an economic meritocracy, in which anyone could prosper. Coming from Birkmann, however, the phrase "anything is possible" took on a different meaning.   Having witnessed the self-centeredness of the American Dream, Birkmann criticized the notion that anything—or anyone—can be bought.   He consciously rejected the grassroots capitalism that exploited hardworking Berliners and at age 19 permanently transferred his residency from Zehlendorf to Lichtenberg.

Cohort members' recollections of British occupation soldiers were understandably less politicized. Whereas American occupation forces sought to establish direct and sometimes long-term personal relationships between individual soldiers and youths, British officers took a more reserved approach to youth rehabilitation.   They allocated meeting rooms for local youth organizations such as the Falcons and the Young Friends of Nature and, upon request, coordinated guest speakers for group meetings. British officials also supported summer camps and other youth group initiatives, but took a comparatively hands-off approach, which was meant to foster the social conditions in which young people could develop critical thinking skills and tolerance.[9]

The French presence in Berlin was notably smaller, and by design, no interviewees lived in the French sector of the city.   Herr Kösel, however, attended school in a French district, and recalled that occupation officials assigned monthly essays in which students were to discuss various aspects of Nazi society. More importantly, Kösel's father worked for French occupation forces, and the Kösels occasionally dined at the French officers' club.   While perhaps not typical of young Berliners' encounters with French soldiers, Kösel's narrative demonstrated how common themes often link memories of temporarily distinct episodes. Specifically, Kösel wove together memories of eating at the officers' club and episodes from his later career resolving insurance claims against all three western powers. Over a period of forty years, wonderful meals and upstanding professional colleagues coalesced into what he described as a generally "comfortable" relationship with soldiers of all ranks.[10]

Cohort members' descriptions of Soviet occupation troops during the *Hungerjahre* were similarly imprecise, even though the Red Army presence was described as forceful—and often violent—during and just after the *Endkampf.* Western Berliners' reticence could be attributed to a lack of contact with Soviet occupation troops; interestingly, the same holds true for many East Berliners, as off-duty Soviet soldiers rarely left their bases. In addition, Soviet officials took a much more subtle approach to youth rehabilitation. Unlike the British and Americans, who assigned youth liaison officers, Soviet occupation authorities funneled their ideals and material support through the KPD and later, the SED (Socialist Unity Party). In addition to circumventing the ugly question of preexisting prejudices and actions, this approach contrasted nicely with what some German communists identified as the imperialistic strategies of the western occupation powers. On the other hand, without the face-to-face encounters deemed crucial by the Americans, East Berliners had fewer opportunities to offset preexisting negative impressions. Finally, specific memories of Soviet occupation seemed much rarer because, in a nutshell, Moscow could never be New York or Hollywood. In other words, during the *Hungerjahre*, most cohort members were far more intrigued by American culture; a general disinterest in things Russian further diluted memories of chance encounters with occupation soldiers.

Descriptions of occupation forces seemed perhaps to be particularly informed by cohort members' interceding experiences. As noted above, throughout most of their adult lives, a visible American presence reinforced West Berliners' recollections, while East Berliners saw much less of Soviet soldiers. That said, the East German State worked to counter anti-Soviet sentiments throughout its forty-year lifespan, through friendship organizations and cultural programs, for example. More so than their western peers, interviewees from East Berlin linked stories or rumors about rape to other incidents that proved "there were both kinds" of Russians.[11] This distinction sometimes corresponded with a parallel differentiation between officers and rank-and-file soldiers; while identifying *Endkampf* fears with the latter, interviewees attributed friendliness, even unexpected courteousness, to particular officers. Miller, for example, initially refused a job in military canteen, fearing such close contact with Russian men. Officials overruled her objections, however, and Miller not only worked but also lived on the base. Looking back, Miller readily acknowledged her early misgivings, but nonetheless emphasized that the Soviet officers completely contradicted her expectations.

They were all old enough to be our father . . . [and] gave us a room with a key, so we could lock the door. . . . We could sleep in peace and they never touched us. [The officer] went and told our parents where we were; I must say they were quite proper, never did anything to us. We had food and . . . were quite comfortable there.[12]

Miller's dispassionate account brushes over what must have been at least a few sleepless nights. More generally, fear, a common theme of many *Endkampf* stories, was notably absent from memories of the Hunger Years. Compared to wartime, or even the first weeks of Soviet occupation, Berliners were in fact relatively safe, and this realization contributed to the euphoria of that first summer. Still, living conditions were far from secure; between the risks they assumed on a daily basis and the heated political atmosphere in which they lived, cohort members could have easily justified feelings of apprehension or fear during the *Hungerjahre*. Such sentiments, however, would challenge the themes of self-sufficiency and confidence that dominated interviewees' postwar narratives.

These themes of confidence and independence may also explain some cohort members' vivid memories of unofficial—even unsanctioned—encounters with foreign soldiers. While local police, health, and youth officials wrung their hands over the veritable Pandora's box of problems associated with the presence of thousands of foreign men in Berlin, cohort members largely ignored these concerns.   Interviewees certainly understood the risks of dealing with the (former) enemy—debt, arrest, injury, or sexual exploitation, for example—but their stories highlighted the beneficial side of such informal contacts.   Even Birkmann, who sharply criticized American attitudes and behaviors, recalled that the GIs offered useful opportunities.

A former colleague went to work for the Motor Pool and told me how incredible it was—he got work clothes for free and lots of food. I did oil changes for them in exchange for bread. . . . They brought in loads of hard coal for their furnaces, and dumped it in the cellars. There was barbed wire all around, but I got through, climbed in the *open* [sic] cellar window and stuffed my backpack full.[13]

Birkmann's complex attitude toward the American presence—simultaneously critical, thankful, and opportunistic—was not unusual.   Rather, it was rooted in the notions of self-sufficiency and independence that structured cohort narratives of the 1940s. Looking back, Birkmann saw no need to excuse his actions; like his peers, he was simply taking care of himself, fulfilling needs that, in his opinion, would have otherwise gone unmet.

Local German authorities recognized that many Berliners took more than wages from their foreign employers.   Municipal leaders also realized that occupation soldiers contributed to the black market and other illegal activities. In their public campaigns, however, officials worked particularly hard to regulate or discourage intimacy between foreign soldiers and German women.   While such relationships were certainly not unique to Berlin, the Hunger Years, or even the postwar era, they did become not only socially but also politically significant in the early years of the Cold War.

While interviewees recalled protectorate relationships—some of which were sexual—during the first weeks of occupation, official rhetoric rarely mentioned these presumably short-term, opportunistic alliances. Like the rapes and looting of the same period, they were simply unfortunate symptoms of the general lawlessness of the *Endkampf*, a brief and bygone era.   Throughout the *Hungerjahre*, however, municipal authorities in both eastern and western districts condemned young *Berlinerinnen* who fraternized with American GIs.

Representatives of the KPD (and, after 1946, the SED) used a variety of tactics to address the problem.   Public appeals warned apparently desperate young girls about the seductive wiles of the American "colonial masters." In a reversal of the communists' usual encouragement of internationalist sentiments, posters encouraged young women to preserve themselves for German veterans. Local health reports, meanwhile, singled out GIs when explaining the causes of high syphilis rates and declining morality among young women.[14] By the latter 1940s, such accusations matched an increasingly overt anti-American political rhetoric with which SED leaders hoped to undermine the western presence in Berlin.

Although a failure in that respect, SED officials' attacks on German-American relations focused on questions that proved even more perplexing to authorities in West Berlin.   They too worried about the impact of American morals (or lack thereof), observing for example that youths flocked to gangster films and that GIs often entered nightclubs with an underage German girl on each arm.   Unlike their SED colleagues, however, western officials could not simply denounce American *unKultur* since, particularly during the 1948–1949 Blockade, West Berlin relied on the United States' material support and political backing. Nonetheless, *Amiliebchen* endured harsh popular and media criticism, depicted as anything from aggressive opportunists to whores or even traitors.[15]

Cohort members often alluded to the same stereotypes in their personal accounts. While more sympathetic to the *Amiliebchen* phenomenon, most distanced themselves from the practice of befriending GIs, often sharing authorities' assumption that the girls sought nothing more than the potentially lucrative material benefits.

The Americans and the British and the French fell over the German women. I don't know, they were blond and pretty and they, well, they sought their pleasure too. They had their own pubs and all, and since the Germans had nothing, they used cigarettes and stockings and such to attract women. . . . Many married and emigrated [*haben 'rübergeheiratet*], like my friend, well, maybe she was better off but you heard about many [girls], that when they got there they didn't find all they'd been promised, after having been, well, here, they were the kings, you know. They had everything, could do everything; a piece of bacon was worth money or a can of meat or sheer stockings, for things like that the women were available.[16]

Tinker, like other interviewees, seemed reluctant to characterize *Amiliebchen* as either victims of foreign aggressors or pragmatic procuresses. Nonetheless, she acknowledged the clear social hierarchy and resulting distribution of power. The western occupiers, and the *Amis* in particular, "were the kings." Everyone in Berlin—authorities, parents, girls, even the soldiers themselves—knew the GIs were gatekeeper to what many *Berlinerinnen*, rightly or wrongly, thought would be a better life.

Tinker also identified generational differences in cohort members' retrospective evaluations of *Amiliebchen*. While interviewees seemed more critical of older *Berlinerinnen*, who had presumably betrayed relationships with, or at least memories of, husbands, they could understand why a peer might desire an American boyfriend. Perhaps recalling their own thoughts and lives, they understood how a young woman, wilting in Berlin's tough *Hungerjahre*, might fall for a generous, handsome, and well-dressed GI.[17]

"Jeder musste arbeiten" (Everyone had to work).

The influence of retrospection on memory is further revealed through Berliners' descriptions of their city's physical reconstruction. Looking back, they marveled at the speed with which Berlin was rebuilt. West Berliners brushed over the long months of incremental progress before the 1948 passage of the European Recovery Plan (known as the Marshall Plan), while East Berliners similarly skimmed over the more than five years until the introduction of a building lottery speeded progress in districts such as Friedrichshain.[18] Yet the simple phrase "everyone worked" expressed the very real effort that went into reconstruction. Although not all identified themselves as rubble workers per se, virtually all Berliners contributed to some kind of reconstruction project. Over a period of more than a decade, voluntary work brigades, youth laborers, and some

60,000 *Trümmerfrauen* cleared away approximately eighty million cubic meters of rubble.

Through the same key words, interviewees pointed to their own multifaceted attempts to meet familial and personal needs. They suggested that despite alleged immaturity or prior exploitation, Berlin's youth found or created economic opportunities for themselves. These usually included both temporary volunteer labor and private-sector employment, since the local job market relied on a successful reconstruction of Berlin's economic infrastructure. The stiff competition particularly hurt young people, since potential employers could be quite selective. Stumpf recalled, for example, that the particularly stiff competition for positions in bakeries and food service meant that the *Abitur*, typically required only of university-track youths, became a standard requirement for would-be apprentices.[19]

Working, in the sense of something everyone did during the *Hungerjahre*, rarely meant finding a *Beruf*, an occupational or professional calling. Even cohort members whose interregnum-era employment evolved into long-term careers seldom anticipated that possibility at the time. Compared to meeting immediate needs, career dreams were an often unaffordable luxury during the Hunger Years. Independence and relative financial security, however, seemed to be a more immediate goal, and most cohort members pursued a series of short-term jobs and independent economic initiatives—legal and illegal—through which they simultaneously met physical needs and nurtured identities rooted in confident self-sufficiency.

Through this same phrase, "everyone worked," some interviewees also criticized contemporary youths' attitudes toward work, observing that today's youth rely on Germany's expansive social net rather than personal discipline or initiative. To cohort members, this modern sense of entitlement contrasted sharply with their own necessity-driven self-sufficiency and flexibility. Tinker, for example, recalled that having never considered a career in education, she rather abruptly decided to answer a newspaper advertisement recruiting *Neulehrer* for Berlin's public schools.

I cleared rubble for a year or so, stood there shoveling, and then one day I read in the paper that they needed teachers. Had to give evidence of an antifascist upbringing and so forth . . . and do a nine-month program at the pedagogical college with all that entailed and then into the schools. Nine months . . . they slowly figured out who was communist and who was SPD and so forth . . . and then they sent us—I was twenty—into the schools. I had a boys' class, huge classes, forty-eight boys. And since they'd all been more or less through the war, they'd seen a lot. . . . I had one, he'd already flunked three times. He was huge, bigger than I, Henry S---. . . . He was the king, whatever he said went and so on . . . he tried to stand up to me at the beginning, and—stupidly, they could've fired me for it—I punched him when he got too fresh with me.

Seeking above all an alternative to physical labor, Tinker enrolled in an intensive teacher training course that neither matched her expectations of higher education nor adequately prepared her to be an educator. She felt no more "called" to teach than to manage her mother's tobacco shop, and in fact did both for the next seven years. The income mattered far more than any idealistic sense of calling or personal desire.[20]

Unofficial employment constituted a central element of youth experience during the Hunger Years. Tinker's under-the-table efforts kept the family's tobacco shop in the black, preserving crucial income and shielding her mother from more strenuous work. More generally, independent economic initiatives helped young Berliners bridge the inevitable gaps between jobs and capitalize on sudden opportunities.

The most well-known forms of "informal" work, of course, took advantage of both an overworked city police force and inconsistent occupation regulations. Archival records, media sources, and historical accounts all highlight black market entrepreneurism, *Hamsterfahrten* (begging expeditions to rural villages) and outright thievery during the Hunger Years. These undertakings were rarely spontaneous initiatives or crimes of opportunity. Instead, most youth scrutinized officials' surveillance habits, analyzed probable risks, and developed practical contingency plans. Mostel, for example, recalled that his clique thoroughly "cased" the American villas they plundered in the 1940s. In one instance, a friend even took a job in the neighborhood so as to gain access to house keys.[21]

The relationship between these less-than-legal initiatives and a cohort-specific identity is multifaceted, of course. The oft-cited practice of begging from farmers, for example, would seem to undermine what I have described as an identity rooted in self-sufficiency, since success depended on the good will and charity of strangers. Most interviewees, however, understood their illegal actions as a necessary response to economic circumstances; doing something, even begging, was more productive than doing nothing. For others, this experience served as a catalyst, driving them to work even harder to avoid such poverty later in life. Birkmann, for example, described being humiliated by prosperous farmers, and recalled swearing to himself, *"Never again, no, never!"*[22]

Even punitive employment constituted part of a wide spectrum of economic initiatives that cohort members understood as proof of their ability to take care of themselves as youth in the *Hungerjahre*. Mostel, for example, spent several months crafting lamps in a youth detention center, earning little more than pocket money for his labor. Whether or not the work contributed to his rehabilitation, Mostel considered it legitimate work, and petitioned to have it included when the government calculated his pension benefits. Although the petition failed, Mostel's attempt underscores the seriousness with which he viewed his work history; the fact that he was serving a criminal sentence at the time did not dissuade him from demanding recognition for the work he did.

All in all, the significance of work in cohort members' self-perceptions extended far beyond material circumstances and economic security.[23] Interviewees typically described themselves as self-motivated youths who valued personal effort and individual achievement in all realms of life. A broad definition of work that included career preparation, temporary jobs, under-the-table employment, and independent initiatives—legal and otherwise—all contributed to cohort members' sense of self-sufficiency. The pragmatism that fueled such efforts also helped individuals justify the illegal nature of portions of their work history.

"Ich hatte keine besondere Wünsche" (**I had no particular desires**).

Their memories of the Hunger Years structured around images of work and deprivation, interviewees often shook their heads at questions about youthful dreams and desires.   Surviving and succeeding in postwar Berlin required considerable effort; postwar youth had little time for wistful fantasies.

You just knew, it was pointless to wish for something because there simply wasn't anything. We just accepted what there was and tried to make the most of it. No point having illusions . . . life goes on even with nothing. . . . There were no dresses at first for example, so a friend made me a nice dress from a pair of curtains.[24]

Just as personal pragmatism informed cohort members' attitudes toward work, so too did virtually all emphasize a no-nonsense approach to material desires and personal dreams. There was "no point having illusions," at least not until the currency exchange and increasing stability of the 1950s made fulfilling some of those dreams possible. Nonetheless, over the course of long discussions, many hinted at earlier aspirations and longings. Although seldom grandiose or even cohort specific, these dreams nonetheless constitute important components of memory and identity because fulfilling them required considerable ingenuity and perseverance. As Barthe described her twentieth birthday party, it became clear even the simplest celebration required considerable forethought, ingenuity, and coordination.

[My sister and I] lived together, on one *Hungerkarte*. And my sister must have told you that we ate birdfeed and such things and used coffee grinds, stirred into a kind of pudding and invented all kinds of things. And I had my birthday in March [1946], and we had many friends here still in Berlin, I said, "I want to celebrate." My father was in the hospital, had a lung infection. . . . Skin and bones. He lay in the hospital and I said, "Nonetheless, I want to celebrate my birthday." So I invited everyone, but said you'll have to bring your own food, we haven't got any. So they brought their sandwiches and all, and one boy, who used to live in our building, he was always on the black market, and he gave me a piece of meat.   That was the best present [laughing]. I thought that was wonderful, you know. And then we had, he'd brought a gramophone and we danced. I mean, we were glad there were no more bombing raids, you know, as a young person one is still so optimistic.[25]

As usual, "everyone worked," contributing what they could to fulfill Barthe's modest wish for a birthday party. And thanks to the individual efforts of each guest—and one blackmarketeer in particular—the evening was a success, becoming a vivid moment in Barthe's memories of the Hunger Years.

Beyond similar accounts of personal or familial celebrations, cohort members shared recollections of a typical (i.e., *nicht besondere*) wish to catch up culturally. With some notable exceptions (such as American music), this was one realm in which youths and officials appreciated each others' efforts. Compared with Nazi-era regulations, for example, postwar censors gave youth access to a treasure trove of literature, at least after antifascist volunteers cleared library shelves of Nazi-inspired works in 1945. There was so much to read, and so little time, recalled Klinkert.

My sister and I used every subway trip, breakfast or lunch break to read. The books were traded around in our class . . . and one girl had *Untergang der Titanic*, and we had to pass it along to someone else and had just one day and one night to read it. Seven or eight hundred pages. Our friend Loni had gotten the book. . . and so we read it, the three of us taking turns . . . in one night.

Klinkert shared a list of more than fifty books that circulated among her friends. Acting of their own accord, the girls read and discussed the works of, among others, John Steinbeck, Pearl S. Buck, Mark Twain, and Jack London. "Our hunger for education was insatiable," she observed.[26]   Since schools were overcrowded and understaffed, Klinkert and her friends simply and eagerly taught themselves.

German youth also made up for lost time at the cinema, and once again, perseverance paid off, as particularly long lines formed wherever American movies were playing. In gaining entrance to a film from Hollywood, young Berliners fulfilled another simple wish: an understandable, if seldom acknowledged, desire to escape the Hunger Years and catch a glimpse, albeit fictional, of American culture. Russian films simply couldn't meet this need.

We just weren't interested, even though they weren't always that bad . . . the way they made the films was just so boring, not to our tastes, just so *Russian*. Even when later they came out with good artistic films, people just weren't interested.[27]

Youth were similarly critical of German films, in part because the productions were simply less glitzy than American movies. Furthermore, complained cohort members, German directors often focused on the problems of postwar life—situations potential moviegoers were only too familiar with.[28]

The popularity of American authors and cinema reiterates the role American culture, real or imagined, played in cohort members' memories of youth. Less clear is the extent to which youths' desire to catch up extended to lost German culture, although both occupation and local authorities certainly felt youth would benefit from a revival of German humanism.[29] Beginning just after capitulation, and continuing throughout the Hunger Years, young Berliners were eligible for free or reduced-price tickets to concerts, plays, and operas, and local artists went to great lengths to revive Berlin's cultural life. These well-documented attempts at cultural reconstruction did not, however, stand out in interviewees' recollections of the period. Rather, they more typically highlighted independent leisure activities—personal interests, individual hobbies, and other independently organized initiatives. Zelle, for example, described himself as an enthusiastic, self-taught musician and amateur radio/gramophone repairman. While these hobbies allowed him to develop useful skills, acquiring the necessary equipment and tools was no easy matter during the *Hungerjahre*.

Finding materials was of course one of the biggest problems, because you couldn't buy anything, not for money or a prayer, there was nothing. And the dealers weren't eager to part with overstocks, because money wasn't worth anything. So I took advantage of other opportunities; for example, a leftover anti-aircraft gun; I took tubes from the electronic parts [and] we built things like transformers or resistors, condensers, etc. . . . It was always different and interesting, one just had to take advantage of whatever opportunities one could get.[30]

Trading parts and information, and finding professionals willing to lend out coveted tools and manuals became Zelle's primary leisure pastime. Like in other realms of life, he cultivated personal contacts and kept a sharp eye out for potential opportunities. Looking back, it's clear that these hobbies also shaped Zelle's future. For example, he met his future wife after repairing her parents' gramophone (impressed with his work, they invited him to their daughter's birthday party). Just as important, perhaps, Zelle's leisure pursuits bolstered his sense of independence and self-determination.

When I think about the [leisure] options for youth today, based mostly on this commercial idea of providing services for consumption, not personal initiative or individual interest, I have to say, we were left alone. We tried to get what we needed, according to our interests: literature, materials, etc. I took up building radios because I wanted to [listen to music]. And I used [whatever] literature I could find and any chance to get the materials, and just did it. Of course it was difficult, but I was never bored and think really, my path was not so wrong.[31]

Zelle, like many of this cohort, described, at least in retrospect, pride and pleasure in having made the most of meager resources. Whatever the circumstances—an upcoming birthday, a fascination with electronics, a love of music—interviewees observed that they and their peers created opportunities, seized the initiative, and "just did it."

For some, asserting individuality led to emigration. Authorities often dismissed such plans as romantic dreams of escapism, and certainly many youths simply wanted to leave rubble-strewn Berlin. Nonetheless, interviewees—even those who left Berlin—rarely spoke in terms of physical flight. Rather, they once again highlighted the self-confidence and initiative required to overcome complex emigration regulations, to begin a marriage, to find a job during the Hunger Years. Over time, these themes of minimizing personal desires and developing self-reliance became key components of this cohort's collective identity. Some interviewees observed that they never wanted more than they could afford, while others seemed saddened, even disgusted, by contemporary youths' presumptuous demands and expectations. While perhaps in part just an intergenerational criticism, such observations are rooted in very real experiences for this cohort. Understanding themselves as having prevailed against difficult circumstances in virtually all realms of life, interviewees reject modern youths' apparent dependence on others—parents, travel agents, and superstars—for entertainment.

To summarize, cohort members often used loaded key phrases to summarize experiences and living conditions during the Hunger Years. Examined closely, memories of the 1940s reveal several common themes. First, as shown in Chapter 3, they often blurred the political turning point of 1945. Second, whereas retrospective narratives of life under Nazism seemed to emphasize the impersonal, the collective, and a lack of agency, recollections of the *Hungerjahre* highlighted individual responsibility and pragmatic action.   Third, this interpretive strategy marks the continuation of a coping mechanism observed in interviewees' *Endkampf* accounts.   The collapse of Nazi society had taught impressionable cohort members to be wary of authorities' promises and to look out for themselves. Understandably reluctant to commit to postwar institutions, interviewees explained themselves as seeking independence and personal security.[32]

Some cohort members mitigated assertions of independence and personal initiative by acknowledging that fate and luck informed both wartime and postwar experiences.   In retrospect, fate helped explain seemingly random tragedies and miracles that might otherwise disrupt a cohesive narrative structure. In stories of the postwar period, fate also served another purpose, explaining encounters or successes that didn't fit the dominant themes of personal initiative and independence.

PRUDENT PRAGMATISM OR POLITICAL APATHY?

The constructive power of memory became particularly apparent when cohort members recalled the political context of their lives during the Hunger Years. This 1926–1933 cohort of Berliners, even before it could redefine itself in the wake of German defeat, found itself divided first by rhetoric, then by political borders. Eventually, of course, this growing political antagonism became a physical barrier, separating siblings and childhood friends; over fifty years of political dichotomies certainly informs interviewees' accounts of political developments in the interregnum period. On the other hand, both East and West Berliners often described themselves as reluctant pawns in a political game over which they had no control—a sharp contrast to strong assertions of individual initiative in economic, educational, and social endeavors.

To a great extent, of course, cohort members' assertions were correct; political developments in interregnum Berlin *were* shaped by outsiders.   That said, however, all the major political parties in Berlin actively recruited youth during this period.   CDU and SPD activists described many of the same problems faced by the KPD, such as the occupation powers' reluctance to license overtly political youth organizations, the *Drang nach Tanz*, and youths' unwillingness to assert political convictions.   Criticized as apolitical in their actions, however, cohort members nonetheless seemed acutely aware of the ideological battle raging around them. The *Berliner Rundfunk*, for example, was immediately linked with the Soviet military authorities, who upon taking Berlin ordered the station to broadcast occupation regulations (which included, paradoxically, that Berliners turn in their radios). Within a year of capitulation, the *Rundfunk* was broadcasting youth radio programs intended to introduce foreign cultures, revive traditional German music, review previously banned literature and—in theory at least—foster political and ideological debates.[33] Although only 41 percent of listeners realized Soviet censors controlled the *Rundfunk* in November 1945 (partly because the station's offices and transmitters were in the British and French sectors, respectively), the station's ideological bias became increasingly apparent. Throughout 1946, listeners heard young activists discuss "The Four Basic Rights of Youth" and perform radio plays such as "Greetings to Moscow."[34] By 1948, the program "You Ask, We

Answer" unabashedly advised youths on questions such as "Can a son of poor parents attend university in the Soviet Union?" and "What's the origin of the word 'comrade'?"[35]

Cohort members in both East and West Berlin recalled the bias of the *Berliner Rundfunk*, which was equally apparent to western occupation officials. Frustrated by Soviet control of the airwaves, U.S. officials established a *Drahtfunk* station (DIAS), which sent signals over telephone wires. The initiative floundered, however, since few private homes had telephone service, and in early 1946, the Americans replaced the hardwired connections with more practical wireless technology. Berliners found the new station, RIAS, more impartial than the existing *Berliner Rundfunk*; retrospective estimates suggest some 80 percent of Berliners regularly listened to RIAS news broadcasts, particularly "*Berlin im RIAS*," a program that explored local developments and political sentiments. Anecdotal accounts suggested RIAS music programs were at least as popular among both Germans and the GIs stationed in Berlin.[36]

On 17 August 1947, British officials authorized a third radio station in Berlin, Northwest German Radio (NDR). Like RIAS, NDR quickly established a solid reputation for news coverage with shows such as "Pulse of the Times" and "Daily Echo."[37] By this time, all three stations also offered specific programming meant to promote youths' political awareness and civic consciousness. Interviewees, however, did not describe listening to such offerings. Although some mentioned British-broadcast English language lessons, most described listening to music and news shows. Radio simply facilitated efforts to catchup culturally and stay abreast of current events.[38]

Interceding Cold War hostilities has likely enhanced cohort consciousness of political bias in the media, although even at the time it was no secret that the SMAD sponsored *Die Täglichen Rundschau* and *Die Berliner Zeitung* while also subsidizing the KPD's *Deutsche Volkszeitung*. For western viewpoints, Berliners read the American licensed *Allgemeine Zeitung* and the British *Der Berliner*.[39] Even this youthful cohort had learned to read between the lines of National Socialist news reports, and after the war, youth became even more critical consumers. "We filtered [news] for ourselves. After every couple words or sentences, [we asked ourselves] 'why is it so, to whose advantage is it?' We took the stuff and *examined* it."[40]

Of course, some forms of political censorship were clear even to those who paid little attention to the media. Rumors that Soviet patrols had suddenly seized particular editions of western papers, for example, suggested that a scathing editorial or incriminating news story had just been published, while few readers questioned the political leanings of the local publisher *Neuer Weg*, whose 1946 publications included *The ABCs of Marxism*, *Socialist Law*, and *A Portrait of Rosa Luxembourg, Mensch und Kämpfer*.[41] An awareness of political bias, however, did not keep Berliners from buying or reading newspapers, according to an American survey from October 1945. On the contrary, Berliners were very thorough consumers: they not only bought newspapers, but also read, shared, and reused them—to line shoes or replace windowpanes, for example. The relatively low cost of newspapers made them good investments for anyone, young or old, who had little discretionary income, had to improvise winter clothing, doubted official rhetoric from any single source, and was curious about foreign cultures and attitudes.

Additional evidence that cohort members were more conscious of political developments than officials believed lay in their memories of specific events. When speaking about the Hunger Years, interviewees frequently alluded to conflicts between Berlin's communist and socialist parties (the KPD and SPD, respectively). The proposed merger of the two into a new Socialist Unity Party (SED) provoked loud and sometimes violent public discourse. From the fall of 1945 through the spring of 1946, political agitators sought to sway popular opinion by plastering the city with posters, collecting signatures, and denouncing opposition leaders in virtually every district.[42]

Most SPD leaders in Berlin welcomed this repoliticization of public life; in a so-called Second Battle for Berlin, they called for free municipal elections in Germany's capital. KPD and SED activists saw this demand as delegitimizing the existing (communist-dominated) administration (which it did), and began a counter campaign. Eventually, the confrontation led to the establishment of two parallel municipal administrations, a division that was solidified during the Blockade and airlift.[43] While a number of interviewees noted this growing political schism, Kreuzberg native Frau Pelsdorf, who took a secretarial job at city hall in 1945, observed the conflict firsthand. Observing crowds marching at the Brandenburg Gate and increasingly violent protests, she and some colleagues quietly began smuggling office supplies and typewriters across the sector boundary to their West Berlin homes each evening. When protestors from the SED and related organizations stormed the building, hoping to dissolve the magistrate and establish a provisional government, friends rescued Pelsdorf from the mob; only days later, she and her officemates became employees of the West Berlin magistrate.[44]

Similar antagonisms marked relations between factions competing for young Berliners' loyalties. While the antifascist youth committees had originally asserted their political neutrality, their pro-communist stance became increasingly obvious by winter 1945–1946. The Prenzlauer Berg youth committee, for example, sponsored talks on communism and materialism, and held "in-depth" discussions of articles in *Neues Leben*. During the same period, the committee's mimeographed newsletter, "*Wir vom Prenzlauer Berg*," focused attention on two political issues dear to the hearts of KPD and SED activists: a resolution supporting a single youth organization (i.e., the FDJ) and the collective mentality necessary for successful group initiatives.[45]

The growing political polarization of the committees can be seen in both archival accounts and personal narratives, and outright criticism of them seemed to grow during the SPD/KPD merger debates.[46] For example, although a World Youth Week commemoration drew some 3,000 youths in mid-1946, observers at a similar rally two weeks later noted that the greatest applause came when CDU representative Dr. Gunther Heinz advised the youth committees to stop promoting the interests of a single group.[47]

Once occupation authorities decided to license youth organizations with overt political agendas, much of this debate shifted to pose the Free German Youth (allied with the SED) against the social democratic Falcons. Over the next few years, these two organizations dominated youth outreach programs (outside the

Jugendämter) in Berlin; to many young Berliners, the FDJ-Falcon debates also epitomized broader ideological debates between East and West.

Not surprisingly, political conflicts were followed most closely by youths raised in the opposing traditions. Frau Burkhardt, for example, had grown up in a strong SPD family. Nonetheless, she explained a life of SPD activism as rooted in an awareness of postwar conflicts with KPD/SED. Burkhardt recalled long talks with her grandfather about the possibility of cooperation between the two parties, and initially advocated this position in her local Falcon group. It was the creation of the SED, Burkhardt noted, that ended Charlottenburg Falcons' tolerance of communist voices.

My grandfather had also been in the *KZ*, sat together with communists and they said, why should the workers' parties be separated? There were many who really thought idealistically that we could work together. But we saw very quickly there was a totalitarian idea behind it, that it was to prepare Germany for Soviet control. . . . A young man from Potsdam, a member of that eastern organization . . . came to us and wanted to spread these idealistic Marxist ideals and we immediately rejected it. And we tried, somewhat illegally, to follow them and rip down their posters, and so forth.[48] Later that year, a SED spy reported on a SPD youth meeting. He observed the dominant presence of older attendees (70% over age 25) and blamed them for not only ruining youth and standing in the way of their socialist maturation, but also attempting to mobilize them specifically against the SED.[49]

This kind of social democratic activism worried SED officials, even in the central youth office (HJA), where they held the majority and were backed by the communist-led magistrate. These authorities feared not only that they would lose the support of young Berliners, but also that youthful committee members would be swayed by "SPD corruption." Twenty-one-year-old youth representative Ilsa Pottgiesser, for example, was criticized as being

strongly influenced by the chairman of the SPD in Zehlendorf. She reports everything discussed in the HJA to them. . . . [Previously] the majority of active participants in our youth work did not question [our] committee's authority. The increasing influence of Western occupation forces [and of] reactionary forces is beginning to change this. There have been more than a few attempts to draw western districts away from the influence of the HJA.[50]

The tug-of-war between the SPD and KPD/SED was the subject of many youth group meetings, so it's certainly not surprising that Burkhardt and other lifelong activists highlight its significance. Unaligned cohort members, however, also noted the tense political atmosphere. Binkert, for example, welcomed the opportunity for ideological exploration produced by the SPD/SED conflicts. Smaller parties, such as the CDU and LDP (Liberal Democrats), also voiced opinions, and the public dialogue, Binkert noted, enabled his clique to study their political options. Each of Binkert's friends would attend one party's local gatherings, after which the youths discussed the pros and cons of various platforms. This practice, although perhaps unique in its methodological sophistication, demonstrated not only an understandably cautious attitude toward political rhetoric, but also that youths could—and did—cultivate their own political awareness without joining a political party.[51]

Nonetheless, such young people were considered apathetic by most city and party officials. Because he refused to join a sanctioned association, Binkert fell into the category of "unorganized youths" who, authorities believed, needed to be "organized" before they could make a positive contribution to postwar society. Thus, even as they criticized the state-sponsored HJ, these officials—at least in the eyes of many young people—were recreating similar conditions; like their Nazi predecessors, postwar officials in East and West insisted that youths unite, join, and accept the ideas of adult political leaders.

Most young Berliners, however, seemed reluctant to endorse any particular structure or ideology. In fact, the initial plurality of political platforms in 1945 and 1946 enabled them to shop around, as did the presence of occupation forces. Because each Allied power had the final word in administering city-wide regulations, opportunities for young people varied from district to district; if chastised in an SED-dominated youth club in Lichtenberg, for example, Binkert could speak his mind at a club in Kreuzberg or Tempelhof. In other words, political conditions enabled young Berliners to use the Hunger Years for noncommittal ideological exploration. In the debates and conflicts, they found opportunities to explore "what was hiding behind all the political rhetoric," seeking the "practical and the realistic" in policy statements; unfortunately for many, this window of opportunity began to close when ongoing conflicts exploded into the Berlin Blockade.[52]

THE BLOCKADE

The Berlin airlift, made necessary by a Soviet blockade of interzonal transit routes in 1948–1949, exemplifies elements of all the previously noted keywords: the foreign military presence, hunger and hardship, competition for loyalties, and above all, youths' own stoic perseverance. Both individual and collective memories received further reinforcement in 1998 (when most interviews were scheduled) as Berliners observed the fiftieth anniversary of the airlift. City officials welcomed retired pilot Gail Halverson back to Berlin, and testimonials from now-elderly Berliners celebrated the compassion and generosity of the American GI.[53]   Local newspapers published archived photographs of children waving to incoming transport planes from atop piles of rubble and interviewed eyewitnesses. Cohort member Frau Rippe, for example, became a local celebrity, offering public readings from her 1948–1949 diary, which, in solidarity with the pilots, she had written entirely in English for the duration of the airlift.

Even prior to this commemoration, of course, the airlift has symbolized Anglo-American support of West Berlin, and interviewees referenced it as an obvious topic of interest to a young American.[54] Public reactions to the June 1947 election of SPD leader Ernst Reuter as Berlin's *Oberburgermeister* had revealed the growing political division of the city, but cohort members typically associated memories of Berlin's partition with either the Blockade or the currency reforms that preceded it.[55] On 20–21 June 1948, the new Deutschmark (DM) became the sole official currency of the western occupation zones (i.e., West Germany), and two days later, the SMAD introduced a different currency in both the SBZ and Greater Berlin. When the western Allies protested this overextension of Soviet authority by declaring the DM-West legal tender in their sectors, the SMAD suspended travel to and from Berlin. Officially, the simultaneous closure of raid, road, and canal routes was blamed on technical difficulties, but the Blockade was clearly meant as a punitive measure.

The Blockade had an immediate and divisive impact on local residents and organizations. First and foremost, West Berliners faced an immediate food shortage. Soviet officials encouraged residents to sign up for food distribution in the eastern sector, but western authorities strongly discouraged such actions, which they saw as playing into the Soviets' hands. As an alternative, Allied pilots began what would become a fifteen-month airlift of some 1.8 million tons of food and other supplies to West Berlin.[56] On the same day (26 June 1948), Berlin's police force dissolved into eastern and western branches, and five days later, the SMAD quit the joint allied Kommandatura. In August, West Berlin union leaders declared their independence from the *Freie Deutsche Gewerkschaftsbund* (FDGB), while academics, frustrated by the growing intrusion of politics into university life, developed plans for a new "Free University" in West Berlin.[57] Finally, on 5 December 1948, residents of the western districts elected SPD majorities to new district and municipal governments; this action created a second mayoral administration, and since neither recognized the other's legitimacy, Berlin, while in theory still under joint occupation, effectively became a divided city.

Although popular accounts evoke images of an almost hermetically sealed West Berlin, both individuals and consumer goods continued to cross sector boundaries throughout almost the entire eleven-month Blockade. For example, some 100,000 West Berliners commuted to jobs in the Soviet sector, and similar numbers of East Berliners worked in the western sectors.[58] In addition, West Berlin's borders with the SBZ remained relatively porous until the construction of the Berlin Wall in 1961 finally cut West Berliners off from the surrounding countryside.

As they blended well-known details about the Blockade and airlift into personal narratives, West Berliners faced a challenge. On the one hand, they recalled stoicism in the face of deprivation; in this sense the Blockade era was simply an intensification of general conditions and personal attitudes during the Hunger Years. Well aware of both personal costs and political consequences, some reminded me that very few, if any, West Berliners accepted Soviet offers of supplemental food.[59] On the other hand, however, cohort members acknowledged a grateful, if reluctant, dependence on western aid. This sense of indebtedness contradicted the themes of independence and self-sufficiency that dominated most interviewees' narratives. The struggle to resolve this conflict could explain why some West Berliners, even as they thanked me for my nation's support, maintained that they personally had received nothing from the circa 250,000 planeloads of supplies flown into Berlin.[60]

For East Berliners, recalling the Blockade presented an opportunity for a retrospective role reversal; for that twenty-two-month period of postwar Berlin history, they—in theory at least—had plenty, compared to their western neighbors. Some even highlight personal efforts to support relatives and acquaintances across the border. Klinkert, for example, described carrying coal briquettes to relatives in the West, since, in her words, "those raisin bombers couldn't drop coal to the city." Instead, she smiled, those frivolous American pilots brought chocolate; it was up to pragmatic Berliners like Klinkert and her sister to facilitate the exchange of such luxury items for more crucial necessities of daily life.[61] Kanter of Prenzlauer Berg echoed these sentiments.

Well, the borders were already there [before the Blockade], but you could go back and forth. And I know we'd always taken coal and potatoes to my aunt in the West Berlin; there was always an element of risk to it, but only a little, really. . . . It was worse for the West Berliners than for us; we lived in the East . . . and had light and electricity and heat. But how they got through it, lots of Easterners gave them support; [with us it was] mostly my father, but I did too [although] I was studying, and didn't have much. But I'm positive the family supported my aunt, my aunts over there, or the aunts came to us. . . . I was studying in Magdeburg, GDR, deep in the GDR; you could see and follow [things] on the radio, television wasn't really, we didn't have a television at home for a long time, you know. But the West Berliners did suffer more then, they did endure something. We only heard the bombers all the time, the planes, every two and a half minutes, now *that* was loud.[62]

Kanter experienced the Blockade less directly than other interviewees, as she spent most of that year in Magdeburg. Nonetheless, like many East Berliners, she had friends and relatives in the western sectors, and certainly understood the practical implications of the Blockade. Typical of East Berliners' accounts of the Blockade, Kanter implied that West Berliners could not have survived had they been truly dependent on airborne shipments of food and coal. Second, Kanter's seemingly incongruous reference to her family's long wait for a television set suggests that Blockade-era memories were tied to a fundamental difference between eastern and western experiences. While their neighbors in the western sectors were compensated for eleven months of stoicism by decades of prosperity, East Berliners endured years of austerity and only a delayed, and frequently very limited, reward after 1989. Post-1989 developments may have even increased the significance of this temporary role reversal; described as the poor little brothers, or criticized by westerners for impeding united Germany's economic growth, easterners might relish images of a period, albeit brief, when they were comparatively well off.

While the Blockade clearly tied each nascent German state into its respective Cold War alliance, the status and future of the capital remained uncertain, at least in the minds of many Berliners. Having seen "the situation in the city [become] the expression and central component of the power relations between the two rival systems," interviewees (from East and West) wondered why the West did not overtly challenge the Blockade. Such unanswered questions, combined with the knowledge that the western Allies had allowed the SMAD to violate prior agreements, led some to doubt the professed Anglo-American commitment to Berlin's security.[63]

Given such political instability, and recognizing that the two superpowers, not Berliners or even Germans, controlled their city's fate, cohort members would have had little reason to leap into civic activism in the late 1940s. On the contrary, the proven strategy of watching out for themselves and avoiding commitment continued to make sense. At the same time, the Blockade, together with the dual currency reform, marked a turning point; by the time the last plane had landed, cohort members were no longer simply Berliners, but rather *Ossis* and *Wessis*.

LEISURE AS ANCHOR

Social and cultural opportunities in Berlin recovered quickly in the Hunger Years, sometimes even drawing energy from the political tensions.   Berliners' efforts to catch up culturally, already mentioned in the context of summer 1945, certainly brightened difficult lives and crystallized intergenerational conflicts about artistic expression and personal values.   However, interviewees' accounts suggested that their leisure initiatives constituted more than a rejection of adult tastes or a quest for unchaperoned space.   During the Hunger Years, young Berliners sacrificed valuable time and tangible resources to develop anchors of personal stability; in some cases, interviewees used hobbies and leisure pursuits to compensate for the lost foundations of social stability.

First among these shaken social underpinnings was the family.   Fondly recalling family outings and celebrations from their early childhood, and proudly noting their own children's achievements, interviewees rarely spoke about family life or parent-child relationships in the Hunger Years.   This often reflected that fact that many German families, already strained by wartime experiences, endured worse hardship during the Hunger Years.   Interviewees frequently suggested that their parents, struggling to make ends meet and psychologically cope with the Nazi past, were simply exhausted and consequently incapable of providing security, sympathy, or advice.[64]

Interviewees' frequent vagueness about their mothers shed led new light on women's roles in rebuilding Berlin.   Both popular and academic histories of postwar Germany celebrate the image of the *Trümmerfrauen*.   However, while the mothers of this cohort typically worked long hours, not only clearing rubble but also at a variety of other tasks crucial to postwar life, interviewees did not recall them as heroines of the postwar era.   Instead, most described their mothers, figures of strength during the war, as suddenly exhausted and vulnerable—as worried, preoccupied women who had little interest in either their children's pastimes or broader social-political questions.[65]   Although popular representations of the period downplay such images, they were substantiated by contemporary observers. Thurnwald, for example, found that more than half of Berlin's housewives worked twelve- to eighteen-hour days; the sociologist lamented that chronic exhaustion prevented women from meeting their work potential.[66]

Cohort members said even less about their fathers, either during or after the war. Thurnwald, however, found many veterans physically or psychologically unable to work. Undiagnosed depression plagued men who had essentially failed to defend family and fatherland.   Many also felt robbed of their authority in the home, since it was nearly impossible to re-create prewar familial relationships. Some returned to never-seen children, to older offspring who rejected parental discipline, or to wives who had remarried or pursued protective sexual relationships in their absence.   In short, parent-child relations were often a hidden casualty of the war that led youths to seek mentors outside the home.[67]

In general, cohort members responded to questions about familial relations with anecdotes from their prewar *schöne Kinderzeit*.   Asked about personal mentors, they rarely recalled heart-to-heart conversations with any adult relative, even though they frequently shared homes with extended families. Instead of a safe haven from the problems of the Hunger Years, interviewees' home lives were typically informed by actual or threatened material scarcity, illness, and interpersonal conflict.

Of course we had arguments. . . . For example, much to the dismay of our parents, since we had at the most one pair of shoes each, my friends and I loved playing soccer. I got a coupon for a new pair [in the summer of 1946] and was so proud . . . I stood in line. . . and finally had decent shoes and [then] played ball for hours. I came home and told my mother that I'd played soccer in the only shoes to my name. That was a huge fight. A total lack of understanding. . . . We got along, but it was hard, so many people in one room. . . . I remember one time, just before Christmas, my grandparents had gone visiting, and we had the whole kitchen to ourselves; we felt like kings. Of course we argued. Food was tight and Mother was very exacting, 200 grams per person, sliced every morning, and when it was gone, that was all.[68]

There are of course exceptions to the model of overtaxed parents and independence-seeking youths. Generally, however, details about family life in the Hunger Years remained cloaked beneath assertions of independence. Whether driven by personal regrets, a desire for distance from Nazi-era identities, or the memories of harried, preoccupied parents, cohort members highlighted their own material, or at least psychological, self-sufficiency.

School constituted a second shaken pillar of stability in young Berliners' postwar lives. Although schools reopened relatively quickly, most offered classes in shifts, so actual classroom time was limited. Furthermore, particularly in eastern districts, many classes were taught by hastily trained *Neulehrer* who were often themselves too young to serve pupils as mentors. In fact, those cohort members who returned to school often used memories to reinforce themes of independence and self-motivation. Klinkert, for example, interrupted an animated account of extracurricular activities to display a stack of worn school notebooks and reports. "We were all very industrious, pushing on towards the university despite the horrible conditions. . . . When we studied, we could scarcely concentrate, but our goal [was to] earn very good grades to pull ourselves out of poverty."[69]

In other words, while school helped secure the future, it hardly made life easier at the time, in part because many youths had to completely change prior educational or career goals. In this way, even their own dreams and expectations could hardly constitute a source of stability. The collapse of the Reich, the postwar economic crisis, and their city's uncertain political status had rendered young people's earlier plans invalid. While most developed effective coping day-to-day strategies, few youths could predict which long-term paths—political, educational, or personal—might prove effective.

The combination of shattered social institutions and difficult living conditions increased the significance of young Berliners' leisure-time pursuits. Although Nazism glorified youth, the war had, in a practical sense, largely eliminated the social category, splitting this cohort of Berliners into defense workers and child evacuees. During the Hunger Years, leisure activities became a way to reclaim youthfulness and a refuge from the instability of postwar society. Furthermore, because so many other anchors of stability and personal identity had been shaken, leisure activities constituted a way to assert initiative and control.

Frau Distel's memories of the American German Youth Activities (GYA) clubs epitomized the long-term significance of postwar leisure.   Distel first encountered the program in 1946, soon after U.S. Army officials had begun encouraging organized fraternization between GIs and young (ten- to twenty-five-year-old) Germans.   Through a network of loosely organized clubs overseen by American military mentors, planners hoped to reduce juvenile crime and introduce young Germans to western ideals of cooperative leadership and democracy. "Unless this can be achieved," warned one guidebook, "the youth of Germany will be a quarreling, hating, mob, susceptible to the next 'strong man' who needs them for non-peaceful purposes."[70]

At its peak, the GYA enrolled more than 600,000 registered members in clubs scattered throughout both the American zone of Germany and Berlin. Distel and her friends first discovered the Schiller Club, one of twelve GYA clubs in the American sector of the capital.   Sponsored by the 7808th Motor Transport Battalion, the youth club offered Distel the chance to pursue her love of music, and by mid–1947, Distel had joined the step-dancing group and club choir. She also enjoyed frequent swimming excursions; the 7808th provided trucks, drivers, and chaperones, on whom the Germans tested their English conversational skills.

Distel spent more and more time at the GYA club, even as she began her professional training at Berlin's *Fachschule für Textilindustrie und Mode* in the fall of 1947. About this time, Distel left the Schiller Club for a GYA club in Lichterfelde Ost, which was a good forty-minute commute (on foot and by streetcar) from Distel's Tempelhof home. Attracted to the Columbus Club by a seemingly endless supply of coal, a large record collection, and a well-equipped sewing room, Distel found herself unwittingly drawn into the club's political scene.

I could care less if the club presidents tore their hair out [over politics].   I was wrapped up in sewing, drawing and dancing and thought everything was wonderful. I had never learned to think critically and did so only when prodded. . . . We were a close group, all seamstresses, and we shared the Club's wonderful old sewing machine.   [One day] I ran into—I don't know why—the perpetually-newspaper-reading Dieter W., the likeminded Ulrich D. [and] Werner K., who I knew from his crass speeches on CRS (Club Radio Service).[71]

In short, the young Columbus Club activists introduced Distel to political theories and practices. She sat through fervent discussions about the club's constitution and the creation of a city-wide club board, and witnessed heated debates between political factions. Most importantly, she recalled, fellow club members compelled her to formulate and articulate her own thoughts and opinions.[72] In 1948, for example, a particularly assertive friend enrolled Distel in an eight-day course at the *Wannseeheim für Jugendarbeit*, one of two youth training centers established by western allies in Berlin to train current and potential youth leaders.[73]   For Distel, the GYA had become a safe place to ask questions and draw her own conclusions about the growing political conflicts in Berlin.

The fact that Distel spent her free time at an American club, however, did not escape the director of her school, which was in Friedrichshain. School officials criticized Distel for supporting western imperialism by buying supplies in her (western) home district. When Distel and some friends began organizing a graduation ball, she was accused of "western decadence." The director advised her to quit the GYA, establish residency in the Soviet sector, and begin working in an East Berlin clothing factory. Distel refused, and was consequently barred from the final examination.

Beyond its obviously negative professional impact, Distel's decision had other long-term implications. The unemployed youth found janitorial work at the Columbus Club and joined other GYAers to political lectures, demonstrations along the *Ku'damm* and RIAS taping sessions. Ulrich, the student who had signed her up for the leadership seminar, led some of these activities. The two later married, and when Ulrich began a political career in Bonn, Distel worked as his secretary.

Looking back, Distel credits the GYA not only as a matchmaker, but also for providing opportunities to develop informed opinions about social and political issues. She also continues to confront Berlin's division in personal life, in 1998 finally winning recognition as a politically disadvantaged citizen.[74] Although the GYA indirectly shattered her early professional goals, Distel eventually won recognition (under the auspices of the 2. SED-Unrechtsbereinigungsgesetz) as a victim of political oppression, and the months spent at fashion school were credited into her pension benefits. Less tangibly, she credits the program with having cultivated political savvy and self-confidence, skills that proved crucial as her husband established a career in the West German capital.

Interestingly, Distel described the threat of expulsion as her own personal dilemma; the decision to remain loyal to the GYA was reached independently. Recalling experiences in the FDJ, Zelle and Birkmann described similar themes. Neither described himself as a political activist in the postwar years, nor—despite the FDJ's increasing dominance of leisure activities—did they describe any pressure to join the organization. In fact, Birkmann initially attended both GYA and FDJ gatherings in Zehlendorf, although he recalled becoming disgusted by the wasteful nature of the GIs and disappointed by the seemingly frivolous activities. He learned more about the FDJ at a summer camp and, finding their ideas "logical," became a "friend of peace." Like Distel, Birkmann's leisure activities and professional development were closely related; he eventually moved from Zehlendorf to Berlin's eastern sector, and while he described the move primarily as a pragmatic career decision, it was facilitated by friends in the FDJ. Moving to Lichtenberg also brought Birkmann closer to a vibrant FDJ group, in which he became more and more active. Like Distel, both Birkmann and Zelle asserted the openness of the early youth groups. However, whereas Distel drew clear links between the GYA and her own political convictions, the former FDJlers downplayed the political nature of the East German organization.   Despite—or perhaps because of—the FDJ's reputation as a monolithic state-dominated institution, Birkmann and Zelle downplayed the organization's political functions; instead, they described the FDJ as simply facilitating their pursuit of personal hobbies and interests. Like the GYA, the FDJ was recalled as a source of stability and friendship and has produced, like their later union involvement, enduring commitments and friendships.[75]

Other young Berliners found a similar anchor in sports, and while authorities welcomed the interest, they restricted the reestablishment of private sports clubs, fearing that Nazi-era organizations would reconstitute themselves and serve as a cover for continued paramilitary training. Consequently, the SMAD initially banned all but communal athletics (coordinated by the district and central *Sportämter*) and interscholastic sports programs.

Herr Heinemann joined his school's track and field team, and in 1947, just as private sport clubs were again permitted in Berlin's western sectors, he won a city-wide shot put competition and was recruited by the recently relicensed Sport Club of Charlottenburg (SCC). He recalled being thoroughly consumed by athletics during the Hunger Years.

We trained in unheated gyms, by the light of so-called Petromax lamps. . . . And we had nothing to eat but still had to give our best; rather we *wanted* to do our best, that was the whole point. We had no clothes, there were no uniforms, my first spikes were a gift from Hermann Schlösske, our coach. He'd been a world-record holder, and gave me a pair of his old spikes. And of course there were no special diets. One time we had meat, dumplings and sauerkraut for dinner. I stuffed myself, naturally, and then went off to track practice . . . and became violently ill.[76]

Smiling at his own shortsighted behavior, Heinemann recalled more concern about the impact of occupation on his athletic training, as British forces (like their counterparts in other sectors) requisitioned most of the functional gymnasiums, playing fields, and swimming pools in their sector. By mid–1946, however, officials had negotiated shared usage agreements and city-wide competitions and festivals had become regular occurrences.[77]

Heinemann dismissed the horrific training conditions as he described what he gained from the SCC. Like Distel, he believed the benefits of membership far outweighed the costs. Heinemann found mentors in his coach and a disabled veteran who had run competitively before the war. "He was at the track every day. If we had worries, he'd take us aside and talk about things. He was a father to us, a voluntary father-figure."[78] Given the overcrowded conditions at home, Heinemann and his friends saw in the SCC not only an athletic club, but also a place to simply relax with friends; in short, Heinemann believed sports kept him off the streets and out of trouble. The SCC youth team also gave Heinemann opportunities to expand personal horizons; he offered enthusiastic stories of trips to national and international competitions. For example, even though the Berliners lost badly in a 1948 meet against a Swedish team, Heinemann, his teammates, and some 15,000 spectators were thrilled that the foreigners recognized them as legitimate competitors (not former Nazis). In 1949, the SCC 100-meter relay team qualified for the national Junior Championships. Lacking train or bus fare, Heinemann and three teammates hitchhiked to the competition in Stuttgart-Feuerbach—a sixty-hour trip. The relay team lost badly, but Heinemann recalled the trip's broader impact; he saw firsthand the material differences between East and West.[79]

Despite a career-ending illness in 1951, Heinemann continued to identify himself as a *Sportler* throughout his adult life. He remained an active member of the SCC, serving in administrative capacities, closely following the club's win/loss records, and socializing with old friends at the club. He described overcoming or ignoring material deprivation in order to keep commitments to himself and his teammates, and was proud of the self-discipline, physical abilities, and friendships that he developed during the Hunger Years. In retrospect, Heinemann concluded, "It was awful, but it was wonderful." [80]

Even passionate, apolitical young athletes, however, could not completely ignore the growing political tensions in the late 1940s. During the Blockade, for example, ties were often broken between sport clubs in East and West Berlin. Herr Schäfer had joined the Treptow-based *Sport Club Poseidon* in 1946, and recalled that the club moved facilities in West Berlin just before the currency reform.   This financial restructuring, in Schäfer's mind, inadvertently undermined the team's stability.   Specifically, swimmers from West Berlin began buying and bringing to practice "these big *Sahne-Bonbons*, which we couldn't afford. They shared with us sometimes, but it was so discriminating . . . and so we all came back here to the club at DAB Treptow."[81]

While the image of such conspicuous consumption and economic elitism—perhaps reinforced by a lifetime of living in the GDR—remained clearly etched in Schäfer's memory, he focused primarily on the benefits of competitive swimming. Like Heinemann, he recalled traveling to competitions, as well as relaxing and talking over problems with teammates. "The other kids hung out on the streets and in the rubble, and we were pretty much always at the swim club. It became a close-knit group."[82]   Schäfer continued swimming competitively while studying at the Humboldt university and, like Heinemann, still had social relationships with former teammates over fifty years later. Unlike his western peer, however, Schäfer tended to tie recollections from the 1940s with later experiences, leaving unclear, for example, distinctions between the DAB and later workplace-sponsored teams and criticizing the GDR for nurturing only the very best athletes.   Schäfer also used sports to identify himself as an opponent of broader SED policies. For example, he identified one club (Werner-Seelenbinder-Halle) as "the *Stasi* team" and recalled heckling team members as a form of political protest.[83]

Finally, cohort members found a social anchor in church-based activities. Although most interviewees criticized religious institutions for failing to address pressing moral issues, a few recalled church and family as mutually sustaining forces of stability during and after the Nazi period. Kanter, for example, credited this reciprocity with helping her withstand Nazi-era discrimination, survive postwar hardship, and endure another half-century of religious repression in the GDR.   Doubts about God led Kanter to her family, while fears about family members were allayed by her faith. Nonetheless, even Kanter asserted that, like other interviewees, she made most important decisions on her own. While the church helped her make sense of the world, it did not shield her from taking personal responsibility for her actions and thoughts.[84]

In general, cohort members' vivid memories of leisure pursuits highlighted three aspects of experience. First, young Berliners saw their hobbies and personal interests as a way to temporarily escape crowded, tension-filled homes, avoid problematic intergenerational conflicts, and find substitute support networks. Second, memories of leisure activities to demonstrated personal initiative; as members of youth organizations, sports clubs, and even the much-criticized "unorganized" clique, interviewees identified themselves as engaged, forward- looking individuals, thereby challenging typical images of skeptical or even lost youth. Finally, citing hard work and personal sacrifice, interviewees also associated their hobbies with a dominant theme of postwar narratives—perpetual hard work. Hobbies and personal interests of the Hunger Years provided a basis for lifelong friendships and identities.

In other words, while images of leisure may seem incongruent with a collective identity rooted in self-sufficiency and hard work, hobbies and peer-group activities played an important role in this cohort's postwar development. With traditional spaces for self-assertion (school, work, family) rendered unstable during the Hunger Years, leisure pursuits took on greater meaning. These individuals saw themselves as particularly distanced from their parents, not responsible for Hitler's rise, and integral to postwar recovery, and leisure initiatives helped demonstrate independence, persistence, and pragmatism.

NOTES

1. Georg Holmsten, *Die Berlin Chronik: Daten, Personen, Dokumente* (Düsseldorf: Droste Verlag, 1984), 402–403.

2. Hilda Thurnwald, *Gegenwartsprobleme Berliner Familien* (Berlin: Weidmann, 1948), 112.

3. Ibid., 43–45, 52–53.

4. Ibid, 89, 135; Bezirksamt Friedrichshain, "Bericht zum Gesundheitszustand beim Schulabschluß," 1947, LAB STA Rep 135/16 Nr. 62.   Also on living conditions: Birkmann, 5–6; Kanter, 7, 11; Mostel, 1.

5. The 16 October 1945 edition of *Der Berliner* announced a plan for the air evacuation of 50,000 children to the British zone for the winter.   A similar 1947 initiative to evacuate14- to 18-year-olds to Nordrheinwestfalen was restricted to fifty orphaned and homeless youths. HJA, "Bericht," 22 October 1947, LAB STA Rep 118 Nr. 117, 38; Senat Berlin (1959), 161; Höcker, 121; Rippe, 6.

6. Most districts introduced school lunch programs, both to supplement caloric intake and to lure pupils back to the classroom.   HJA der Berlin Magistrat, Abt. Sozial, "Rundschreiben 104/47," 9 November 1947, "Winterspeisung für Jugendliche," LAB STA Rep 118 Nr. 773; Pelsdorf, 12.   In 1947, the city magistrate could afford to designate only RM 20,000   to be divided equally between needy children and youth. "Rundschreiben des Hauptjugendamt," #108/47 26 November 1947, LAB STA Rep 118 Nr. 773.   Beginning in fall 1947, only children nine and under received milk coupons (for skim milk). Infants received for whole milk, and the Red Cross provided milk to children suffering from tuberculosis. Thurnwald, 86; BA Lichtenberg, "Schulwesen Bericht," 1 December 1947, LAB STA Rep 147/12 Nr. 21.

7. Schäfer, 12. Lichtenberg Schulwesen, "Bericht für September," 9 October 1947, LAB STA Rep 147/13 Nr. 21; Magistrat Abt. Sozialwesen, "HJA Rundschreiben Nr. 95/47," 3 September 1947, LAB STA Rep 118 Nr. 773.

8. Birkmann, 2, 6, 11–12. See also: Robert P. Grathwol and Donita M. Moorhus, *Berlin and the American Military—a Cold War Chronicle* (New York: New York University Press, 1999).

9. Arno Klönne, "Kulturkampf: Bemerkungen zur Schul- und Jugendpolitik der Besatzungsmächte in Deutschland nach 1945," *Jahrbuch für zeitgeschichtliche Jugendforschung 1994/95* (Berlin: Metropol Verlag, 1995), 28–39. Also Walter Schumann, *Being Present: Growing Up in Hitler's Germany* (Kent, Oh: Kent State University Press, 1991) 169–70; Thomas Fleming, "Besatzer und Besetzte," in Jürgen Engert, ed., *Die Wirren Jahre Deutschland 1945–1948* (Berlin: Argon, 1996), 10–49.

10. Kösel, 10–12.

11. Even easterners who seemed otherwise critical of Soviet policies typically emphasized this distinction. It would be interesting to explore if East Germans depicted their relationships with Soviet soldiers (or lack thereof) differently before 1989.

12. Miller, 6–8.

13. Birkmann, 2; Mostel, 1. On stealing from occupation forces, see also: Barthe, 5; Stumpf, 1; Miller, 9–10.

14. Jugendkommission Sitzungsprotokol, 12 October 1949, LAB C Rep 900 IV L-2/16 Nr. 481; BA Friedrichshain, "Bericht zum Gesundheitszustand beim Schulabschluß," ibid.; Gesundheitsamt Friedrichshain, "Streifenberichte," 23 April and 30 April 1947, LAB STA Rep 135/16 Nr. 60; KPD Berlin, "Bericht," September 1945, LAB I/20/040, 13, 16; FDJ Bezirk Mitte, "Bericht," 20 March 1948, SAPMO DY 30/IV 2/16 214.

15. See Johannes Kleinschmidt, "Amerikaner und Deutsche in der Besatzungszeit—Beziehungen und Probleme" in *Besatzer—Helfer—Vorbilder. Amerikanische Politik und deutscher Alltag in Württemberg-Baden 1945 bis 1949. Dokumentation des Symposiums vom 11.10.1996 im Stuttgarter Rathaus.* http://www.lpb.bwue.de/publikat/besatzer/us-pol6.htm (6 June 2003).

16. Tinker, 17, 21–22.

17. Tinker, 18. See also Rippe, 3, 11, 14–15. Maria Hohn, "GIs, Veronikas and Lucky Strikes: German Reactions to the American Military Presence in the Rhineland Palatinate during the 1950s" (Ph.D. dissertation, University of Pennsylvania, 1995); ibid., "Frau im Haus und Girl im Spiegel: Discourse on Women in the Interregnum Period of 1945–1949 and the Question of German Identity," *Central European History* 1993 26(1): 57–90; Lore Kleiber, *Fremdgängerinnen: zur Geschichte binationaler Ehen in Berlin von der Weimarer Republik bis in die Anfänge der Bundesrepublik* (Bremen: Ed. CON, 1990).

18. Reconstruction efforts in East Berlin progressed faster in the 1950s, when the state introduced a building lottery, in which volunteers could earn a ticket (for the right to live in one of the new buildings) for each shift worked. Vast housing blocks along the Frankfurter Allee were among the products of this effort.

19. Stumpf, 2, 5. Traditionally not necessary for many apprenticeship programs, the *Abitur* is sometimes translated as a high school diploma, but in fact demonstrates a higher level of proficiency. Also on being misqualified for work: Barthe, 8; Senat von Berlin (1959), 221.

20. Tinker, 10–12. Also Miller, 9; Mostel, 13; Pelsdorf, 5.

21. Mostel, 1. Also Birkmann, 2–3.

22. Birkmann, 6. Also Mostel, 30; Völker, 2; Rainer Karlsch, "Kohle, Chaos und Kartoffeln," in Engert, 104–108.

23. The relationship between work and German identity may contribute to post–1989 antagonisms between *Ossis* and *Wessis*, both of whom seemed to compare their own hard work with the other side's dependence on superpower support. For more on the significance of work, see: Elizabeth H. Tobin and Jennifer

Gibson, "The Meanings of Labor: East German Women's Work in the Transition from Nazism to Communism," in *Central European History* 28:3 (1997), 301–42.

24. Tinker, 23–24, 29. Also: Schäfer, 27; Heinemann, survey, 2; Pelsdorf, 16.

25. Barthe, 6–7.

26. Klinkert, 1; Letter from Klinkert to Redding, 4 February 1998, 1–2; Birkmann, 9.

27. Tinker, 24. After turning off the tape recorder, Binkert and the Dinkels enjoyed an animated discussion of American films from the 1940s, flipping through a hundred-page film almanac containing photos, short biographies, and film credits of ninety American stars whose wartime films were released in Germany in the early postwar period (cover missing, no date or title, suspected late 1940s). Also: Stumpf, 13–14; Völker, 4; Schenkel, 88–91.

28. For examples, see: *Ein alphabetisches Titelverzeichnis von Filmen der DEFA nebst Personenregister* (Oldenburg: Verlag University Oldenburg, 1993).

29. Arno Klönne notes that while the GIs were warmly welcomed by most young Germans, neither Soviet nor western authorities welcomed the cultural invasion. Far from promoting consumer capitalism as the path to political democracy in the early postwar years, the writers of western youth policies, argues Klönne, saw the revival of German humanism as fundamental to the recovery of this lost generation. Arno Klönne, "Kulturkampf: Bemerkungen zur Schul- und Jugendpolitik der Besatzungsmächte in Deutschland nach 1945," *Jahrbuch für zeitgeschichtliche Jugendforschung 1994/95* (Berlin: Metropol Verlag, 1995), 38.

30. Zelle, 13–18.

31. Ibid. Also: Mostel, 6, 14; Völker, 8.

32. Miller, 11; Winkert, 12.

33. Harold Hurwitz, *Die Eintract der Siegermächte und die Orientierungsnot der Deutschen 1945–46* (Cologne: Verlag Wissenschaft und Politik, 1984), 85, 105; Berliner Rundfunk, "Jugend voran" (aired 17.6.45), DRA, B202-00-06/0406, DRA; ibid., "Das Leben ruft unsere Jugend" (aired 8.12.45), B202-00-06/0484.

34. Hurwitz, 105; Berliner Rundfunk, "Junge Welt" (aired 22 December 1946), DRA, B204 01 01/0027; Jugendfunk Berlin, "Arbeitsplan 16-31.8.1946," SAPMO DY 24 802.

35. See the schedule for "Sie Fragen, Wir Antworten" (aired 10.6.48 and 15.7.48), DRA, B204 02 06/0005 and 0015.

36. British and American officials had hoped for joint regulation of the *Rundfunk* and initially (in July 45) proposed leaving the station in Soviet hands, provided each nation could broadcast an hour of unrestricted programming each day. Extensive debates, during which French officials also demanded unrestricted airtime, failed to shake the Soviet position that all three western Allies share a single sixty-minute timeslot. Hurwitz (1984), 84–87, 104–105; Miller, 20; Schneider, 17; Tinker, 23. Also Johanna Schenkel, "Lust und Leid und Liberty," in *Die Wirren Jahre Deutschland 1945–1948*, ed. Jürgen Engert (Berlin: Argon, 1996), 60–62.

37. See: Peter Schultze, *Eine freie Stimme der freien Welt. Ein Zeitzeuge berichtet* (Berlin/Bonn: Westkreuz Verlag, 1995).

38. Nordwestdeutscher Schulfunk, "Sendeplan für die Zeit von 19. April bis 10 Juli 1948" (poster), LAB Rep 120 Nr. 245, 29; Berliner Rundfunk, "Schulfunk Programm 2–14.6.47," LAB Rep 120 Nr. 245, 1–2; ibid., "Schulfunk Program 1–15.11.47," LAB Rep 120 Nr. 245, 18–25. See also: Birkmann, 7; Schäfer, 21; Deutsches Rundfunkarchiv, Historisches Archiv Collections B202-00-01, B204-02-01, and B203-02-06.

39. Hurwitz (1984), 86–87; "Enclosure One: Newspaper Questionaire" (undated), NA OMGUS 135/2–4, reproduced in ibid., 95.

40. Birkmann, 8–9.

41. Jugendsekretariat der SED, Letter to Verlag Neuer Weg, 17 June 1946, SAPMO DY 30/2/16 94, 188–89; ibid., Letter to SMAD Abt. Propaganda, 12 June 1947, SAPMO DY 30/2/16 221–26. On political literature for youth, see: Correspondence between Joachim v. Dobrzynski and Zentralsekretäriat der SED, Abt. Parteischulung, 20 May 1947 and 6 June 1947, ibid., 63–64; Correspondence between Hans Helmut Doerr and Verlag Neuer Weg 21 July 1946 and 9 September 1946, ibid., 65–66. Also: Birkmann, 8–9; Kösel, 14.

42. The SPD Berlin demanded a referendum on the proposed merger which party members in the western sectors overwhelmingly rejected on 31 March 1946. Richie, 643. Also Burkhardt, 4; Birkmann, 6, 8–9.

43. The SMAD, for example, subsidized media campaigns and confiscated pro-SPD newspapers and literature. Roland Gröschel and Michael Schmidt, *Trümmerkids und Gruppenstunde* (Berlin: Elefanten Press, 1990), 21–22.   Also: Henry Krisch, *German Politics under Soviet Occupation* (New York: Columbia University Press, 1974).

44.   Pelsdorf, 5.   Also Hirsch, speech transcript, undated, Heimatmuseum Charlottenburg, 1; Mostel 19–20.

45. "Wir vom Prenzlauer Berg," 16 February 1946, SAPMO DY 30/IV 2/16 211,138–43; "Tätigkeitsbericht der Abt. Jugend für Dezember 1945," SAPMO DY 30/IV 2/16 211, 158–61; "Monatsplan des Bezirksjugendausschuß Prenzlauer Berg," June 1946, Binkert private collection; "Monatsprogramm des Abschnitts 65," June 1946, ibid. See also: "Programm des Jugendausschuß Charlottenburg," SAPMO DY 30/IV   2/16/211,   12;   Jugendausschuß   Charlottenburg,   "Sprachrohr   der Charlottenburger Jugend," Hirsch private collection (also in LAB Rep. 207, Acc 3075, Nr. 5079 II Fol.27); Abt. Für Volksbildung Friedrichshain, "Bericht des Jugendausschußes," May 1947, LAB Rep. 135/1 328, 108–13.

46. In Prenzlauer Berg, the KPD counted 2,200 active youth and 18,000 "passive" (i.e., not regularly involved in KPD or JA programs) in November 1945.   KPD Bezirk Berlin, "Tätigkeitsbericht der Jugend- und Sportabteilungen der VBL Prenzlauer Berg," November 1945, SAPMO DY 30/IV 2/16/211 B1 162–67.

47. Senat Berlin (1961), 404, 461.

48. Burkhardt, 4. Because none of my interviewees described themselves as antifascist activists or founding members of the FDJ, that point of view is not represented here, but has been discussed by East German scholars.   See: Helga Gotschlich, ed., *Links und links und Schritt gehalten. Die FDJ: Konzepte, Abläufe, Grenzen* (Berlin: Metropol Verlag, 1994); Helga Gotschlich, Katharina Lange, and Edeltraud Schulze, eds., *Aber nicht im Gleichschritt: zur Entstehung der Freien Deutschen Jugend* (Berlin: Metropol Verlag, 1997).

49. "Bericht SPD Jugendversammlung," 4 October 1946, SAPMO DY 30/IV 2/16 213, 20–22.   The youth magazine *Horizont* was frequently—and often justifiably—identified as fostering anti-Soviet sentiment. Also: "Bericht über die Jugendarbeit innerhalb der Partei," 2 February 1946, SAPMO DY 30/IV 2/16 211, 149–51.

50. "Kurze übersicht über die Tätigkeit und Zusammensetzung der Berliner Jugendausschüße," 2 June 1946, SAPMO DY 30/IV 2/16 213.

51. Binkert, unrecorded conversation with Dinkel.   Also Birkmann, 6, 8–9; Burkhardt, HMCH Interview, 2; Kanter, 17; Kösel, 4–5; Miller, 19; Schneider, 18; Zelle, 10.

52. Völker, 8.

53. As the story goes, Halverson met a group of Berlin children and was shocked that, unlike children in the western zones, they did not even ask him for candy. Upon

return to his base in West Germany, Halverson crafted parachutes from handkerchiefs, tied them to candy bars, and showered the children with the treats during his next approach to the city.   Other pilots soon joined the effort; the Candy Bomber initiative grew, and eventually, coupons for CARE packages were also airdropped over parts of Berlin.

54. See: "IPM Allierte in Berlin—Meinungen und Einstellungen, 1985," in Gerd Langguth, "Wie steht die junge Generation zur deutsche Teilung?" in *Politische Studien Nr. 289* (1986), 524, 537.

55. Already in 1945, the SMAD had compelled western allies to ship supplies to Berlin, refusing to supply goods from the Soviet Zone.   Georg Kotowski, "Geschichte Berlins seit dem Zweiten Weltkrieg," in Langguth, 48–69.   On 24 January 1948, the Soviets stopped an interzonal train for eleven hours; on 5 April, the western Allies blamed a Soviet fighter pilot for the crash of a British passenger plane en route to Gatow.   The Soviets left the Kontrollrat on 20 March 1948; in June they also walked out of the Berlin Kommandatura.

56. Citing "shortages," Soviet authorities also halted the shipment of coal from the Soviet Zone to West Berlin, a step that significantly hurt economic development in the western sectors.   Text der ADN Meldung, 24 June 1948 in Forschungsinstitut der deutschen Gesellschaft für auswärtige Politik, e.V., *Dokumente zur Berlin Frage 1944–1962* (Munich: Oldenbourg, 1962), 72.   Although the Blockade was lifted on 12 May 1949, according to the New York (Jessup-Malik) Agreement of 4 May, the airlift continued until 30 September. Also: Kösel, 15; Kanter, 21.

57. The Free University was founded on 4 December 1949.   On its history: Siegward Lönnendonker, *Freie Universität Berlin. Gründung einer politischen Universität* (Berlin: Duncker and Humblot, 1988).

58. Ann and John Tusa, *The Berlin Blockade* (Toronto: Hodder and Stoughton, 1988), 275; Fulbrook (1992), 158.

59. Reports from the time indicated that about 100,000 West Berliners accepted aid (ration cards) from the SMAD. Udo Wetzlaugk, *Berliner Blockade und Luftbrücke 1948/49* (Berlin: Landeszentrale für politische Bildungsarbeit, 1998), 54, 74. Also: BA Kreuzberg, "Jahresbericht 1949," 1950, Kreuzberg Museum Archive, 54.   This report says 10,600 residents registered with the SMAD, and of those, 9,400 later rejected (or pretended to reject) Soviet aid.

60. Although British forces were an integral part of the airlift (providing ca. 30 percent of the flights), and French troops also supported the effort, it is remembered primarily as an American undertaking. Senat von Berlin (1962), 64; Birkmann, 15; Mostel, 30.   Generally on the Blockade, see: Gerhard Keiderling, *"Rosinenbomber" über Berlin: Währungsreform, Blockade, Luftbrücke, Teilung - die schicksalvollen Jahren 1948/49* (Berlin: Dietz Verlag, 1998); Uwe Prell and Lothar Wilker, *Berlin Blockade und Luftbrücke 1948/49 Analyse und Dokumentation* (Berlin: Arno Spitz Verlag, 1987).

61. Birkmann, 2, 6; Klinkert, 20.   Although organizers were initially concerned that coal dust would damage the planes' engines, they quickly resolved this problem, and the airlift did fly in vast amounts of coal. A number of East Berliners commented on the coal shortage in West Berlin and how they helped alleviate it.

62. Kanter, 19–20.

63. Udo Wetzlaugk, *Die Alliierten in Berlin* (Berlin: Arno Spitz Verlag, 1988), 48.

64. Bergemann, 19; Birkmann, 13; Heinemann, 10, 13; Kanter 10, 17; Miller, 17; Mostel, 1, 30–32, 36; FDJ Bezirk Mitte, "Bericht," 20 March 1948, SAPMO DY 30/IV 2/16 214; Thurnwald, 172–73,178, 181–88.

65. Kontrollratsgesetz Nr. 32: "Beschäftigung von Frauen beim Bau und Wieder-aufbauarbeiten," 10 Juli 1946, cited in Meyer-Schulze, 188.   This postwar image

contrasts sharply with that cultivated by the NS regime. See: Irmgard Weyrather, *Muttertag und Mutterkreuz: der Kult um die "deutsche Mutter" im Nationalsozialismus* (Frankfurt: Fischer Taschenbuch Verlag, 1993).

66. Heinemann, 10, 13; Kanter 5, 6, 10; Mostel, 28,. 36; Roberts, 57–62; Thurnwald, 35–37, 174–75.   Also: Beate Hoecker and Renate Meyer-Braun, *Bremerinnen bewältigen die Nachkriegszeit* (Bremen: Steintor, 1988); Sybille Mayer and Eva Schulze, *Wie wir das alles geschafft haben. Alleinstehende Frauen berichten über ihr Leben nach 1945* (Munich: Verlag C.H. Beck, 1984).

67. Tinker, 5, 12, 21–22. Also: Birkmann, 5–6; Mostel, 1–4, 9, 32.   On the impact of war on personal relations, see also: Barbara Heimannsberg and Christoph J. Schmidt, eds., *Das kollektive Schweigen. Nazivergangenheit und gebrochene Identität in der Psychotherapie* (Heidelberg: Asanger 1988); Sybille Mayer und Eva Schulze, "Krieg im Frieden. Familienkonflikte nach 1945," in Jutta Dalhoff, Uschi Frei, und Ingrid Schöll, eds., *Frauenmacht in der Geschichte* (Dusseldorf: Schwann, 1986).

68. Schäfer, 9–10.   Public officials lamented widespread familial breakdown and cited the literal and psychological dissolution of families as a key cause of rising youth crime rates. Was weiss der Lehrer von der sozialien und politischen Gruppierung der Jugendlichen LAB Rep 15 Acc 1431 Nr. 23/4–5, p. 5; "Berichte über die Tätigkeit des Jugendamtes" (statistical summaries),16 April 1946, 17 September 1946, 20 June 1947, LAB STA Rep 118 Nr. 763; Mayer and Schulze, 221; Thurnwald, 201–208.

69. Klinkert, 1, 5–6; Klinkert survey, 4; Kanter, 7–8.

70. Training and Education Branch, OPOT Division, Headquarters, EUCOM, eds., *German Youth Activities, Army Assistance Program Guide* (undated, presumed 1948), 9.   Also: Karl-Ernst Bungenstab, *Umerziehung zur Demokratie? Re-education-Politik im Bildungswesen der US-Zone 1945–1949* (Düsseldorf: Bertelsmann Universitätsverlag, 1970); Gerhard Emskötter, "Jugend und Besatzungsmacht," in *Nordwestdeutsche Hefte* 1947 Heft 7 (Berlin edition), 24–28; Karl-Heinz Füssl, *Die Umerziehung der Deutschen: Jugend und Schule unter den Siegermächten des Zweiten Weltkriegs 1945–1955* (Paderborn: Schöningh, 1995), 148-67; "Wir wollen mit ihnen leben," in Neue Zeitung 6 October 1947, 5.   Reports from specific clubs in Berlin: Archiv des Diakonischen Werkes der EKD ADW, Hb-B 62; "Auflistung der Zeitungsartikel über GYA Clubs," Privatarchiv Müller (includes both articles from the 1940s and 1950s as well as commemorative reports from the 1990s); "Der Gong, Eine Clubzeitung des German Youth Center Special Troops" (Distel private collection); Office of Military Government for Germany (U.S.), Education and Cultural Relations Division, Group Activities Branch, "German Youth Between Yesterday and Tomorrow, 1 April 1947–30 April 1948," Tracy Strong Collection I/238, FU Berlin.   For participants' perspectives on the GYA see: Birkmann, 3; Mostel, 6–7, 16–17, 19–20.

71. Distel unpublished paper, private collection.

72. Distel, 19–20, 22–29; *Zeitschrift der Berliner Jugendclubs* April 1949, 3 J g Nr. 3 (cover photo depicts Distel promoting a fashion show).

73. At the *Wannseeheim*, a committee of six Germans and an American youth officer developed seminars for actual and potential youth group leaders. Although the center also trained youths to lead cultural activities, most courses were intended to introduce lay leaders to different pedagogical theories and practices.   "Wannsee Center for Youth Work, " Tracy Strong Collection 17/65, FU Berlin; "Festschrift zum einjährigen Bestehen des Wannseeheims für Jugendarbeit," ibid., I/136;   Füssl (1995), 138; Distel, unpublished manuscript, 30–31, private collection.

74. Distel's expulsion was finally judged to have been a form of political mistreatment; as a result, the months she spent at the fashion school will now be calculated into pension benefits.

75. Birkmann, 2–4, 6. 9–10, 12, 14; Zelle, 17–18.

76. Heinemann, 3.

77. Interviewees recall undertakings such as the August 1946 *Sportfest der Berliner Jugend im Post-Stadion* and the September 1948 *Jugendspiele im olympischen Geist* (sponsored by Hauptsportamt and RIAS in Olympic stadium because Germans were not permitted to go to real Olympics) *Senat Berlin (1959)*, 299, 641.

78. Heinemann, 17.

79. Heinemann's relay team qualified again in 1950. They chartered a bus for the trip to Kassel where he used starting blocks for the first time. The team took second place and was rewarded by the SCC with a *Schnitzelessen*. Heinemann, 3–4.   U.S. occupation forces also sponsored interzonal soap box derby and vocal competitions. Mostel, 7.

80. Heinemann, 13, 14.

81. Schäfer, 12.

82. Schäfer, 21. Interestingly, Schäfer also mentioned competing against a Swedish team.

83. See also Heinemann, 7. The *Stasi* was the now infamous state security agency of the GDR.

84. Kanter, 10, 17. Also Völker, 5–6.

Interlude II

Young Criminals

Public authorities' fears that young Berliners would resort to a life of crime after 1945 shared much in common with their concerns about girls. In particular, the rise in juvenile (i.e., 14–18-year-old) convictions during and after World War I confirmed the beliefs of most German reformers, criminologists, and academics that the political, social, and economic consequences of modernization had set off a crime wave among youths.[1]

Juvenile delinquency remained a widespread social concern throughout the Weimar era, and definitions of criminal behavior also changed. Emergency decrees passed to cope with political crises during the Brüning and Papen administrations, for example, not only gave greater power to policing authorities, but also criminalized previously tolerated activities and contributed to a 10 percent rise in juvenile delinquency between 1930 and 1932.[2] Research conducted during this period suggested that apprentices and unskilled workers, both groups characterized by frequent unemployment, low pay, and general dissatisfaction, were most likely to become juvenile offenders.[3]

Such observations boded badly for Berlin in the years following World War II. For one thing, the vast majority of young Berliners had sacrificed educational or employment opportunities during the war. Furthermore, Allied bombing raids and the final battle of Berlin had devastated the city's economic infrastructure; there simply weren't jobs, let alone decent wages, for those returning from wartime service or evacuation. Finally, most Berliners, young and old alike, were desperately short of food and other basic necessities in the first months and years after defeat. Knowing this, local officials anticipated climbing juvenile crime rates, and they recognized that colleagues in other war-torn nations faced

similar problems. Nonetheless, they believed unique local conditions during and
after the war had left young Berliners at increased risk.

There can be no doubt that crime is rising among young people. This is true not only
in Germany, but in all countries that took part in the war. The most important
question is: Do all of these youths have a criminal disposition? The second question
is: Which strategies can best help young people? The presence of the black market
seems to be decisive in terms of upbringing. The working population is angered by
the luxurious lifestyle of the black marketeers, while the most of them . . . earn less
than they need to live. This fact means no household is prevented from the necessity
of becoming, at one time or another, buyer or seller on the black market. . . . The
general situation is particularly dangerous for our youths, who, after so many years of
Zwang und Rastlosigkeit, need calm and a secure, if modest, basis for their
development. . . . The black market offers an opportunity for everyone who has no,
or no longer, intact morals, to buy all the food they lack daily, if they have enough
money. All the stolen food in all Berlin can be sold on the black market, and it is
possible to trade anything there.[4]

While addressing broad questions of youth rehabilitation in western Europe
and the United States, this report highlighted several problems as unique to "our
[Berlin] youths." For example, German youths carried the scars of years of
political exploitation, a fact deemed particularly significant since contemporary
theories of juvenile delinquency highlighted the role of psychological
development in shaping—and for that matter, reshaping—juvenile offenders.
Furthermore, German (or at least Berliner) youths faced temptation—in the form
of the black market, pubs catering to occupation force, and ruins just waiting to
be looted—on every street corner.

The report from the church mission office, however, was not simply a plea
for sympathy at the plight of Berlin's youth; rather, it also held them
responsible for the broad social consequences of their actions. Specifically, the
report blamed young Berliners and their apparently successful black market
ventures for angering the "working population." Never mind that it was
unemployment that drove many young people to petty theft and *Schwarzhandeln*
in the first place. Criminally minded youths were both ruining their own lives
and demoralizing their gainfully employed neighbors. In other words, the EKD,
along with other authorities seeking to curb juvenile crime in the postwar years,
understood young lawbreakers as both products and perpetuators of immorality
and lawlessness.

Young lawbreakers themselves rarely took time to engage in such
philosophical debates; they had, not surprisingly, a more immediate concern:
meeting their personal needs without getting caught. Frau Tinker summarized
this perspective quite succinctly.

And then the black market got going, because there was nothing, so there was this
trading business, black markets everywhere and the police got wise to it —German
police already—and announced raids everywhere; you had to be careful to not get
caught in a raid, you know, if there was one. . . . Everyone had saved something [to
trade]. But back to the raids, I remembered them because we were still quite young, as
I said, not so mature as now, for us everything was, well, we were raised differently.
We weren't so, we didn't know so much about life . . . at any rate we were a bit behind,

so, today they know already at 13 or 14 what a boy is and what a girl is, but I didn't know at 19, before the rapes started I had no idea what it could be. . . .

Well, that changed quickly afterwards, when the young people went out dancing and you learned about everything really fast, and then you were always afraid [of a] raid, and luckily you were clean, and then the police cars came out front and . . . then into the cars, get in, get in, get in, all the women that they thought—and perhaps also were—into prostitution. I don't know, but anyway we always got away, we were never taken in. They'd have to go to the police and be tried and examined and who knows what all. We never had to do it, perhaps we were too young.[5]

Tinker, like many of her cohort, considered herself a sporadic delinquent, not a habitual criminal. She highlighted not the illegal nature of dance hall and black-market activities, but rather young Berliners' ability to recognize and escape the authorities trying to restrict their freedom and moneymaking endeavors. Instead of describing her own particular escapades, she offered a compilation of general knowledge linking—as did most official reports—music, sexuality, and crime.[6] Tinker exemplified the most common kind of young criminal in postwar Berlin; she was an opportunist, and her presence bolstered crime statistics, but she hardly constituted a serious threat to her neighbors or Berlin's economic development. In the eyes of many officials, however, she was only a slippery slope away from the organized youth gangs described as terrorizing the city in the months and years after World War II. The criminal exploits of these cliques were reported in often graphic detail in the press, became fuel for rumors and public paranoia, and were also discussed at length by municipal authorities.

Comrades Geschke and Jandretzky,
I know you have enough problems to solve, ask you however, to give particularly more attention to the *Jugendverwahrlosung* and its reduction. If something doesn't happen soon from the side of the Magistrate, we will soon be overwhelmed. In six days, we at one branch of the police department have received three cases of bandit break-ins—mostly youths. [While] taking the reports, it always becomes clear that the youths meet and plan their robbery sprees in one of the many cafes. In many cases, they hang around the streets of their districts and don't know what to do with themselves. . . . All the gang-related thefts that I have dealt with, were planned in cafes. The causes usually [include] no regular employment, no money, no guidance. . . . At the moment, we have the case of a five-member band from Lichtenberg, most of the rascals 16-year-olds. The oldest one, Edgar Kaminski, 19 years old . . . has no idea what a disservice he's done. . . . On top of that, according to the law, he's no longer a youth. Thus begins a life of crime. . . . At long last, help the youths with positive steps. Close 2/3 of the cafes, and convert them into youth centers directed by real social workers. If you have no work for them, let them take day hikes or play sports. . . . If something doesn't happen soon, our youths will be nothing more than thieves and occupation whores.[7]

Trying to combat youth crime, Officer Strehl is clearly frustrated by the lack of options available. While magistrate officials and political activists such as Geschke and Jandretzsky (both in the KPD) might lament the "youth problem," the alternatives they offered—primarily low paying work programs—were idealistic at best.

Through his experiences on the streets, Strehl offered more pragmatic suggestions. Juvenile delinquency had long been associated with dance halls, and most authorities assumed a connection between the 1945 *Drang nach Tanz* and youth crime. Although communists were most likely to directly link American music and immorality, colleagues and activists across the political spectrum recognized that Berlin's loud, crowded nightspots offered safe havens in which youths could plan their attacks.

Strehl's ideas reflected the prevailing attitude that, if caught early enough, and incorporated into supervised activities and structured organizations, most asocial youths could be rehabilitated, and some dance halls were in fact converted into youth centers as early as September 1945. New or unlicensed clubs sprang up as fast as old ones could be closed down, however, and while local *Jugendausschüsse* offered the very opportunities Strehl suggests, participation rates were less than encouraging. Observers complained that committee activists simply couldn't relate to young Berliners' lives or concerns.[8]

Efforts to reduce youthful delinquency were also hindered by conflicting definitions of criminal behavior. Most young people understood snitching fruit from a neighbor's tree, cheating unsuspecting occupation soldiers on the black market, and even stealing from one's employer as essential for survival. Furthermore, the fruits of such endeavors were generally welcomed and rarely questioned by cohort members' parents. In this atmosphere of tremendous need and understaffed police forces, young Berliners such as Herr Dinkel developed elaborate schemes through which to support themselves.

So, there I was back in Berlin and . . . looked for my old clique. There was nobody left, not until 1946 or early '47, except one colleague. So we joined up with others and started up with them in *Café Nord*. It was a very large café, a former department store, mirrors, pillars, etc., perfect for it and the owner was from the first *Café Nord*, during the war. He took over this hall after the war, and that's where we went dancing. . . . I earned 60 marks a week for 80 hours [of work]—10 Ami cigarettes and the money was gone, so you tried to deal, buy cigarettes cheap someplace and then evenings, if I wasn't at *Café Nord*—[where] I even sold to the waiter—I sold on *Alexanderplatz*, just like the Vietnamese these days. You had to keep a sharp eye out, or you'd get caught. It was illegal. . . . [Later] I went with my friend Helmut to Hamburg, we wanted to get on one of the boats to America, but we couldn't pay the ticket, so we signed on as sailors, the *third* backup crew, for if the first got sick and the second... and the boat wasn't even built yet! That's how badly people wanted to go. . . .

I couldn't get any work as a tailor in Hamburg. So at night along the *Reeperbahn*, we met a Pole who provided us with goods—ties. We had a great business. You needed a tie to get into the bars. Clothes could be bad, but a tie, or you couldn't get in. There were lots of people who wanted to get into the bars but didn't have ties. So we stood out there with our ties. Sold ties and cigarettes and slept someplace during the day, on the grass. Summer '47. We stuck with it three or four weeks . . . but couldn't support ourselves in Hamburg. My one friend lost his shoes, stolen in the train station when we were sleeping . . . and I used the last of my money to buy him shoes—you had to have shoes. . . . Everything happened in the train station, where you could buy or sell anything. . . . We got money then by registering [falsely] as returning prisoners of war. They didn't want photo identification, just thumbprints, and with the allowance [the social workers gave us] we bought tickets back to Berlin.

So then I appeared at home in Berlin again and my father said nothing, just "So there you are again, still have your money?" [Which I didn't] so, well, back to *Café Nord*, and sometimes I went sailing. A friend of mine had a sailboat; I'd made a suit for him once and he took me sailing and I loved it. He must have earned money like crazy already in those days. And I wanted a sailboat. Ok, had to earn some money. So I went with a pal back to Hamburg and we started [smuggling]. Bought things in Hamburg, brought them over and sometimes sold them already in Magdeburg and then back again. Then came the currency reform and we had to pay half in West marks, half in East. . . . I was caught once by the Russians at the crossing to West Germany. Had 400 West Marks in my glove—a huge sum of money, the whole boat cost 1000 Marks—they took and checked everything else, but not that. So I went on and got caught again on the return. Not exactly caught. It was in a swampy area and we could see ahead the lights—flashlights—and heard shots, and the whole crowd had walked into a trap. I let myself drop to the ground, lay in the swamp 'til morning and I was alone.

[Then I found] a boat, belonging to a West Berliner, an older gentleman who wanted to get rid of it anyway, so we bargained . . . he wanted 1000 marks; I had maybe 300 as down payment. So I paid that. Then went *Hamstern*, it was during the blockade by then. I went to Nauen, through Nauen to the little villages, where I could get a *Zentner* of potatoes for 30 marks. Bought three *Zentner*, carried it with a little hand wagon, repacked it in two 1 1/2 *Zentner* sacks, and when the train pulled it, I put it on the lowest running board. Tied it on, leaned up next to it, and tied myself on [too]. At the first station, the platform was up here, and the board down lower, I had to wait 'til the train moved on. But in Nauen it was an open platform. So, with the sack [I] marched off to the *S-Bahn* to the other platform, tied it on and back for the other bag, then to Wilmersdorf. There were young boys at the station, 10–12 years old. They'd made themselves little wagons. . . . I gave them ten marks, they loaded it up and took it to the artists' colony. I sold the potatoes there; bought them for thirty marks [East] a *Zentner* and sold them for thirty marks West. The exchange was I don't know 1:5 or 1:6, so you could earn a lot. It worked wonderfully, I left home [around four], got back so five or six in the evening, washed up and [was] off to *Café Nord*! I took my father along once—it was a total catastrophe! He lost his backpack along the way and . . . [he] cost me too much time.

[Once] they stopped and searched us.[9] Took the potatoes. They gave us our sacks back, but kept the potatoes. So then we got the idea [to get off] before the train pulled into the station. On the platform, they had put so many police, that there was practically one in front of every door. We never would've gotten through, would've been caught. But, if you climb out the backside of the cars, underneath there's a little lever, and if you pull on it, it sets off the emergency brake, and if you push it back down, no one can tell where it was pulled. If you pull the brake *inside*, they can tell where it was pulled, it hangs down, but there underneath you can't tell. But the train had to get up steam again, had to wait a bit, so we climbed down and took off through the woods to the *S-Bahn*, where there were no police. But then the police figured out what was going on, so the next time, one of us climbed out, pulled the brake, but we stayed inside. So the police were out there in the woods and we got through to Nauen and there were no one there! (laughter)

We couldn't do that very long though; it was over. One day they caught me; I had a backpack, no sacks, that didn't work anymore, it was too much because you already had to be a bit careful there running through the woods. I never would've made it with my three *Zentner* of potatoes. They saw me, and I jumped on [the train] and [the cop] right behind me. I had to hold on with two hands, but he had a hand free and tried again and again to get me. But I didn't jump down. Somehow I got him, and at the end of the platform he flew tumbling off. . . . After that I couldn't show my face there again. I got home and my mother didn't recognize me. Both eyes [swollen] shut, black and blue all over. My mother really let me have it. And the last bit of money I somehow scraped together; my friend loaned me some too. So then I went to work repairing my boat.[10]

Authorities would have wrung their hands over Dinkel's inability to complete his apprenticeship and sharply criticized his obvious preference for a life of criminal behavior. For Dinkel himself, this unsanctioned capitalism became a way of asserting and establishing independence and self-reliance. First, he described himself as unsuited for the regulated life of a tailor's apprentice, a comment that suggests some combination of a lifelong personality trait, juvenile impatience, and a rejection of the attempted overregulation he recalls from the Nazi era. Second, Dinkel explained his illegal activities as a more lucrative substitute for an apprentice's low pay and long hours. Like so many other Germans in the mid-1940s, Dinkel felt he could not spare the long-term investment of technical training. Although it seems that most of his earnings in fact went toward his sailboat, he articulates a common theme: an immediate need for long-unavailable material goods. Dinkel did invest time and energy in investigating and discussing with friends the new political and economic parameters in which he found himself. After a period of trial and error, Dinkel learned to function as an essentially successful self-employed entrepreneur.

Dinkel detailed his illegal exploits in a very straightforward manner, as if it constituted simply one stage of his work history, much like an apprenticeship or internship. If anything, he seemed proud of his entrepreneurial accomplishments; the import business earned a sizable profit, enabling Dinkel to pay off his debts. His only regret had nothing to do with the illegal nature of his activities, but rather the shame of admitting to his father—his first and only investor—that the Hamburg venture had been a waste of time and money.

In fact, Dinkel's black-market memories revolved almost exclusively around his efforts to acquire a boat, a boat for which Dinkel paid hard-earned cash, in which he invested hours of labor, and on which he courted his future wife and cemented other lifelong relationships. Although it's unclear if he actually stopped smuggling after completing the boat payments, Dinkel described that moment with finality: "then I went to work on my boat." He stored his boat at a dock in West Berlin for twenty-five (West German) marks a month. About the same time, he embarked on a long career in the DEFA's costume workshop and began paying rent to his parents. In the eyes of youth officials, Dinkel had finally yielded to the rules of postwar society; he had turned from his immoral ways to embrace a legitimate occupation. Dinkel, however, emphasized his self-reliance throughout this period. He was intent on making his own way in postwar Berlin; the smuggling, the boat, and eventually the full-time job were all stepping-stones to the personal and financial independence he so desired.

Dinkel's upbeat recollections of his criminal career contrast sharply with those of fellow interviewee Herr Mostel, who epitomized the categorically asocial young Berliner in the early postwar period. Lacking a stable home environment and susceptible to the influence of other young lawbreakers, Mostel sank ever deeper into criminal habits.

It was a dark period, 1945–46, and while some people made crooked deals or racketeered, a fellow apprentice, two school friends [and I] took another path. They'd lived in Zehlendorf, in a building that had been commandeered by the Americans, so they were familiar with the neighborhood. One even had a key to one of the kitchen doors, so they got in and cleared out the pantry. And then in another house, we took what we could get from the hall and the kitchen; a criminal act, strictly speaking, but when you're hungry, what can you do? It was such a turbulent time that not even the Americans knew what was up and what was down. A German special commission was established to follow these cases, because they [the Americans] never caught anyone breaking in. Fact was, [the commission] conducted house searches of the people . . . they knew lived or had lived in those buildings . . . with the *Kripo* [criminal police], they searched and found things that normally the people weren't allowed to have. American cigarettes and clothing and so on and so forth.

And because I lived in the East—the others all lived in Zehlendorf—I had a long way to go and left part of my loot in a little wooden box, with my name in it. They [the investigators] didn't have a key, and so broke it open, and there was my name. The result? They looked for me, and because this special commission *had* to find people, they went to the company where we worked. But precisely on that day I had a doctor's appointment, because I had bad hands and feet from frostbite, and when I stopped by in the evening to excuse myself and pick up my pay and turn in the doctor's note, the boss said, "Hey Dieter, they're looking for you and so on, go on and clear things up," and then I knew what was up. They were all gone [but] I had a terribly bad conscience because I didn't want to trouble anyone. So I went out to *Baumschulenweg*, in the East, where one of my former colleagues lived. I'd gotten him to give me an old revolver; [it was in the box] and what, was I supposed to turn him in?! I could've just as easily found the revolver digging around [in the rubble] just like he did. So I went out there and told him it didn't matter, don't worry, you or me, either of us could've found it, so it was all right. But then he told his father I'd stolen a bicycle. And the father said, "Listen here, that's not so bad, go tell the police," so I went with this man to the police on *Baumschulenweg* . . . and I told them, yes I was wanted and so on and so forth, nothing else. So then they brought me from *Baumschulenweg* to *Alexanderplatz*, and after three days this special commission picked me up. If they'd known, the Eastern [police, that I had] a revolver, a SS dagger [and] a flag, they would've sent me someplace where I would've never got out.

They sent me to the *Ringstraße* [detention center] where I sat from the end of December through mid January or mid February; we had a trial and mid February we were transferred to the *Jugendhof* [youth facility]. One, two, three, four, five of us, there were. Of the five I knew three, two we hadn't met 'til we had the [court] date. . . . So we set out from the *Ringstraße*, it was the bitter winter 1947, and we were over eighteen [but] this judge [named] Seehof, from the American military court gave us a break and said, "Ok, we'll see how you do," and so we were the first ones older than eighteen who ended up in the *Jugendhof*. It was an American institution, administered by Germans, although the barracks where we lived were the German army's. I have photos. . . . That was the blockhouse, where we were put first, with this watchtower, and then after about four, five weeks we came out into the regular camp. There, the boys who had jobs on the outside could go out, some, not all of them. . . . And we had our room, wooden bunk beds stacked atop each other. Four to six in a room, the bedrooms were bitter cold, we had three sleeping bags on top of each other and these American soldiers' coats, dyed black for the POWs . . . we laid those on top and slept then twelve or fifteen to a room.

. . . There was a barrack where we made lamps and wall lights from rubble, the city commander even got one. Those wall lamps, we made maybe, oh, fifteen or twenty, and Mayor Reuter got one and Judge Seehof and, yes, I had one too. We were allowed to make one for ourselves. We didn't get any money. . . . It's like this: The children who are locked into the *Jugendhof* today, they have to work too and they get money for it—not much, but their social security gets paid. They didn't do that then. I wanted to get the time recognized [for pension purposes—KAR], but didn't win [the case], oh well. Water under the bridge. So we worked there, and as a thank you, a guy named Riese, the director, took us sailing sometimes, imagine that!! . . . There was a group, Eberhard Group, they called themselves, it was an organization for Jewish-Christian or Christian-Jewish cooperation, and they took a group of mute people rowing [and camping] in the *Grunewald*. . . . And I was out for two weeks with this group, and then we were supposed to return to the *Jugendhof*. [But] some people from this Eberhard Group put in a good word for me, so I could stay out four weeks, all the way into October; 1947 was a long summer and it was still warm in October. So we stayed out there in tents, and I met a Mrs. Epstein . . . who wrote a recommendation for me and because of that, I was released already in 1948, although I'd gotten a five-year sentence. . . . I was lucky, got out mid April, and between April and July had to appear before this [parole officer]. . . .

There were also small children in the *Jugendhof*. . . . They had been mascots for the Americans, little children, who were abused sexually and they were rounded up and came to the *Jugendhof*. There was a Mrs. Sottchek, who'd had to quit her studies in the Third Reich, somehow she was medically undesirable or something, and she took care of the children. . . . My father died in 1946, more or less my fault, because [he] got so upset because they wanted to arrest me. . . . He had a hemorrhage and was gone. My mother remarried 1952, an old friend, also from the *Wandervögel* . . . he'd lost his wife in 1945. . . . So after the war, I had only a short relationship with my parents. My father was a sick man, he'd made two parachute jumps in 1937 and got a lung infection, and it never really healed. . . . My father had to inhale calcium dust (?) and do breathing exercises with a therapist and did all kinds of things, went to a spa, and then they wanted to, there's a word for it, shut down one lung. . . . [The doctor] healed him up again, but through the poor nutrition my father was very sickly, and I was the one who more or less pushed him into the grave. . . . Later on, I got along all right with my mother, but not then, during that time, nor with my father. I somehow drifted away from home. First, when I was in the *Jugendhof*, my mother was alone. And that was bad enough. But later after she married, we got along a bit better. Although there was always this thing with my stepfather.[11]

Unlike Dinkel, whose recollections of delinquency seem to be a stepping-stone to financial solvency and adult independence, Mostel's account fits into a life narrative largely informed by a theme of impropriety. Over the course of two multihour conversations, Mostel described numerous acquaintances from all walks of life who had profited from illegal or immoral actions.

Mostel also showed much more regret for his actions, blaming his criminal activities for permanently upsetting relations with his parents. He recognized his father's extensive efforts to help him find apprenticeship and employment opportunities during the war, and acknowledged not ever really appreciating this support. In fact, Mostel recalled having engaged in "stupid behavior" throughout the mid-1940s, and believed his eventual arrest literally broke his father's heart. Mostel's mother also tried to keep him on the straight and narrow—the first time he brought home a revolver (in May 1945), she made him get rid of it. Ultimately though, her efforts also failed. Although the two "got along a bit better" in later years, Mostel noted that the relationship was permanently scarred by his illegal behavior as a youth.

Although Mostel spent a number of months at the *Jugendhof*, he said little about the rehabilitative pedagogy he encountered there. At the time, local authorities proudly described the institution as a "new kind of home" where "new paths to reform convicted youths are pursued," but Mostel recalled only unpaid work and Spartan living conditions. Upon his release in 1948, he faced exactly those dangers predicted by HJA director Erna Maraun, who lamented the lack of "ongoing counseling and housing for released minors, who often no longer have stable home situations and must be given refuge in the homes or families of their employers."[12] Nonetheless, Mostel's stay in the *Jugendhof* did seem to set him on a new path. Shortly before his parole, he began participating in events at the local German Youth Activities club. This American-sponsored organization facilitated Mostel's reintegration into public life, even providing the half-orphan a place to sleep for several difficult months.

Like Dinkel, Mostel's adult identity also seems to have been strongly influenced by his shady past. However, whereas Dinkel described himself as an alert opportunist, Mostel portrayed himself as a victim of circumstances. For every Mrs. Epstein or other positive role model, Mostel seems to have encountered another adult who pursued suspicious—if not outright criminal—behavior, frequently without any legal repercussions. In Mostel's eyes, the world was (and is) anything but just. Economic success is rooted not in persistence and fair play, but rather in personal connections and good luck.

In sum, authorities understood that necessity drove some youths to criminal behaviors. Unable to change the socioeconomic conditions that produced crime, the officials focused on punitive regulation, a practice which reinforced public fears that cohort members would develop (or already had) permanent criminal dispositions. Youths themselves, however, had no trouble understanding apprenticeships, part-time jobs, black-market activity, and even theft along a continuum of economic activity necessary for survival during a period when legitimate opportunities were scarce. Although personal experience may not have convinced cohort members that successful adults played by the rules, most did abandon illegal schemes as more legitimate opportunities became available in the 1950s.

NOTES

1. In August 1914, a general amnesty led to a deceiving drop in youth crime statistics; previous records were erased, pending crimes left unrecorded, and current sentences suspended or converted to probation. Waite, 352.

2. The NSDAP took advantage of such statistics, promoting itself as the party that would crack down on crime. Stachura, 139; Humphries, 175.

3. Wagener, *Einwirkungen von Krieg und Revolution auf die Mordkriminalität der Jugendlichen* (Berlin, 1932) 14, 34–35, in Waite, 356–57.

4. "Youth in Danger. Youth Crime in Berlin." Gesamtverband der Berliner Inneren Mission (undated, appears to be fall 1946) Archiv des Diakonischen Werkes der EKD GV 14.

5. Tinker, 6.

6. Roland Gröschel and Michael Schmidt, *Trümmerkids und Gruppenstunde* (Berlin: Elefanten Press, 1990), 19. If arrested, girls (who constituted 10–20 percent of juvenile offenders) were typically tested for STDs; boys were not.

7. Copy of letter from Comrade Paul Strehl to Geschke and Jandretzky, Berlin 24 September 1945, SAPMO DY 30/IV 2/16 212, 140–41.

8. Not until ca. 1950 would a professionally trained cohort of social workers bring coherence and consistency to programs for youth in Berlin. SAPMO DY 30/IV 2/16/211, 204–6; "Bericht des Zentralen Jugendausschußes Berlin," 9 August 1945, SAPMO DY 30/IV 2/16 212, 210–15; P. Weiß, "Fragen an Ella Kay," *60 Jahre Gesetz für Jugendwohlfahrt 1922–1982* (Berlin: Hauptjugendamt: 1982).

9. Although Dinkel clearly discussed his plans with other like-minded youths, it is unclear how frequently he worked with a partner.

10. Dinkel, 6–9.

11. Mostel, 1–4, 9, 30, 32, 36.

12. Erna Maraun, "Jahresbericht über die Tätigkeiten des Hauptjugendamtes 1946–47," LAB 120 3004.

4

Normalizing Abnormalcy

The year 1949 marks the establishment of two German successor states, a turning point which would shape Berliners' lives and identities through the end of the century. Although interviewees rarely mentioned such political declarations directly, they associated the year 1949 with efforts to resolve—for better or worse—the crises of the Hunger Years. Instead of highlighting key words or moments in the post-Blockade years, interviewees described the 1950s as a time of reestablishing personal normalcy. After the drama and crises of Hunger Years, which culminated in the Blockade, the early fifties were a time of steady progress; after nearly a decade of turmoil, cohort members yearned for and successfully pursued normal lives, characterized by steady jobs, stable relationships, and material security.

These attempts to claim a sense of normalcy, however, collided with the implications of political division, which destroyed any hope of a quick return to the Berlin of prewar memories. Consequently, Germany's postwar division compelled this cohort to develop new perceptions of normal life in Berlin. Over time, cohort members' expectations, experiences and recollections both shaped and were shaped by these new constructions of normalcy, a divided normalcy that structures memories of the 1950s and Berliners' contemporary identities.

PERSONAL NORMALIZATION

Five years after Germany's defeat, cohort members still faced major material hurdles in both their daily lives and their efforts to assert independence and self-sufficiency. Crowded multigenerational or multifamily living arrangements were still the norm, while unemployment remained particularly high among young people.[1]   Authorities continued to be plagued by numerous hurdles as they sought alternatives for young Berliners. In 1950, for example, Kreuzberg officials complained that perpetual budget shortfalls not only kept them from expanding social programs for youth, but also delayed new school construction and prevented the district from acquiring needed educational materials. Worst of all, Kreuzberg was compelled to cut the district government's budget midyear by another 20 percent.[2]

Despite such documented economic problems, however, interviewees tended to downplay the previously dominant theme of hardship when recalling post-Blockade experiences. While key words such as "everyone worked" (see Chapter 4) would have accurately encapsulated this period for most cohort members, they instead relied on phrases such as "*es wurde dann besser*" or "*es ging endlich aufwärts*."[3]   In other words, they described the beginning of a returning normalcy, suggesting that the hard work and deprivation of the Hunger Years started producing tangible rewards in the 1950s.[4]

As a first indicator of returning normalcy, cohort members noted the increasing availability of consumer products. West Berliners, for example, talk of a sudden economic turnaround after the Blockade, using images of suddenly filled shop windows often associated with West Germany following the 1948 currency reform. Even though Berlin's business community struggled to attract investors, cohort members also recalled greater personal prosperity; after years of going without and making do, they finally had money for "luxuries"—a motorcycle, a formal evening gown, or a new (as opposed to well-worn) bicycle.[5]

This sudden material revival, which has become an integral part of both the Federal Republic of Germany's and West Berlin's postwar recovery stories, was unparalleled in either the GDR or East Berlin. Nonetheless, cohort members from eastern districts also highlighted the increased availability of consumer goods. Many shopped in the western sectors, using money saved by buying subsidized basic food items in their own districts to purchase more expensive or luxury items on trips to the West. On a more fundamental level, improving material circumstances meant, recalled Birkmann, "[that] after about 1949, I no longer thought constantly about food."[6]   Instead, cohort members began acquiring the accoutrements of a normal life.

After years of deprivation, their perceptions of normalcy were shaped by diverse, even contradictory, factors. First, cohort members drew on memories of prewar life—the nostalgia-filled *schöne Kinderzeiten*. Second, expectations of what was normal for modern young people came from foreign (i.e. often American) movies and books. Klinkert, for example, who together with her sister had to support and nurse their invalid mother during this time, remembered being glad she could finally emulate the fictional heroines the girls knew so well from novels and films.

As young ladies, we wanted better clothes and shoes, better living conditions and furniture [of course]. Things got better and better and we eventually got everything we wanted through our own industriousness, endurance and discipline.[7]

Beyond suggesting what material possessions "young ladies" deserved, Klinkert's statement exemplified how interviewees tied personal prosperity to

the established theme of self-reliance. Just as they had survived the Hunger
Years thanks to their own efforts, so did they earn—"through industriousness,
endurance and discipline"—the possessions that made their lives better, and more
normal, in the 1950s.

Normalization also meant opportunities to resume or finally begin
educational and professional paths upset by the war and its aftermath. While
school administrators still struggled to find and maintain suitable facilities, the
supply of teachers had increased—by the reinstatement of many originally
dismissed teachers in the West and by rapid teacher training programs in East
Berlin and the Soviet Zone. That said, the renormalization of public school life
brought with it numerous changes, such as co-ed classes and the lowering of
financial barriers to the university-track *Abitur*. Students in the East were also
impacted by the SED's "democratic school reforms." In theory, this would
replace the traditional class-based selection system with an *Einheitschule*, in
which all pupils, regardless of social-economic background, received the same
basic education.[8] While the SED's system favored youth from working-class
families, it put new barriers before youths from more educated families, who
considered university education "normal" for their children, yet were
unredeemably "bourgeois" in the eyes of the SED leadership. Beginning in
1949, however, even these young Berliners could pursue higher education by
seeking admission to the nascent Free University in Dahlem. Such new
educational opportunities contributed greatly to cohort members' perceptions of
returning normalcy. East Berliner Schäfer recalled that instead of wondering if
they should even bother applying to university, he and his friends discussed
which subjects to pursue.

They'd eliminated the *Schulgeld*, so that problem was solved. We passed the *Abitur*,
and [then came the question of] what to study. We had no idea what kinds of things
one *could* study, just that it was hard to get into medicine and that it was hard to get
admitted to the Technical University in Dresden; other than that, we weren't so sure
[about anything]. So we went to the *Uni* and just looked around . . . sat in on a lot of
lectures [and] looked through the catalog.[9]

While some revived long-neglected educational dreams, other interviewees
described normalcy in terms of abandoning frequently improvised employment
histories of the Hunger Years to pursue long-term careers. For Herr Hirsch, this
shift occurred in the winter of 1949–1950, when as a *Jugendpfleger* trainee, he
took a job in the Charlottenburg *Jugendamt*. When the department more than
doubled its paid staff and moved to a newly built *Jugendheim*, Hirsch found
more spacious, heated offices and, encouraged by the new professionalism,
devoted more time and energy to his work. The young man who had volunteered
with SPD youth during the Hunger Years had begun a lifelong career in the
district youth bureau.[10]

More generally, interviewees suggested that personal living arrangements
finally began to approximate normalcy in the early 1950s. West Berliners
acknowledged that the American Marshall Plan, as well as support from the
nascent West German government, speeded reconstruction projects. However,
East Berliners seemed to more often emphasize this aspect of normalization, in
part because many of them made hands-on contributions to the restoration of

devastated neighborhoods.   Specifically, they mentioned the *Nationales Aufbauwerk* (NAW), a massive building campaign along the *Frankfurter Allee*, one of the main avenues through East Berlin. In honor of Stalin, the street was to be renamed and rebuilt as a showpiece of socialist architecture.   Initial plans had been drawn in 1948, but between the painstaking work of clearing rubble, political developments (the Blockade), and the need to accommodate the SMAD's stylistic demands, construction did not begin until 1952.[11]

For East Berliners, the NAW constituted a long-awaited attempt to alleviate a severe housing shortage. Most cohort members understood the building project as a chance to secure "normal" living arrangements, that is, apartments in which they could finally live on their own.   Encouraging these sentiments, the SED government also told German youth they had a social and national duty to volunteer as manual laborers at the NAW site. Like thousands of other students, apprentices and factory workers, who often worked ten-hour days, Birkmann devoted numerous evenings to the project. For each three-hour shift, he earned a lottery ticket for a drawing that would distribute the projected 2,000 new flats to local residents.

In 1950 we cleared the city center for free. Every factory had a site. I gave up 3 percent of my pay for lottery tickets, even though nothing came of it. [We] worked shifts along the *Stalinallee*. [Was it] voluntary? It was a question of conscience. There was pride in it, working as many shifts as possible.[12]

While state officials promoted the work as an obligation, Birkmann suggested he was more motivated by both the spirit of competition and his own self-interest, an investment made in the hopes of winning the housing lottery.   In his narrative, a state-sponsored building project became a way of asserting a willingness to work for personal gain.   Zelle, who also volunteered for the NAW, recalled similar sentiments; volunteering for NAW was the only way to create the living space Berliners so obviously needed and desired.[13]   Zelle's assertions of pragmatic self-interest, like Birkman's, tended to downplay official pressure to contribute to the national project.   After a brief exchange with his wife, however, he revised his account.

There was a gentle pressure. But not like one was absolutely *required* to do it. We did that kind of thing a lot. For example, sometimes [we would be] called to help with the potato harvest, and of course we did it. Even though it was somewhat ridiculous since the travel time was much longer than the work time.[14]

Zelle's reconsideration of the NAW put the project in a different, retrospective context. It exemplified not only how Berliners rebuilt their city, but also a plethora of other, unnamed service projects to which Zelle contributed as a citizen of the GDR.   Seen pragmatically, some of these initiatives were "somewhat ridiculous."   Nonetheless, concluded Zelle, participation was expected and normal in the nascent GDR.

Cohort members enacted a final aspect of normalization as they took on more age- and gender-specific roles and expectations. A proper marriage, as opposed to a wartime *Ferntrauung* or the necessarily austere ceremonies of the

Hunger Years, was one such goal, and while men rarely mentioned such events, female interviewees described the celebration in detail.

We got married, with—as much as possible for the times—all the bells and whistles. . . . One could go to the west to buy things, [at the] 1:7 exchange rate; [you] had to pay a lot . . . but could get the things you wanted. And I had a pinkish, light pink organdy dress with a wide calf-length skirt, and of course a white veil . . . it was actually a little much for me. . . . My mother and mother-in-law and everyone who came, if they'd had their way, I'd have ridden off in a buggy afterwards, which I really didn't want. So we walked, it wasn't far. . . . We even had a honeymoon, to Bad Sarow, not far from here.[15]

By forming their own family units, cohort members began replicating not only normal social structures, but also routines recalled from childhood, such as family outings and holiday gatherings. Starting families also led to a certain renormalization of gender roles. Some young women stayed home full time with their children; others emulated their mothers' wartime lives, juggling familial responsibilities and either formal or casual employment. Interviewees' descriptions of improvised daycare arrangements and efforts to keep children from bothering tired husbands or disagreeable in-laws certainly fit "normal" images of twentieth-century motherhood.[16] Men, on the other hand, rarely spoke about their children, highlighting instead their efforts to provide for their wives and family.

Just as cohort members sought a return to normalcy in the early 1950s, so did youth authorities try to move beyond crisis-management strategies of the Hunger Years. As part of these efforts, youth officials reconsidered definitions of "youthfulness," often struggling to reach consensus. For example, while some Kreuzberg social workers believed twenty-five-year-olds still needed youth-specific counseling, the district *Jugendamt* was only officially accountable for its work with minors. Centrist politicians also questioned grouping twenty-five-year-olds with "youths," since "they have generally taken on adult roles and responsibilities."[17] Just a few years earlier, local *Jugendämter* had considered older youth particularly at risk precisely because of the adult roles many had assumed during the war; by the early 1950s, however, officials believed young people had sufficiently come to terms with Nazi-era experiences.[18]

Youth organizations faced similar questions. The FDJ continued issuing membership cards for activists well into their thirties, even as it expanded recruitment efforts among a rising younger cohort of Young Pioneers.[19] The Falcons grouped members into children (ages 6–14) and youth (ages 14–20), but similarly relied on older, more experienced leaders; twenty-nine-year-old Heinz Westphal, for example, was elected managing director of the youth organization in 1951. As membership climbed, questions of self-definition challenged group leaders, who sought to balance the interests of new young recruits and older members.[20] Such debates would have seemed superfluous during the Hunger Years, when youth organizers struggled to overcome material shortages and lamented young Berliners' apparent apathy.

STRUCTURAL NORMALIZATION

Although cohort members focused on the gradual normalization of their personal lives after the Blockade, external forces also began reimposing structure on the chaos of the Hunger Years. A declining disease rate, for example, indicated that sanitation and nutrition had improved. Despite tuberculosis outbreaks and annual polio epidemics, Berlin seemed to have overcome its postwar health crisis; after all, even the United States endured polio scares every summer. Berlin's youth officials were especially encouraged by a notable drop in so-called social diseases (STDs); even if they remained fascinated with all things American, German girls seemed to be recovering some moral standards.[21]

Second, as noted above, the normalization of a war-torn city administration included a shift in youth policies, shifting attention from rehabilitative crisis management to more general social programs. In West Berlin, this process was led by Ella Kay, who had begun working with young people in the interwar period. Kay recognized that postwar youths' needs and expectations differed from those of earlier eras. Reflecting on her career of service to youth in West Berlin, she observed,

I had learned that youth don't want to be taken care of. They want to be recognized. . . . With much help from the youth organizations, I developed [a new kind of] *Jugendamt*. Youth need a place that belongs to them and in which they belong. The independent *Jugendamt* gives them much security and self-recognition.[22]

Through the reconstituted *Jugendamt*, Kay and others in West Berlin's social democratic leadership introduced a new policies that more closely reflected this cohort's image of itself as independent, capable, and searching for stability in an insecure postwar society. By grouping *Jugendhilfe* and *Jugendpflege* together, for example, youth officials shifted from a strategy of reactive discipline and rehabilitation, rooted in expectations that the cohort was sinking into immorality and illegal behavior, to one that recognized youths as individuals and offered them encouragement to pursue their own dreams and goals. In short, *Jugendpflege* (implying the nursing of the injured or sick) became *Jugendförderung*, which, according to one of Kay's colleagues,

aims simply to help youths use their free time in a meaningful way, to ensure good health, through games, athletics, hiking and camping, and, through inexpensive cultural options, to . . . foster a taste for the beautiful and the reflective.[23]

In practice, this meant including representatives of various youth groups on central advisory boards and soliciting young Berliners' ideas for new programs. Responding to youths' input, for example, a training course for new social workers required more practical experience of applicants.[24] Kay also established better-staffed, more independent *Jugendämter* at the district level, where social workers had long observed that the ideals of the antifascist youth committees were "not exactly beloved" or effective.[25]

Despite the ongoing budgetary concerns noted above, Kreuzberg officials exemplified the successful transition from crisis management to normalcy, beginning in April 1949, when the district replaced its communal sports program (established according to Soviet guidelines in 1945) with the traditional and more popular network of private sport clubs (*Vereine*). Although this shift sometimes entailed little more than changing the club's name, it symbolized returning normalcy by reviving the city's proud legacy of independent sport clubs.[26] More generally, Berlin's reconstruction had progressed to the point that districts could dedicate more funds toward leisure facilities. Between 1950 and 1954, for example, even budget-strapped Kreuzberg completed, among other projects, a new *Haus der Jugend*, five roller-skating rinks, thirty playgrounds, and a boathouse filled with canoes and kayaks that were built by young people themselves. Home to seven youth centers in 1949, all of which were "in a shockingly neglected state," Kreuzberg offered nineteen by 1954, each complete with lounges, ping-pong tables, radios, board games, and assorted other supplies.[27]

Other western districts matched Kreuzberg's efforts, using financial support from the West German government, which had announced a new Federal Youth Plan in 1950. About half of the DM 18,000,000 budget was dedicated to traditional—and very necessary—*Jugendpflege* programs for needy, orphaned, and at-risk youth in Berlin and the Federal Republic. However, the Federal Youth Plan also funded initiatives intended for more typical young Germans such as international exchange programs and youth periodicals (including the Landesjugendring's *Blickpunkt*).[28] The western Allies supported *Jugendförderung* initiatives in Berlin through monetary and in-kind donations to the *Landesjugendring* and the *Jugendämter*. In June 1950, for example, American City Commander General Major Taylor designated DM 97,000 for summer travel and camps for youths.[29] OMGUS also continued its support of the GYA program until closing the clubs and donating the facilities to German authorities in the mid-1950s. American-sponsored Rhine cruises may have seemed an unnecessary luxury, but they demonstrated that occupation forces no longer saw Berlin's youth as troublesome ex-Nazis but rather as normal, fun-loving young people.[30]

In East Berlin, social institutions gradually came to resemble the Soviet model, with state regulations increasingly dominating educational, professional, and leisure opportunities. Politicians consolidated ideas introduced in the earlier *Jugendausschüsse* into the "Law Concerning the Role of Youth in the Establishment of the GDR and the Advancement of Youth at School and at Work, in Athletics and Recreation." Passed on 8 February 1950, this "first youth law" clarified the relationship between the SED state and its young citizens; it protected their rights in four realms—politics, work and recreation, education, and happiness—but also required youth to support the government in creating a new kind of German society.[31]

The FDJ also evolved from an organization of activists to one that shaped the lives of average youths. Whereas the 1946 FDJ identified neighborhood groups as the primary unit of organization, a new 1949 constitution relocated these core units into the workplace, school, and university. FDJ leaders had learned they could more effectively organize youths where they spent most of their time; it made sense to offer ideological and cultural programs where they already "worked and learned."[32]

Not surprisingly, the FDJ's interpretation of normalization also included ever-closer ties with the SED. The organization's 1949 constitution included goals that paralleled those of the SED's "Building Socialism" program, and FDJ officials began a tradition of matching shifts in SED policy. In 1952, for example, the FDJ adopted new statutes to match the party's "New Course" program. Although youth activists had always worked closely with party leadership, coordination between the FDJ and SED became more apparent after 1950, when the youth organization publicly acknowledged the dominant role of the SED.[33] Not unlike Kay and her coworkers, youth officials in the East no longer focused on rehabilitating war-maimed youth; instead, programs were designed to "instill in young people a democratic national consciousness [and] a new morality and work ethic" and converting the FDJ into a "socialist mass organization."[34]

In both East and West, the new structures limited the range of acceptable attitudes and limited opportunities to pursue personal initiatives. This is most clear in the centrally regulated FDJ. For example, the organization encouraged local groups to express support for SED policies and antiwar resolutions by sending their own theoretically spontaneous and individually composed statements to the party leadership. Letters from unrelated groups, however, typically mirrored each other virtually word for word. In many instances, school directors simply distributed mimeographed copies of a single letter to each classroom; pupils' input consisted only of signing their names to the common text.[35] Together with the state-sponsored workers' union, the FDJ replaced private athletic clubs with an extensive system of *Betriebssportgruppen*; tied to the workplace, this new "truly democratic sport movement" was far more than a fitness program. It would foster competition (thus increasing production) and promote antifascist, anti-imperialist attitudes.

Cohort members rarely spoke of political pressures or ideological uniformity within the FDJ, but did observe that the organization increasingly controlled leisure opportunities and resources. Zelle recalled welcoming this institutionalization, as it facilitated his development as a musician, since he couldn't afford to buy an instrument. Having joined an FDJ-sponsored band, he borrowed a friend's guitar until suddenly, "one day there appeared a bass guitar; the FDJ factory group had bought it. And that, it did pull me in somewhat. . . . They also enabled me to take music lessons. That was when (1951–52) a bassist from the Philharmonic . . . no the German Opera, he taught at the music school on the side . . . [and] the factory paid for all my lessons."[36]

Although less obvious, a growing standardization of social institutions and youth organizations also began limiting young people's autonomy in West Berlin. The guiding principles of Kay's *Jugendamt neuer Prägung* described previously, for example, cloaked a common desire among officials to gather unorganized young Berliners (who still constituted a vast majority of the cohort) into an orderly network of youth groups. Despite the much-lamented effects of Nazi-era experience, most social workers still believed formal organizations could best ensure young Berliners' welfare. In other words, while cohort members asserted autonomy, youth authorities preferred conformity.[37]

Another West Berlin institution, the *Landesjugendring* (LJR), limited youths' options in the early 1950s. Established in 1947, the LJR was intended to coordinate the activities and represent the common interests of the *Bund Deutscher Jugend* (BDJ), *Demokratischer Jugendverband* (DJV), Falcons, FDJ, and church-affiliated youth associations. The LJR did win some concrete advantages for Berliner youths, including reduced-price rail tickets, supplemental vacation time, and improved social benefits. Simultaneously, however, the LJR was plagued by political disputes among members, even after the FDJ dropped out in 1948. In addition, the Ring faced accusations of discrimination from both the smaller member organizations and independent youth groups. For example, when the LJR took on the task of distributing municipal funds, it used membership figures to determine how much money each organization should receive. On the one hand, larger groups needed more money to support activities. On the other hand, argued some representatives, the larger groups already collected more money in the form of membership dues; using the extra funds to develop even more sophisticated programs, these groups would draw members away from smaller groups, which would eventually be eliminated for a lack of material resources. The fact that the already dominant Evangelical Youth and Falcons more than doubled in size between early 1949 and mid–1950, while the Catholic Youth nearly tripled in membership, gave credence to such predictions.[38] Meanwhile, independent youth associations and local cliques such as "The Bad Boys," "The Gray Bears," and "The Merry Sparrows" had little hope of ever recruiting enough members in enough districts to qualify for Ring membership and financial support.[39]

In short, the once loosely defined parameters for youth initiatives became more institutionalized—and thus limited—in the early 1950s. The gradual normalization of policies, institutional practices, and funding procedures in effect steered young Berliners toward the larger youth organizations (such as the Falcons or FDJ), encouraging individuals to accept its regulations and ideals, which were in turn coordinated with municipal guidelines, than to strike out independently. As a result, about 70 percent of West Berliners between the ages of fifteen and nineteen belonged to one of the nine youth organizations represented in the LJR. Such indications of increasing conformity, however, did not stop cohort members from asserting themes of self-determination and independence during this period of increasing normalization. Kestler, for example, while acknowledging the FDJ's influence in the educational realm, asserted that he was admitted to East Berlin's university purely on merit. Although he did join the FDJ, it was not due to social pressure. Rather, he explained that the GDR's political strategies simply made the most sense to him at the time.

I joined the FDJ at 19, after I was accepted at the University, it was related to the development of attitudes in opposing directions. On the one hand "democracy," [sic] which was very interesting with the many groups and political directions and so forth. . . . And then I had a flyer that talked about the demand for a unified Germany, but then when the [FRG] was founded, it became clear that remilitarization would follow, and it was clear to me to choose the eastern path. Well, and then as it became obvious that remilitarization could occur only with the help of the old military and in part the Nazi civil service . . . and all the teachers came back, and so forth . . . and those were all reasons that we got more interested in communist ideology, socialism, and such. . . . I did not join FDJ out of opportunism or anything. I was admitted to the University even though I wasn't in the FDJ.[40]

For Kestler, FDJ membership and university enrollment were certainly connected, but not because one facilitated the other. Rather, both demonstrate his own ability to analyze a situation and determine a logical course of action. Birkmann explained his increasing involvement in the FDJ in similar terms. On the one hand, he explained that, following a tip from an FDJ activist, he moved from Zehlendorf to Lichtenberg in order to land a desirable job, and once there, quickly found new friends in the local youth groups. On the other hand, however, Birkmann acknowledged no causal relationship between the two developments; one was a purely professional decision (he couldn't find a job in West Berlin), and the other was the obvious result of having found an organization with logical answers to pressing questions.[41]

Of all interviewees, only Frau Kanter, whose narrative follows a theme of clear-sighted nonconformism, spoke directly about the FDJ's increasing domination of opportunities for youth.

And then the FDJ started coming into the [parish] youth groups, because the FDJ of course was charged with recruiting socialist-minded youths, and a good many of even catholic young men were at first attracted to the FDJ, because they thought, "well the basic idea isn't bad." But we figured it out pretty quickly. And then the FDJ started usurping things, [just] like the Nazis; one was red and the other brown. . . . I said [to my father], "we were left in the wrong boat yet again."[42]

A family of socially conscious Catholics, the Kanters had experienced similar problems during the Third Reich, when the Nazis limited the activities of church youth groups. Kanter recognized strategies of the HJ in the FDJ and, although disappointed that so little had changed, held to her own convictions despite the new regime's aggressive overtures. Offered a three-year scholarship to the Women's College for Financial Studies in Illmenau (ca. 150 miles southwest of Berlin), Kanter was tempted by the prospect of advanced education and a better job. After reviewing the curriculum, however, she changed her mind.

[I brought home] a big binder, with everything in it; everything related to finance [was] at the very back and in front [it was] all Marxism, Leninism and so forth. And my father said, "You won't be able to stand it, no one could. If you go there for three years you'll be red, lost to us."[43]

More than a career opportunity, Kanter described the scholarship offer as an attempt to convert her—the intelligent, charismatic daughter of an unfortunately Catholic family—to socialism. She also recognized the parallels with her prewar life, in which the HJ and BDM tried to undermine youths' ties to the church. This too was a kind of normalization; hostile societal structures were again testing her personal convictions.

EXPERIENCING DIVISION

This whole process of normalization, of course, occurred within a context of heightening tensions between the Soviet Union and the western Allies, and Berlin had become a focal point of the simmering ideological conflict. As the superpowers gradually integrated the two German successor states into opposing

economic, political, and military alliances during the 1950s, the prospect of
normalizing Berlin's status seemed increasingly unlikely. In 1952, West Berlin
was formally integrated into the Federal Republic's financial system and then
quickly incorporated into the European Coal and Steel Community. [44]   In 1954,
the Federal Parliament introduced the so-called Berlin Clause, through which
future federal legislation would also apply to West Berlin. That same year, the
United States, Great Britain, and France led NATO in recognizing Berlin as the
sovereign territory of a member state.[45]   Similar agreements bound the
GDR—with Berlin as its capital—to the Soviet Union and other Eastern Bloc
states.   The Warsaw Treaty, for instance, guaranteed mutual friendship,
cooperation and protection for Albania, Bulgaria, Hungary, the GDR, Poland,
Romania, the USSR and Czechoslovakia. Separate treaties asserted the mutual
recognition of national sovereignty between the GDR and USSR, and clarified
the role of Soviet troops on German soil.[46]

The increasing alienation of East and West found concrete expression in
Berlin, where the divided magistrate, the new, provocatively named "Free
University," and repeated SMAD restrictions on movement in and out of West
Berlin all foreshadowed a long-term division of the former capital.[47]   While
residents had shrugged off minor disputes as simply *"Berliner Wetter,"* there was
an unavoidable sense of permanence surrounding the construction of a new Outer
Railway, *Autobahn Ring*, and shipping canal, which would enable both private
and commercial traffic to completely circumvent the western sectors of the
city.[48] Still, the SED continued to at least nominally recognize Berlin's official
status as an occupied territory under joint administration. Consequently, the
GDR's constitution was initially not validated for East Berlin, and early
legislation distinguished between the GDR proper and its capital. Welcoming
GDR president Wilhelm Pieck to Berlin, mayor Friedrich Ebert carefully noted
his city's unusual position:

We respect this [joint occupation] status as we do all orders signed by the four
powers. We Berliners make no demands of either you, Mr. President, or the nascent
government of the German Democratic Republic. We are proud to be the capital of the
Reich [sic] and will do all we can to completely fulfill our resulting moral
responsibilities towards the GDR.[49]

Suggesting acceptance of Berlin's ongoing special status, the East German
constitution prevented East Berlin's representatives from voting in the national
legislature until 1958. Furthermore, although the national courts convened in
East Berlin, the judiciary initially had no authority in the city; local cases of
national interest were tried by the SMAD. As a further concession, the SED
tolerated the presence of local SPD groups in East Berlin, although the Social
Democrats were not allowed to advertise or recruit new members.

Nonetheless, even after the Soviets lifted the Blockade in spring 1949,
Berliners could hardly have ignored eastern challenges to joint occupation status.
The SED announced most important policy changes in its "national capital,"
including the 1950 *Jugendförderung Gesetz*, and the heavily publicized National
Front Program, which advocated referendums on questions of unification, a peace
treaty, and occupation troop status.[50] Furthermore, the government informed
East Berliners that their most important obligation—other than rebuilding the

capital—was convincing their western neighbors to abandon the "insanity of Reuter-politics."[51] The FDJ also made Berlin's future the responsibility of local residents, particularly after the organization relocated its central offices to a prominent *Unter den Linden* address in 1950. Officials maintained that the FDJ welcomed all peace-loving youths who supported a united, antifascist, and anti-imperialist (i.e., anti-Western) German state, and organized frequent demonstrations for "peace and unity" in Berlin. Such events, however, often led to loud, even violent, confrontations with prowestern activists. The fact that West Berlin police sometimes used force to break up demonstrations was never lost on the SED; rather, the party widely publicized such occurrences to prove that western officials opposed both unification and peace.

The role of youth in this new socialist state was defined in overtly antiwestern terms. On 17 January 1950, the SED announced a competition through which young activists would prove themselves "Ready to work for and defend the Peace" against western threats. A few weeks later (8 February 1950), the government passed a new law, clarifying the "Participation of Youths in the Construction of the GDR and the Promotion of Youths in School and the Workplace, in Athletics and Recreation." One section of the document explained the state-sponsored athletic program as preparing peace-loving youth for military service.[52] At the same time, the government attacked American "unculture," which, as Wilhelm Pieck explained, sought to undermine the socialist system by seducing young Germans with graphic depictions of pornography and violence.[53]

In practice, these policy statements meant that interviewees were repeatedly encouraged to hunt down imperialist "agents, spies and saboteurs." One song even encouraged young friends of peace to join young socialists from around the world and "storm Berlin."[54] To justify such aggressive action, authorities pointed accusing fingers westward.

Boys and Girls of Berlin, guard the peace!
The *Kammerherr* of the Schöneberg town hall, Ernst Reuter and his bodyguard . . . get new orders from the three Western city commanders every day, instructing them how to put down those advocating peace, those who do not want our capital to become a life-long refuge for mad skirt-chasers from Texas and Chicago, who don't like the fact that West Berlin factories are already again producing war materials, that 40,000 unemployed young West Berliners have become Foreign Legionnaires, sacrificing themselves . . . for the warmongers somewhere in Korea, Indochina or Vietnam. . . . Berlin belongs to Berliners, just as Germany belongs to Germans. And that's why Berlin's youth must stand in the front line of the battle for peace and the democratic unity of Berlin, uncovering the warmongers and enlightening the population about the American imperialists' scandalous plans.[55]

Western rhetoric, although not always as colorful, could be equally aggressive, explaining youth policies as "psychological rearmament" deemed crucial to West German national security.

The external defensive readiness of [West] German youths is not conceivable without securing them morally and politically. The best weapon of future young German soldiers will lie in his strength of character and in his conviction that he is prepared to defend a free world.[56]

Like their eastern counterparts, political leaders in West Berlin supplemented strong antiwar rhetoric with public demonstrations and commemorations. In 1950, for example, western authorities organized a May Day celebration rivaling that organized by the SED administration. Held at the Platz der *Republik*, the event drew more than half a million Berliners, who rallied around the slogan, "Against Unity in Chains, for Peace and Freedom"—a clear challenge to the SED's own rhetoric of unity and peace.[57]

Members of youth organizations, in particular the Falcons and FDJ, felt the deepening political rift in their meetings, newsletters, and activities. Having to some extent vied for members immediately after the war (since both organizations asserted leftist origins and goals such as unity and antimilitarization), the two groups had used political incidents to criticize each other even before the FDJ quit the *Landesjugendring*. Still, through the late 1940s, Falcon leaders saw the *Pfadfinder* (scouts) as their primary competitor. In contrast, former Falcons described ongoing intellectual exchanges with FDJ members during this period.[58]

This reasonably tolerant coexistence vanished in the years following the Blockade, as political tensions undermined not only interorganizational dialogue, but also each organization's internal structures. Already in mid-1950, for example, sixty-nine Falcon activists from Berlin's eastern districts rejected ties to western Falcons "because [of] the leading functionaries' provocative actions and dependence on the SPD leadership." The self-proclaimed "progressive Falcons" elected their own officers and enrolled 300 members by September, advocating peace with the Soviet Union, the unification of German youth, and closer cooperation with the FDJ.[59]

More broadly, law enforcement officers were given greater latitude in repressing undesirable activities. For example, an East Berlin court sentenced Gerhard Sperling, chair of the Lichtenberg Falcons, to twenty-five years in prison for distributing political leaflets in the *S-Bahn*.[60] Meanwhile, the mayor of Kreuzberg authorized police crackdowns on demonstrations led by "organizations belonging to the SED"; on one occasion in 1950, officers took over a hundred FDJlers into "protective custody" for congregating outside the *Görlitzerbahnhof*.[61] Although Kreuzberg FDJlers protested what they saw as sanctioned police brutality, the mayor's strategy was effective; the Kreuzberg FDJ lost nearly half its card-carrying members by the end of the year.[62]

It was not just FDJlers and Falcons who recalled the consequences of political and economic division. Binkert, for example, abandoned a promising career in the Prenzlauer Berg *Bezirksamt* to join the 675,000 East Germans who "voted with their feet" by crossing the German-German frontier between 1949 and 1952.[63] For Frau Barthe, economic concerns took priority. After marrying an East Berliner, she maintained her Kreuzberg residency status so as to receive maternity benefits in the stronger currency.[64] Even Herr Zelle, who remained in the East and seemed satisfied with his personal life and career, recalled being angry when the political conflict threatened his favorite hobby.

I apprenticed in an export firm [in the eastern sector] until 1952 and then was hired right after that, 1955. We had to swear not to go into the western sectors, which was fine, [it wouldn't have] bothered me. *But* I had developed a hobby, water sports, we bought a boat and then this oath thing came down from the party elite, from the Central Committee to [our] office.

Zelle refused to sign the oath, not out of ideological convictions, but simply because he wanted to sail his boat in West Berlin waters.[65] West Berliners also faced difficult choices. As noted in Chapter 4, Distel sacrificed a diploma—and a career—in order to maintain her ties with the GYA.   Barthe did stay in Kreuzberg until her child was born, then yielded to pressure to transfer residency to East Berlin, even though receiving her salary in the weaker eastern currency meant she could no longer afford the higher quality western baby items.

In sum, political and economic division subverted, in both large and small ways, cohort members' efforts to construct normal independent lives.   The politics, rhetoric and consequences of division made it virtually impossible to re-create prewar normalcy. "Normal" life—as represented in memories, books, and film—entailed routine, not perpetual inconvenience or the underlying fear that political conflict might escalate into armed confrontation. In other words, given imposed social and political parameters, this cohort could not *return* to normalcy; instead, it had to *create*, over time, a new definition of normalcy.

COMPETING FOR YOUTH: THE WORLD FESTIVAL GAMES

The Third World Festival Games of Youth and Students, according to organizers' estimates, drew more than two million youths and young adults from 104 nations to East Berlin between the fifth and the nineteenth of August 1951.[66] The *Weltfestspiele* (WFS) included athletic competitions, music and dance concerts, art exhibits and displays highlighting young people's scientific achievements. As "not only the largest athletic, but also the largest cultural event of postwar Germany," the festival also drew attention to what was becoming normal in divided Berlin; participants could witness what Berliners negotiated every day: duplicate administrative structures, divergent living standards, and a confrontative political atmosphere.[67]

According to official rhetoric, the WFS would demonstrate young Germans' dedication to peace, international solidarity among working peoples, and cooperative achievement.   Young socialists from around the world would converge on East Berlin to share common ideas and diverse cultures, thereby smoothing the GDR's path into what was becoming a global socialist community.   Inspired by the material and ideological renewal of a city and people only recently freed from fascist exploitation, visiting delegates from Germany and elsewhere would return home eager to carry on the struggle for world peace and international solidarity.

The Greater Berlin World Festival Games Preparatory Committee seemed undaunted by logistical hurdles that included the ongoing housing crisis and a lack of public venues; Germany's youth, they decided, would simply build what was needed. Months before the festival, the committee had already mobilized thousands of young volunteers, recruiting not only FDJlers, but also members of the SED, Freie Deutsche Gewerkschaftsbund (FDGB—the state-sponsored union) and *Gesellschaft für Deutsch-Sovietische Freundschaft*.[68]

The young East German state welcomed the WFS, since the festival presented an opportunity to promote a long list of ideological campaigns, educational initiatives, and work programs. According to Erich Honecker, for example, an intimate understanding of Marxist-Leninist-Stalinist teachings constituted "a crucial element of preparations for the Third World Festival Games in Berlin, since a clear understanding of the connections between theory and practice was necessary in the struggle for peace, unity, and happiness."[69] Honecker also described the festival as a chance for German youth to thank Soviet mentors who had both sheltered them from capitalist exploitation and guided them toward socialist solidarity.[70]

In fact, virtually all state-sponsored youth initiatives were recast as essential to the success of the WFS. The FDJ publication *Junge Generation*, for example, told members that electing qualified officers and establishing special antimilitarization action committees constituted "important" and "the best" preparations for a successful festival.[71] Amateur choirs, theater companies, and dance troupes were reminded to "reflect the struggle for peace, a love of homeland and the joy of work" in their 1951 productions. Youths without demonstrated talents were encouraged to study classical German literature and music, memorize songs and texts of the International League, and earn proficiency badges such as the Athletic Achievement Award Level I and the Award for Good Knowledge.[72] Increased productivity in the workplace was also explained as yet another necessary precursor to the 1951 festival; professional competitions, in which apprentices took on extra work while racing to complete their schooling, would both serve the Five Year Plan and demonstrate youths' commitment to a prosperous, peaceful future.[73] Above all, festival promoters reminded youth to focus on their common goals as citizens of a new German state.

We want to prove that the new German youth is mastering culture and science. . . . It is not only to the new, however, that you must devote your whole strength, intellect and abilities. Only through developing and protecting our classical roots, as well as their applications and developments, can you meet the prerequisites of our great plan. You must nurture not only our national legacy . . . but the whole world literature. . . . Carry on tirelessly the battle against formalism, the cultural barbarism promoted in the western parts of our homeland. In all you do, choose the great, wonderful, inexhaustible theme—peace.[74]

The SED, FDJ, and related organizations had, of course, promoted these ideas since their inception during the Hunger Years. As the WFS approached, however, young people in every field were reminded that technical achievements, cultural accomplishments, and political agitation efforts all demonstrated a commitment to peace and progressivism.[75] Even traditional rural festivals became opportunities to collect donations and promote awareness of the fast-approaching WFS.[76]

Young Berliners, who would host the festival, found slogans, appeals, and action programs everywhere they went in the "democratic sector," while the *Berliner Rundfunk* broadcast special semiweekly updates on the preparations.[77] Throughout the spring and early summer, local youths collected donations of food and bedding, recruited neighbors to house foreign visitors in spare rooms, organized decorations, and rehearsed their own contributions. During the festival itself, Berliners hosted delegations in school gymnasiums and factory cafeterias, escorted visitors to events, and themselves participated in cultural programs, athletic contests, and carefully choreographed mass marches. After more than forty years of socialist demonstrations and work initiatives, Klinkert still enthusiastically recalls her round-the-clock efforts of the early fifties.

We were on the go for cultural [performances] and in between we always did the neatest homework. On Saturdays and Sundays. And then sometimes rubble work, harvest work, yes, we did everything. But whenever someone said, "are you coming? Will you take part?" "Yes, yes, we'll be there." Then, 1951 . . . the World Festival Games were organized here in the East, and we, well, first, 1950 was the dress rehearsal, the *Deutschlandtreffen*. . . . We performed with the choir and the dance group, in the streets and in factories and in 1951 it just got crazier, we did everything, weeks of preparations, laying mattresses on the floor in schools and straw for when the youth came . . . we didn't come home for weeks, we even slept at the office, you know?[78]

Klinkert and her sister cleared rubble, joined several folkdance groups, and sang in the district choir. In return, each girl received a pair of new shoes and the knowledge that they had demonstrated their commitment to world peace and somehow contributed to Germany's reintegration into an international community.

Participants' accounts also demonstrate how the spirit of the *Weltfestspiele* supported local reconstruction efforts. For example, although youth volunteers had served on municipal construction crews since 1945, Herr Birkmann explained Berlin's *Wiederaufbau* by describing the Construction Sunday campaign of the early 1950s, while Klinkert associates the National Reconstruction Project with preparations for the WFS, even though construction did not begin until after the festival. The two initiatives were intertwined, however; seeking to mold Berliners' cultural identity and encourage a new work ethic, they both won popular support for the SED's goals of redefining Germany and winning international recognition.

Both campaigns also used notions of pride and obligation to attract youths, but what actually motivated young people to take on extra responsibilities? To volunteer another three or four hours after a full day's work? To sleep, stomachs growling, on the floors of factory lunchrooms? Despite many interviewees' skeptical critiques of political rhetoric and mixed emotions toward the now-defeated GDR, the rallying cries of "Never again war!" and "Stop imperialist aggression!" found—and continue to find—great resonance among cohort members; several interrupted their recollections to voice concerns that contemporary youths cannot conceptualize war. Problems of imperialist aggression, nuclear weapons, and in particular America's role in Korea punctuate their recollections.

The desire to satisfy long-standing curiosity about foreign cultures also motivated young Berliners to participate in the WFS. Except for vacation camps and bike tours sponsored by *Jugendämter* or the larger youth organizations, postwar youth had few opportunities to explore the world outside Berlin, let alone beyond Germany's borders. The 1951 World Festival Games brought the world to them, and images of a colorful, musical, international community of youth punctuated participants' recollections.

The youth of the world paraded through the streets with their *Schallmeien* and traditional costumes. . . . [It was] the first time since the war we had seen foreigners from other lands; we couldn't go there, so it was fascinating, the Asian faces different and the *Negers* [*sic*], and we were a part of it all. We converted the big hall (of the workplace) into a Hall of Peace and hosted the delegations. My sister and I were selected as servers—not everyone was picked, of course . . . Koreans, and Romanians and Bulgarians, it was all very simple, we served cookies and some cheap wine; they danced for us and we got by with our few words of Russian or English. . . . Friendship without language.[79]

More than political slogans or solidarity, participants highlighted the chance to meet other cultures face-to-face and to enjoy "normal" youthful activities—eating, talking, and laughing together. Like Klinkert, who recalled dancing and flirting with her foreign guests, Birkmann observed that the visitors had apparently forgiven and forgotten the war.

I chaperoned four choirs, rode with them every day to lunch in the (hall at) police headquarters and took them to their performances. It was considered FDJ *Dienst*; we got off work and went all over the city, wherever the performances were. . . . It was magnificent when they sang . . . we sat up on top of the busses, the best seats. . . . The delegations visited each other all the time. We were with the Hungarians, and the atmosphere was something else! The German always needs a bit of alcohol, but those Hungarian girls . . . they were so vivacious, they would just grab the German guys and spin away (dancing)! We collected commemorative kerchiefs . . . it was wonderful, the other young people recognized us as *vollwertige Menschen*; that was our first international recognition.[80]

Both Klinkert and Birkmann downplayed both language barriers and the documented difficulties that arose as waves of visitors came and went throughout the WFS. Instead, they emphasized the spirit of the festival, which they described as overwhelmingly positive and enthusiastic. The WFS represented to them, as they looked back on it, a returning normalcy on both interpersonal and international levels. They echoed organizers' calls for peaceful solidarity and intercultural exchange, but found it in personal encounters, rather than the carefully planned official program offerings.

Similarly, interviewees did not suggest that the existence of West Berlin shaped their experiences of the *Weltfestspiele*, even though archival records indicate that local authorities devoted considerable thought to this situation. Festival organizers instructed local volunteers to avoid sector boundaries, except during a few scheduled demonstrations, and to discourage visiting delegates from leaving the "democratic" sector. In particular, festival organizers worried about delegates from throughout the GDR; they clearly did not want young Germans to compare conditions in the decadent West with those in the democratic East, or to take home tales of western prosperity.

Nonetheless, beyond the sanctioned demonstrations along sector boundaries, an estimated 500,000 festival participants visited West Berlin at least once.[81] The West Berlin Senate had anticipated this opportunity to showcase its own ideas and values. It organized its own WFS Youth Bureau, in which representatives of more than twenty-five departments and organizations, including HICOG (U.S. High Commissioner for Germany) and the Federal Ministry for German-German Questions, developed a parallel cultural program of films. In the weeks prior to the festival, the bureau printed brochures, posters, and press releases advertising free films, cultural performances, art exhibits, and political events, including a UNESCO display on human rights and live taping sessions of popular radio programs.[82]

Western "welcome centers" were flooded with visitors, especially in border districts such as Kreuzberg.   The Saturday before the festival began, the district's WFS action committee opened five youth clubs and a central youth office to visitors and, responding to popular demand, set up three more centers on 9 August.   In addition, WFS delegates were offered free admission to the annual Kreuzberg Festival and Sports Week (11–19 August).   Action committee officials considered their efforts successful when local volunteers counted more than 950 visitors a day.[83]

While enjoying the free or reduced-price performances and athletic events, WFS delegates also sought other attractions in West Berlin.   Youth Bureau staffers, for example, noted widespread interest in daily newspapers, satirical journals, and *Der Tip*, a published calendar of cultural events; some visitors, in fact, pursued these publications for three or four hours at a time.   Welcome center volunteers also noted an overwhelming demand for snacks and warm meals; when asked about the WFS, German delegates often complained of being hungry, explaining that organizers seemed to save the best food for the foreign visitors.[84]

Although the Youth Bureau understood that free food and entertainment would attract visitors, western officials strove to engage WFS delegates in political discussions.   Like their counterparts in East Berlin, western organizations took the political side of the festival very seriously, issuing daily evaluations of each district's efforts to promote pro-western attitudes.   Welcome center volunteers took notes on their conversations with visitors, which were compiled in daily reports that revealed the extent of East German propaganda.   Delegates had been warned, for example, that western food might be poisoned and that West Berlin police would probably harass WFS delegates.

Ideological differences sparked political confrontations and sometimes even violence.   At one Kreuzberg welcome center, where volunteers identified 2 percent of visitors as communist party hard-liners, police arrested four suspected spies.   During a large peace march on 15 August, Kreuzberg police pushed an organized column of some 3,000 uniformed FDJlers (rumored to include Erich Honecker himself) back from the sector boundary at *Schliesische Brücke*, arresting sixty-two protestors in the process.   On same day, officers used physical force to break up 4,000 marchers in *Neukölln* and resorted to a water cannon to end a protest in Wedding.[85]

Although official SED accounts sharply criticized such theoretically unprovoked police actions, they clearly anticipated potentially violent confrontation. The leader of the Saxon delegation, for example, advised delegates to break formation and link arms after crossing the sector border, keeping girls in the middle of each row.[86]   Young Berliners were similarly unsurprised when peaceful protests turned violent, since clashes between political forces in East and West had become an expected element of most public demonstrations and holidays. In their eyes, the political nature of the WFS confirmed what was already apparent—Berlin had been divided by two opposing ideologies. Cohort members' pursuit of "normal" adult lives entailed accepting the parameters imposed by this division.

Beyond confirming ideological differences, the WFS opened doors to the world beyond Berlin and demonstrated the SED state's expectations of young Germans. To Birkmann, the festival also solidified a postwar, adult identity. After having spent years skeptically questioning, exploring eastern and western sectors, and mulling over political slogans and speeches, the WFS confirmed that *his* Germany was the true "friend of peace." After the festival, Birkmann became increasingly involved in both FDJ and union activities, embracing a relationship between youth and state that in exchange for service and loyalty offered the chance to be carefree, to celebrate *Freude und Frohsinn*.[87]

NORMALCY AS CONSTRUCT

This discussion of the World Festival Games illustrates the simultaneous role of expectations and retrospection in East Berliners' narratives. Both Klinkert and Birkmann described an anticipation of normal relationships, which was at least briefly fulfilled in their personal contacts with foreign delegates to the festival; both Berliners highlighted opportunities to socialize and feeling accepted as peers, not perpetrators of war. Beyond this fulfillment of expectations, however, a sense of retrospective normalcy informed accounts of the 1950s. "Of course, we [twins] would be a part of it," said Klinkert; looking back, participation in such large-scale initiatives was commonplace, and unquestioned, throughout a lifetime of obligatory volunteerism.

East Berliners' recollections of the workers' strike of 17 June 1953 also demonstrated how definitions of normalcy reflect expectation and retrospection. Zelle, who had gotten married four days earlier, offered vivid memories of his political and personal circumstances during the strike.

I had applied for two weeks vacation but was denied, because [things] were already restless. . . . And then, the week before the 17th of June came the announcement of the New Course, so that a lot of these new measures [announced earlier that spring] were revoked, in exchange for raising the workers' quotas or something. . . . And since I hadn't gotten any vacation, I had to work. . . . They used me as a courier between the different export firms. And I did that until it wasn't possible anymore, with the demonstrations and tanks on the 17th. I was home in the evening, and from the balcony we could see the whole length of the *Landesbergerallee*, one tank after another headed downtown. And then on the next day, "state of emergency." I went to work anyway, and then someone threw a sheet of paper down from a balcony—a school child [had] ripped a page from a notebook or something . . . and the soldiers construed *that* as some kind of [political] action—typical of the time. We could go *into* the house, but no one could leave . . . my mother-in-law had her shop around the corner, and couldn't get there. She'd closed the store and come to see us as soon as she heard what was going on, and couldn't get back out. That is, well, later she went through the courtyard and through other yards and got back to her building. It lasted two days and then it was over. We were just glad when the tanks left.[88]

Zelle expressed no surprise at the developments that produced a state of emergency in Berlin; if anything, the aggressive response to civilian demonstrations was "typical of the time"—certainly no reason for him to stay home from work. His family carried on with their lives as best they could, using their familiarity with the neighborhood's interconnecting *Hinterhöfe* to outmaneuver officials. Although Zelle described being relieved when the strike ended, he offered few clues as to his sympathies or personal opinions.

Frau Miller similarly distanced herself from the political conflict behind the strike. While the uprising seemed to reinforce her opinion of both the Red Army and the SED government, Miller, like Zelle, emphasized the existance of a private sphere beyond the reach of political strife or rhetoric.

[The year] 1953 was the uprising in East Berlin. 17 June. And we were glad, we thought, "Wow, finally we'll get free from the Russians." You know, those poor soldiers that came, they had no idea why they were there. They were just boys, sitting outside our yard, and behind them tanks. My sons were five and six [years old] then, and the gooseberries were in season; they gave the [Russians] berries. . . . And then as the Russians were leaving, they brought a whole stack of wood, right into my front garden. . . . Yes, and well, June 17th was a total flop. They see it differently now, that it could've been a third world war and so on, but we'll never know the whole story. . . . I went to work [that] September; they put me in the [SED] Party office. . . . I had to laugh [about] the reports they wrote, how they all fought to save the factories and such. That the workers had to literally *defend* the factories . . . nonsense, all of it nonsense. They portrayed it as though everyone wanted to storm the factories. At any rate, I [typed] it all up and was quite amused by it all.[89]

Amused, but distant. Outspoken as she was, Miller said nothing about the false reports, but rather chuckled quietly to herself. By 1953, she seemed to suggest, East Berliners expected tainted reports of political events and knew enough not to challenge official rhetoric.

Both Miller and Zelle, like other cohort members, had learned from a young age to guard their tongues. The strategy of avoiding overt political or ideological commitments had served them well during both the war and the Hunger Years; it continued to make sense in the early 1950s. Over time, this public silence became a normal, lifelong coping strategy for many East Germans. It shielded Miller, Zelle and others from unwanted attention from an increasingly paranoid state. As a central feature of their narratives, it helped them assert independence from a subsequently delegitimized regime.

For West Berliners of this cohort, the cautious independence born in the Nazi era and cultivated in the later 1940s shifted into a somewhat guarded allegiance to the West combined with an ever-present awareness of the tenaciousness of their city. For example, although they diplomatically thanked me for America's support, most denied having personally received financial or material aid from the U.S.

For the cohort as a whole, acceptance of real parameters merged with a pragmatic sense of distanced individuality. Over time, *Ossis* and *Wessis* each developed new perceptions of normalcy.[90] In other words, the "returning normalcy" of the early 1950s described by interviewees is largely a retrospective definition. Memories of specific events—personal and public alike—have been reshaped by at least three common factors. First, sociopolitical parameters that were new in the 1950s have become normalized because they would remain relatively stable for almost four decades—the majority of cohort members' adult lives. Although the specific form and extent of division obviously evolved over time, Berlin's division as such became a normal part of life.

Personal decisions made in the 1950s have often been similarly normalized by subsequent experiences. While getting married, having a child, or choosing between career and education were certainly significant commitments at the time, they have become anchors for subsequent developments. Kösel's summary of this era exemplifies the integration of significant decisions into smoothly flowing narratives. Having been forced out of the Humboldt University in 1947, Kösel struggled to find work, housing, and a viable alternative to university study. Just after the Blockade, however, his life started to sort itself out; Kösel got a full-time job, began night school, and proposed to his girlfriend. Taken together, these developments formed the basis for the next four and a half decades.

I worked myself up [the ladder] a bit and then went to the Free University, finished my night school degree . . . which I could use in my later training, and then gradually and steadily climbed until I was finally [in 1988] administrative director at the AOK [Allgemeine Ortskrankenkassen—a major health insurance provider], and then retired. I had reached a goal, that, even with a full degree, I might never have achieved. Now what else? [In] 1954 I married my wife . . . it's been forty-four years now, we've been together. We live alone together in our old age, take lots of trips, and *took* lots of trips. . . . Not that we're waiting to die, not at all, but we've made the best out of life. . . . Things got normal after the airlift was lifted 1950 I think . . . actually beginning '50–'51 [living] conditions got back to the way one expects them to be."[91]

While acknowledging the difficulty of beginning a family and a career just after the Blockade, Kösel presents the 1950s as normal by linking experiences to later developments. Zelle uses a similar strategy to connect his purchase of a tandem bicycle in 1952 with returning normalcy. Originally, Zelle and his wife used the bicycle to escape the overcrowded apartment in which they sublet two rooms. They later moved into their own flat, but kept the bicycle, using it throughout the years on family camping trips throughout the countryside.[92]

Beyond the normalizing power of lifelong hobbies and careers, subsequent revelations have informed memories of the postwar years. For example, although the extent to which the state security of the GDR (the *Stasi*) monitored daily life surprised many East Germans after 1989, Frau Miller emphasized that she never doubted its omniscient presence along the Stalinallee; *Stasi* spies were normal, she suggested, even in the early 1950s.

I lived on *Parkstraße* with coal heat, no bath, two rooms and a kitchen; we paid 90 *Pfennigs* [per square meter]. . . . We were glad that we even had a flat in those days and I wouldn't have moved into those [new NAW flats] where everyone spied on everyone else. I knew from a colleague who lived there, people would say, "Ah, I see *you* read the *Berliner Zeitung*, not the *Neues Deutschland*." And I told myself, "You just stay put."[93]

While Miller's suggestion that she had always seen through SED propaganda and espionage probably became more assertive after 1989, the dissolution of the East German state left others more defensive about their past. It was often hard to tell if interviewees were speaking of unions, the FDJ, or even the SED when they described their leisure activities in the 1950s. Kestler, Zelle, and their peers have learned that since 1989, what was for many a normal part of life in the GDR has become at least potentially problematic.   Recognizing that membership in *any* of the GDR's mass organizations could be interpreted as complicity with an evil and failed regime, they asserted that, at least in their day, joining such organizations was neither unusual nor limiting but simply enabled them to enjoy normal pursuits.

Finally, a basic awareness of narrative structure probably also informed cohort members' interpretations of the 1950s as a time of returning normalcy. Most know through experience, for example, that stories balance moments of tension with periods of calm, eventually building to a climax. Following this rough structure, cohort members typically set the scene of their personal stories in prewar Nazi Germany, followed by the drama and tension of the war and the Hunger Years. Portraying the early 1950s as the denouement of a tumultuous youth helped this cohort transition into the next chapter of their life stories, a period in which division was indeed normal.[94]

NOTES

1. In 1950, more than 166,000 of an estimated 309,000 unemployed West Berliners were under the age of twenty-four; officials predicted another 23,000–33,000 youths would join local unemployment lines upon graduation from school. "Die Jugend in West-Berlin," 5, cited in Roland Gröschel and Michael Schmidt, *Trümmerkids und Gruppenstunde* (Berlin: Elefanten Press, 1990), 130–31. Total unemployment in West Berlin also reached a post-Blockade high that same year.   Georg Holmsten, *Die Berlin Chronik: Daten, Personen, Dokumente* (Düsseldorf: Droste Verlag, 1984), 417.

2. Ausschuß für Volksbildung Kreuzberg BVV, "Ausschuß Protokoll," 11 November and 15 December 1949, LAB Rep 206 Acc 3070, Nr. 3561; Ausschuß für Volksbildung Kreuzberg BVV, "Ausschuß Protokoll," 18 July 1950, ibid.   Some optimistic officials hoped to make up the shortfall through a lottery, but this idea was dismissed as unrealistic.

3 Lit., "then it got better" and "it's finally going better".

4. See Dorothee Wierling, "The Hitler Youth Generation in the GDR: Insecurities, Ambitions and Dilemmas," in *Dictatorship as Experience*, ed. Konrad Jarausch, 307–24 (New York: Berghahn Books, 1999), 314–15.

5. Schneider, 13; Klinkert, 24; Pastler, 21; Zelle, 21–22. Also: Wolfgang Ribbe and Jürgen Schmädeke, *Kleine Berlin-Geschichte* (Berlin: Stapp Verlag, 1994), 206; Erich Wildberger, *Ring über Ostkreuz* (Hamburg: Rowohlt Verlag, 1953).

6. Birkmann, unrecorded interview.

7. Klinkert survey, 3. For Klinkert, the simultaneous coming-of-age and material prosperity were especially important, since her family had struggled economically ever since her father's death in 1938.

8. A further paragraph stipulated that education would become the sole responsibility of the state. Adopted in the SBZ in 1946, this "Democratic School

Reform" paved the way for the SED and FDJ to regulate education even before the founding of the GDR.

9. Schäfer, 13–14. Also: Bistop, 12–13.

10. Hirsch, 1–2. Also: Birkmann, 4.

11. The Bonitz plan dates from 1948, and in 1949 the street was renamed the *Stalinallee*. The first new flats along the boulevard were occupied in May 1952, although the first lottery distribution did not occur until 30 January 1953. Achim Hilzheimer, *Von der Frankfurter zur Stalinallee. Geschichte einer Straße* (Berlin: Heimatmuseum Friedrichshain, 1997); Simone Hain, "Zwischen sowjetischer Europapolitik und linkem Nationalismus. Ein Versuch, sich der Stalinallee zu nähern," in Bernd Wilczek, ed., *Berlin—Hauptstadt der DDR 1949–1989. Utopie und Realität* (Baden-Baden: Elster Verlag, 1995), 33–51; Holger Kuhle, "Auferstanden aus Ruinen: Der Alexanderplatz," in ibid., 52–72.

12. Birkmann, 14. Also: Tinker, 25–26, Hain 47–48; Wierling (1999), 315.

13. Zelle, 20. See also: "Plan zum Nationalen Aufbauwerk Friedrichshain," 1953, LAB STA Rep 135/1 492; Walter Hauer, "Stalin-Allee du bist uns Künder," undated lyrics, ibid.

14. Zelle, 20. See also: "Werbung für das Aufbauwerk," 1954, LAB STA Rep 135/1 492; "Jeder Berliner 1x im Monat auf der Baustelle," 1954, ibid.; "Plan zum nationalen Aufbauwerk Friedrichshain," 1953, ibid.

15. Tinker, 13–14. Also: Birkmann, 4; Dinkel, 10; Mostel, 38, Pastler survey; Pestopf, 1–2.

16. Pastler, 25; Barthe survey.

17. Bezirksamt Kreuzberg, "Jahresbericht 1949," 1950, 74, KMA; "Sitzungsprotokoll, 10. Sitzung der Ausschußes für Jugendfragen der SVV," 3 March 1950, LAB Rep 1 Acc 889 Nr. 149. More generally on the subdivision of this cohort: Gröschel and Schmidt, 136–52.

18. One East Berlin official did observe that, while legally defined as adults, many 18- to 21-year-old offenders remained socially and psychologically immature. Magistrat, "Einladung zum Gespräch," 11 June 1951, LAB STA Rep 101 463. Facing similar difficulties, West Berlin officials experimented with transferring older offenders to youth facilities.

19. The Young Pioneers was technically an independent organization, but depended on the FDJ for local leadership.

20. Bodo Brücher, *Die sozialistische Jugendbewegung Deutschlands. Politisch-pädigogischer Konzept und Realität sozialistischer Jugend und Erziehungsarbeit in den Nachkriegsjahren* (Werther i. W.: Paegelit Verlag, 1995), 26, 30–31.

21. Bezirksamt Kreuzberg, "Jahresbericht 1949," 1950, 59, KMA.

22. Ella Kay, quoted in P. Weiß, "Fragen an Ella Kay," in *60 Jahre Gesetz für Jugendwohlfahrt 1922–1982* (Berlin: Jugendamt Berlin, 1982), 63–66. The new *Hauptjugendamt* (formerly *Abteilung für Jugendfragen*) was established on 18 January 1949, and led by Kay until 1962. The SVV approved the establishment of independent *Jugendämter* at the district level on 2 January 1950. Senat von Berlin, *Berlin, Ringen um Einheit und Wiederaufbau 1948–51* (Berlin: Heinz Spitzing Verlag, 1962), 93, 542.

23. Bezirksamt Kreuzberg, "Jahresbericht 1949," 74–75, KMA. Also Hirsch; taped interview, 12 April 1989, HMCH. Some political leaders, most notably in the CDU and FDP, opposed this new focus on youth, fearing it would lead to cuts elsewhere. "Sitzungsprotokoll des Ausschußes für Jugendfragen der SVV," 3 March 1950, LAB Rep 1 Acc 889 Nr. 149.

24. Youth representatives rarely had voting privileges in these committees. Gröschel and Schmidt, 164; Hirsch, recorded speech, 3 July 1989, HMCH; Bezirksamt Kreuzberg, "Jahresbericht 1949," 64, 76.

25. Ibid., 64. For example, under Kay's influence, the *Jugendamt Charlottenburg* doubled its staff, and was finally offered a relatively spacious, heated office with rooms for outreach activities in the same building. Hirsch, taped interview, 12 April 1989, HMCH.

26. Bezirksamt Kreuzberg Abt Volksbildung, "Tätigkeitsbericht January–March 1949," 20 April 1949, LAB Rep 206, Acc 3070, Nr. 3561.

27. Bezirksamt Kreuzberg Abt. Jugend, "Bericht," 4 December 1953, LAB Rep 206 Acc 3070 Nr. 3579/1; Horst Simanowski, "Bericht über die Arbeit der Abteilung Jugend des Bezirksamt Kreuzberg 1951–54," Heimatsammlung Kreuzberg; Bezirksamt Kreuzberg, "Jahresbericht 1949," 76, KMA.

28. Gröschel and Schmidt, 165–66. Some of this money did support trips through the countryside around Berlin. Kreuzberg officials, for example, encouraged young travelers to demonstrate the material benefits of western-style development to their peers in the Soviet zone. Ausschuß für Volksbildung Kreuzberg, "BVV Protokol," 2 June 1950, LAB Rep 206 Acc 3070, Nr. 3561.

29. *Ringen*, 696. Kreuzberg reported similar contribution to their *Jugendförderung* program of DM 10,000. Bezirksamt Kreuzberg, "Verwaltungsbericht June 1950," 17 July 1950, LAB Rep 206 Acc. 3092 Nr. 3477; *Berliner Abendblatt*, Zehlendorf edition, 4 December 1996, 3. The western Allies remained reluctant to approve the SVV's "Gesetz zur politischen Entlastung der Jugend" of 20 February 1947. *Ringen*, 137, 139, 293.

30. Gröschel and Schmidt, 165–67. See especially the chart reprinted from the "Bundesjugendplan Berlin 1952/53."

31. "Gesetz über die Teilnahme der Jugend am Aufbau der DDR und die Förderung der Jugend in Schule und Beruf, bei Sport und Erholung" in Gesetzblatt der DDR Nr. 15 (21 Feburary 1950), 96, cited in Roswitha Brandtner, "Die FDJ und das erste Jugendgesetz der DDR," in Helga Gottschlich, Katharina Lange and Edeltraud Schutze, eds., Aber nicht im Gleichschritt: zur Entstehung der Freien Deutschen Jugend. (Berlin: Metropol Verlag,1997), 189–90. Many of these rights had already been alluded to in the 1946 proclamation "Basic Rights of Youth," announced during the FDJ's first parliament in Brandenburg; Herr Birkmann mentioned this proclamation as influential in his decision to join a socialist youth group in Zehlendorf.

32. Freiburg and Mahrad (1982), 37–40. The 1952 constitution rendered the *Wohngruppe* virtually obsolete. Ibid., 42. See also: "Magistratsbeschluß, Verordnung zur Förderung der Jugend," 22 February 1950, LAB STA Rep 101, 451.

33. In 1952, for example, the FDJ adopted new statutes to match the Party's New Course. FDJ policies were again altered in 1955 for destalinization, and another four times to parallel later transformations in the SED. Erich Honecker, *From My Life* (New York: Pergamon Books, 1981), 174.

34. 4. Pädagogische Kongress der DDR, Beschluß: "Schulpolitische Richtlinien für die deutsche demokratische Schule," 25 August 1949, quoted in *SBZ von 1945 bis 1954*, 109; SED Parteivorstand, Beschluß: "Schulpolitische Richtlinien," 24 August 1949, quoted in ibid., 108; Freiburg and Mahrad, 42, 153–4. Neither resolution offers examples of such activities.

35. Collection of signed resolutions from various East Berlin schools, October 1950, BBF FDJ 72; III Einheitsschule Treptow, Protestresolution, 20 October 1950, BBF FDJ 72 67–77, 79. *Ringen*, 105.

36. Zelle, 15. Also: Klinkert, 15–16.

37. Kay, in Weiß; *Ringen*, 93, 542.

38. Table: "Mitgliederzahlen der Jugendverbände in West-Berlin 1949 und 1950," Gröschel and Schmidt (1990), 156. Table: "Anteil der in den LJR-Mitgliedorganisationen organizierte West-Berliner Jugendlichen," ibid., 157. To their credit, Falcon representatives to the LJR did propose alternative ways to distribute funds.

39. Bezirksamt Kreuzberg, "Jahresbericht 1949," 74. In order to gain a seat in the LJR, an organization had to already be represented in six of the twelve district-level Rings. On ties between the Falcons and the *Jugendring*, see Hirsch, recorded interview, 12 April 1989, HMCH. The GYA clubs similarly became more institutionalized. All the Berlin clubs joined together into the AJAS (*Arbeitsgemeinschaft der Jugendklubs im amerikanischen Sektor*), but were refused membership in the LJR. LJR, "Sitzungsprotokol," 14 March 1950, LAB Rep 13 Acc 1046 Nr. 8, 3.

40. Kestler, 13–15; Birkmann, 7.

41. Birkmann, 4.

42. Kanter, 17. Kanter was not alone in criticizing the FDJ assault on parish youth groups. See Fred Stumpel, undated open letter to FDJ, SAPMO NY 4090/516, 49–56. On relations between church and the SED, see: Horst Dahn, *Konfrontation oder Kooperation?: das Verhaltnis von Staat und Kirche in der SBZ/DDR 1945–1980* (Opladen: Westdeutscher Verlag, 1982); Robert Goeckel, *The Catholic Church and the East German State: Political Conflict and Change under Ulbricht and Honecker* (Ithaca: Cornell University Press, 1990); Helmut Nitsche, *Zwischen Kreuz und Sowjetstern Zeugnis des Kirchenkampfes in der DDR 1945–1981* (Aschaffenburg: P. Pattloch, 1983).

43. Kanter, 14–15.

44. Gesellschaft für Auswärtige Politik, e.V., *Dokumente zur Berlin-Frage 1944–1962* (Munich: R. Oldenbourg Verlag, 1962), 177–79. See also: Hans Herzfeld, *Berlin in der Weltpolitik 1945–1970* (New York: Walter de Gruyter, 1973), 313–22.

45. "Kabinettsbeschluß der Bundesregierung über die Fassung der Vorschriften zur Erstreckung von Bundesrecht auf Berlin (Berlinklausel)," 6 February 1954, in Forschungsinstitut der Deutschen Gesellschaft für Auswärtige Politik, e.V. 169–76; "Erklärung der Vereinigten Staaten von Amerika, Großbritanniens und Frankreichs auf der Londoner Konferenz vom 28 September bis zum 3 Oktober 1954," ibid., 216–17; "Entschließung des Nordatlantikrates vom 22 Oktober 1954 über die Zustimmungserklärung der übrigen Parteien des Nordatlantikvertrags zu den auf der Londoner Konferenz abgegebenen Erklärungen der Bundesrepublik und der Drei Mächte," ibid., 226–27.

46. "Schlußkommunique der Warschauer Konferenz vom 14 May 1955" in Forschungsinstitut, 238; Moskauer Vertrag vom 20 September 1955 über die Beziehungen zwischen der DDR und der Sowjetunion," ibid., 239–40; "Vertrag über die zeitweilige Stationierung sowjetischer Streitkräfte in der DDR vom 12 März 1957," ibid., 249–51. In general: Bark (1972), 187–207.

47. In 1950 and 1951, eastern officials flatly rejected overtures by West Berlin mayor Ernst Reuter to reunite the magistrate, and a year later denied entry permits to United Nations representatives who had hoped to defuse tensions. See Dorothea Dornhof, "Der Traum von einer Gelehrtenrepublik. Die Anziehungskraft Berlins auf Emigranten und Intellektuelle," in Wilczek (1995), 94–112. On the Free University, see Karl-Heinz Füssl "Die amerikanische Umerziehungs- und Neuorientierungspolitik in der Retrospektive ihrer Akteure," *Bildung und Erziehung* 40 (1987) 2, 201–26.

48. Tusa, 47–48, 51. One British barracks, for example, was raided annually by Soviet soldiers. In 1951, the SMAD instigated what was known locally as the second blockade of Berlin. Soviet guards stopped commercial trucks and postal shipments leaving West Berlin for the FRG, and in late summer, when the SMAD announced tolls on West German vehicles moving through the GDR. Officials negotiated a resolution to the crisis by year's end.

49.   Constitution of the GDR, 7 October 1949, quoted in Heidelmeyer and Hindrichs, *Documents on Berlin 1943–63* (Munich, Oldenbourg Verlag 1963), Document 113. Speech, Friedrich Ebert (Berlin, 11 October 1949) printed in *Neues Deutschland*, quoted in Rexin, 73. See also (on recognition of status of Berlin) Statement by General Chiukov, 11 November 1949, quoted in Heidelmeyer and Hindrichs, Document 116.   Not until the early 1960s would East German administrative officials refer to Berlin as "the *German* capital," referring more frequently to the "democratic Sector" or "democratic Berlin."

50. *SBZ 1945–54*, 120–21; Bark (1972), 296–99.

51. Speech, Otto Nuschke (Berlin-Köpenick, 5 October 1949), printed in *Neuer Zeit*, 6 October 1949, cited in Bark (1972), 94.

52 *SBZ 1945–54*, 120. On the role of sports in the GDR, see: "Auszüge aus dem Protokoll Nr. 40 der Sitzung des Zentralrates der Freien Deutschen Jugend am 13.12.1949," SAPMO DY/34 23219.

53. Wilhelm Pieck, "Freizeit vom Feind ausgenutzt," (1950) in Rolf Badstübner and Wilfried Loths., eds., *Wilhelm Pieck. Aufzeichnungen zur Deutschlandpolitik 1945–1953* (Berlin: Akademie Verlag, 1994). Evemarie Badstübner-Peters, " 'Lassen wir sie tanzen . . .' Nachkriegsjugend und moderne Freizeitkultur in SBZ und früher DDR," in Gotschlich, et al., eds. (1997), 72.

54.   The refrain of the original song read, "Was kümmert uns die Grenze und die Grenzgendarmen . . . .Die freie deutsche Jugend stürmt (storms) Berlin." The text was changed to "die Freie Deutsche Jugend grüßt (greets) Berlin" in April 1950. Mählert and Stephan, 81.

55.   "Aufruf der FDJ Berlin," SAPMO NY 4090/515, 283.   See also: "Kurzkommentar des Tages" (aired 29.5.50), Deutsches Rundfunkarchiv, Standort Berlin, Historisches Archiv B204-02-01/0023; *Berlin Sowjet Sektor*, 34.

56. Bundesinnenministerium, working paper (1953) in Erwin Jordan and Dieter Sengling, *Jugendhilfe. Einführung in Geschichte und Handlungsfelder, Organisationsformen und gesellschaftliche Problemlagen* (Munich: Juventa Verlag, 1988).

57. Holmsten, 419.

58. Brucher, 24; Lindemann, 79; Gröschel and Schmidt, 238–39; Hirsch, taped speech (3.7.89). After 1945, the *Pfadfinder* groups, some of which traced their roots to before World War I, were incorporated with other traditionally middle-class organizations into the *Bund Deutscher Jugend* (BDJ); in 1948, the western Allies rejected the licensure application of an independent *Ringgemeinschaft Deutscher Pfadfinder*. Beginning in 1950, the Frankfurt-based rightwing *Bund Deutscher Jugend* began openly recruiting in Berlin. The more centrist Berliner scouts took the name *Deutscher Pfadfinderbund, DeutscherPfadfinderinnenbund*, but soon splintered into smaller groups. Examples of earlier incidents between FDJlers and Falcons include the late 1947 arrest of sixty-one FDJlers in the American and French sectors and the shooting of Wolfgang Scheunemann at the Brandenburg Gate by East German police during Ernst Reuter's speech on 9 September 1948. "Bericht über einige wesentliche Ergebnisse in der Tätigkeit der FDJ, November 1947–Oktober 1948," 1 November 1948, SAPMO NY 4090/515, 240–44. In mid-1948, as part of the LJR

dispute, Falcon chair Heinz Westphal demanded the FDJ distance itself from certain provocative actions of its Berlin leader, Heinz Keßler. "Protokoll der Jugendringsitzung 7.7.48," SAPMO DY 24/115 O64, in Heims and Popp, 97. Lindemann locates the Falcons' shift from antifascism to anticommunism in the mid-1950s; indications of the change, however, were evident earlier. Lindemann, 71.

59. "Protokoll der Mitgliedervollversammlung des Landesverbands Berlin der sozialistischen Jungedbewegung, 'Die Falken,' " 8 July 1950, LAB C Rep 900 IV L-2/10/397. Also: draft report on the organization, "Progressive Falken," 28 August 1950, ibid.; letter, "Sozialdemokratische Aktion to members of the SPD," May 1950, ibid.; Ausschuß der nationalen Front der Hauptstadt der DDR, "Die fortschrittlichen Falken werden dabei sein," (flyer) ibid.; letter, Fritz Hofer to the Berlin SPD and Falcons 22 May 1950, ibid.; letter, Klaus Scharf to Berlin Falcons membership (1950), ibid.; *Ringen*, 343.

60. The flyer included a quote from Rosa Luxembourg: "Freedom is always the freedom of those who think differently," Brucher 23, 24. Jurgen Gerull, a Falcon leader from Treptow, received a two-year sentence in May 1949 for distributing *Der Telegraf* in the eastern sector. Even Heinz Westphal was imprisoned briefly.

61. Two letters, Kressmann to SED Kreuzberg, 22 August 1950, LAB C Rep 900 IV L-2/10/397; Polizei Inspektor Kreuzberg, "Bericht an Kressmann," 3 September 1950, ibid.; "Bericht," 5 September 1950, ibid.

62. FDJ Berlin-Kreuzberg, "Bericht," 20 November 1950, BBF FDJ 72. 169–73; Lindemann (1987), 125. About the same time, an SPD secretary in Lichtenberg complained that district officials were making it increasingly difficult to invite political speakers from western districts, sometimes even canceling scheduled meetings at the last minute. Lindemann also noted that parents in both East and West Berlin protested against the increasingly violent nature of political demonstrations, saying they would prefer less controversial, nonpolitical groups. Ibid., 126. Also: "Bericht über einen Brief des SPD Sekretärs Lichtenberg," 4 August 1950, LAB Rep 206 Acc 3070 Nr. 3642, II. In both districts the competing parties complained that their posters had been repeatedly torn down by provacative elements from the other side. Letter, Agnes Heinrich to Kressman, 18 July 1950, ibid. The FDJ had been banned in the FRG in 1952, but continued so-called Westarbeit in Berlin throughout its existence. A final attempt at rapprochement came in 1954, when representatives of the FDJ and the Falcons held a series of "secret" meetings. Not surprisingly, negotiators agreed on questions of demilitarization and mutual understanding, but found it impossible to establish any other common ground. The impasse was rooted, according to one FDJ participant, in the "obvious influence of the rightist SPD leadership." Wolfgang Steinke and Joachim Herrmann, "Bericht: Fühlungsnahme zwischen den FDJ und Falken," 25 October 1954, SAPMO NY 4090/516, 144–51.

63. Ribbe, 209–10. Between 1949 and 1951, 54,500 of these refugees took up permanent residence in West Berlin. Tusa (1997), 39; Herzfeld (1973), 326.

64. Barthe, 8–9.

65. Zelle, 9–10. He did not elaborate on the consequences of his protest.

66. BBF FDJ 182 Bl 94–95 *Junge Welt* 23 July 1952; Holmsten, 424.

67. "Schafft die Aktionseinheit gegen Remilitarisierung und Krieg—die beste Vorbereitung für die III. Weltfestspiele" *Junge Generation* 5:2 (February 1951), 86. Also: Bark (1972), 200–203.

68. There were also festival preparation committees in the schools, Volkspolizei, and various sociopolitical groups. Most of these organizations had already cooperated to host the 1950 *Deutschlandtreffen*, when some 700,000 youths descended upon Berlin. Gröschel and Schmidt, 170. "Groß Berliner Komitee zur

Vorbereitung der Weltfestspiele Arbeitsausschuß," 25 May 1951, LAB STA Rep 135/1 104; "Bildung des Festkomitees der Weltfestspiele in Friedrichshain," *Junge Generation* 5:3 (March 1951). See also: Bark (1972), 130–36; Heinz H. Lippmann, "Die Weltjugendfestspiele 1951 in Berlin," in Lippmann, ed., *Porträt eines Nachfolgers* (Cologne: Verlag Wissenschaft und Politik, 1971); *SBZ 1945–54*, 120. "Sollzahlen der Kreise in der Mitgliederwerbung. Anlage 1 zum Bericht der 34. Sitzung des Sekretariat des Landesvorstandes der FDJ," 16 February 1950, SAPMO DY/24 1334; "Deutschlandtreffen Veranstaltungsplan," SAPMO NY 4090/515, 271–72.

69. Erich Honecker, "An alle Mitglieder der FDJ," in *Junge Deutschland* 5:1 (January 1951), 1. Honecker recounts the past five years as systematic steps towards WFS. Honecker, "5 Jahre Freie Deutsche Jugend," in *Junge Generation* 5:3 (March 1951), 99–106.

70. Honecker, speech at the Wiener Tagung des Weltjugendrates, quoted in Tomoschat, 7.

71. Walter Oberthür, "Schafft die Aktionseinheit gegen Remilitarisierung und Krieg—die beste Vorbereitung für die III. Weltfestspiele," *Junge Generation* 5:2 (February 1951), 84–87; Dieter Schmotz, "Neuwahl unserer Leitungen—eine wichtige Aufgabe in der Vorbereitung der III. Weltjugendfestspiele," ibid., 80–83.

72. Hans Schoenecker, "Bereitet die III. Weltfestspiele der Jugend und Studenten für den Frieden vor," *Junge Generation* 5:3 (March 1951), 108–13; Otto Kretschmar "Jede erfüllte Selbstverpflichtung—ein Baustein für den Frieden," *Junge Deutschland* 5:4 (April 1951), 182–83; Gustav Vieweger, "Entfaltet das Jugendwandern," *Junge Deutschland* 5:5 (May 1951), 243–46; Zentralrat der FDJ, "Mit Stalin für die Erhaltung und Sicherung des Friedens," ibid., 5:3 (March 1951), 97–98.

73. Klaus Rosenthal, "Der III. Berufswettbewerb der deutschen Jugend," *Junge Deutschland* 4:8/9 (September 1950), 369–70. The campaigns were not always positive in tone and officials publicly chastised groups unable to meet these theoretically self-imposed standards. See "Die Arbeit der FDJ Gruppe an der Kunsthochschule Weißensee," *Junge Generation* 5:7 (July 1951), 339–42; Erich Honecker, "5 Jahre Freie Deutsche Jugend," *Junge Welt* 18/51, quoted in *Junge Generation* 5:3 (March 1951), 99–106.

74. Redaktion, "An den Kongress der jungen Künstler," *Junge Deutschland* 5:3 (March 1951), 127.

75. Heinz Quaas, "Die Aufgaben unserer Betriebsgruppen im Schwermaschinenbau," *Junge Deutschland*, 5:4 (April 1951), 169–70.

76. "Jugendfreundin Ilse Jaschos vom Landesvorstand Thüringen macht Vorschläge für die Geldsammlungen zum Festival," ibid., 187.

77. Hauptschulamtbericht, "Der demokratische Magistrat sorgt für die Kinder," 4 August 1951, LAB STA Rep 101 463; "Berlin ruft die Jugend der Welt," *Junge Deutschland* 5:6 (June 1951), 257.

78. Klinkert, 17, 19. For a less enthusiastic evaluation, see: Kanter, 13–14.

79. Klinkert, 18. Also Kühn, 13. Bistop was the only cohort member I spoke to who traveled outside Germany around this time. Having received a State Department stipend, he spent a year as an exchange student at Dickinson College in Carlysle, Pennsylvania. Bistop, 13–14.

80. Klinkert, 18; Birkmann, recorded interview.

81. This is a western estimate, distinguishing between individuals (500,000) and visits (more than 1,000,000), since some delegates visited several different centers. "Bericht des Berliner Jugendbüros über die Maßnahmen in Westberlin anläßlich der

III. kommunistischen Weltjugendfestspiele in Ostberlin in der Zeit vom 5–22 August 1951," LAB B Rep 013 Acc 1160, 72.

82. Ibid.   According to Martin Faltermaier (editor of *deutsche jugend*) the *Bundesjugendplan* was conceived in response to SED initiatives prior to the 1950 *Deutschlandtreffen*.   Similarly, in 1951, the *Bundesministerium* seemed to be reacting to WFS rhetoric.   Martin Faltermaier, "Nachdenken über Jugendarbeit," in Gröschel and Schmidt (1989), 165;   Arbeitspapier des Bundesinnenministerium, 1953, in Erwin Jordan and Dieter Sengling, *Jugendhilfe. Einführung in Geschichte und Handlungsfelder, Organisationsformen und gesellschaftliche Problemlagen* (Munich: Juventa, 1988), 62.

83. "Bericht über die Sonderaktion aus Anlass der Kommunistischen Weltjugendfestspiele im sowjetischem Sektor in Berlin" (5 October 1951) LAB Rep 206 Acc 3070 3579/2.

84. "Lagebericht 4.8–8.8" in Berliner Jugendbüro, "Anlage zum Bericht 8.8.51," LAB B Rep 013 Acc1160, 72.

85. Berliner Jugendbüro, "Geheimbericht," 15 August 1951, LAB B Rep 013 Acc 1160, 72.

86. Robert Bialak, quoted by Heinz Lippmann, cited in Ilse Spittmann and Gisela Helwig, eds., *DDR Lesebuch* 1949–1955 (Cologne: Verlag Wissenschaft und Politik, 1991), 141.

87. Lit. "Joy and Cheerfulness." These were among the guaranteed rights of East German youth.

88. Zelle, 23–24.

89. Miller, 12.

90. Tusa, 48. Also Konrad H. Jarausch, Hinrich C. Seeba, and David P. Conradt, "The Presence of the Past," in Jarausch, ed., *After Unity Reconfiguring German Identities* (Providence: Berghahn Books, 1997), 39.

91. Kösel, 2–3 and 8.

92. Zelle, 21–22. Also Distel, 6.

93. Miller, 13. Also: Kösel, 14.

94. See Helga A. Welsh, Andreas Pickel, and Dorothy Rosenberg, "East and West German Identities: United and Divided," in Jarausch, ed. (1997), 103–36.

INTERLUDE III

Bordercrossers

Officials were quite vocal about the problems constituted by girls and young criminals in postwar Berlin. Because both groups had long been identified as problematic, youth welfare authorities could draw on past experience and research as they attempted to rehabilitate these troublesome young people. Furthermore, the existence of *kriminelle Jugend* and *verwahrloste Mädchen* was accepted, perhaps even expected, as a symptom of social crisis. Even as officials debated regulatory measures, most inherently believed that, as daily life normalized, the problems of unbridled sexuality and crime would decline.

The same could not be said for bordercrossers, who were understood as products of the particular sociopolitical parameters of postwar Berlin. Quadripartite rule imposed international borders upon the more natural boundaries of Berliners' daily lives. By the late 1940s, even though socioeconomic conditions had begun to improve, political developments meant that Berlin's bordercrossers were becoming more, not less, problematic. Of course, this was not the first time or place that changing political borders had divided communities. Nor were postwar Berliners the first people to ignore or sometimes exploit such boundaries. However, unlike troublesome girls and criminal youths, bordercrossers had never worried the public nor frustrated government officials to the extent they did in postwar Germany.

One hurdle to eliminating the bordercrosser problem was that the category encompassed virtually the entire population of Berlin. Daily routines regularly sent people of all ages across sector boundaries, which, especially in the districts of Friedrichshain, Prenzlauer Berg, Kreuzberg, and Wedding, separated residents from neighborhood shops and markets. Over time, bordercrossers became associated with increasingly undesirable activities and—unlike girls and criminals—became more problematic in the 1950s, as inter-Berlin borders stood between increasingly different and hostile political realities.

Grenzhändler, those who sold goods on or along sector borders, constituted one major subgroup of bordercrossers. Many Berliners acquired this status inadvertently, simply by reopening shops after the war. Other, more entrepreneurial Berliners recognized the advantage of starting new businesses along sector boundaries. Western cinema operators, for example, could expect larger audiences in theaters near sector boundaries, since American films (banned in the East) were far more popular than those produced by the DEFA or Soviet Union, and because the West subsidized tickets for East Berliners.[1]

Although running a business—or spending money at one—near sector boundaries was perfectly legal, local authorities viewed owners, employees, and patrons of such establishments with suspicion. Berliners who regularly crossed sector boundaries, argued officials, were also more likely to engage in illegal transactions across those administrative borders. Furthermore, those with personal or economic connections in other sectors were more likely to become permanent *Umsiedler*. Like the *Grenzgänger*, this second group of bordercrossers caused headaches for municipal authorities, but found sympathy among most residents. As a well-known cabaret song (performed by *Die Insulaner*) explained, would-be *Umsiedler*, who simply wanted to move across town, faced unprecedented hurdles.

> Willst Du heut' umzieh'n sonstwohin
> Vom Osten nach/m Westen rin,
> Dann mußt Du Dir zehn Stempel klau'n
> Und jemandem den Kopf abhau'n,
> denn freiwillig gibt niemand seinen Kopf zum Tauschen her. . . .
> Ne wissen Se, 'n bißchen verrückt ist ja ganz schön,
> Aber so was Verrücktes so was Verrücktes,
> Kann ich nicht versteh'n[2]

Berliners' frustration stemmed from the ongoing housing shortage in their city. Resources were so tight that each sector maintained a strict headcount of legal residents. In theory, at least, anyone who wanted to move had to negotiate a trade with a household in the desired sector. While exceptions were made to unite newlyweds or to permit minors, retirees, and the unemployed to join family members, many resented the bureaucratic restriction of their domestic mobility.

The underlying problem, obvious to residents and officials alike, was that many more Berliners wanted to move from East to West than vice versa. Glad to approve requests for elderly *Umsiedler*, eastern officials were reluctant to authorize moves for able-bodied young people, who were needed for physical and economic reconstruction. But East Berliners were not the only Germans seeking new homes in western districts. Germans from throughout the Soviet zone correctly believed it was easier to transverse the inter-German border in Berlin; claiming persecution or simply hoping to continue to West Germany, these refugees further strained assistance and housing programs in western districts.

The currency reforms of mid-1948 and the consequent Soviet blockade of West Berlin further politicized the actions of both *Grenzhändler* and *Umsiedler*.[3] Supporting the intersector economy constituted, in the eyes of many officials, an expression of ideological disloyalty. This was particularly true after 20 March 1949, when western authorities declared the FRG's new currency to be the sole legal tender in West Berlin. Thereafter, SED officials described all western-bound bordercrossers—particularly the roughly 50,000 residents of East Berlin and the Soviet zone who worked in West Berlin—as contributing to "currency speculation, corruption and economic damage [in the] antifascist, democratic [Soviet sector]."[4] The SED also accused the West of buying East Berliners by paying part of their salaries in the stronger western currency and establishing special currency exchange bureaus for these workers (*Lohnausgleichskassen*).[5]

Along with the higher political and economic stakes came, from the western side, a formal definition of *Grenzgänger* that included three distinct categories.[6] Frau Pelsdorf represented the first group, Berliners who lived and received ration coupons in the West but worked (i.e., earned wages) in the East.

[In] 1947 I started working, and already then the demonstrations from the eastern side started. At the town hall, where I worked. They demonstrated between the new *Stadthaus* and the old *Stadthaus*; a reporter from RIAS, he stood up in the window . . . and they cut his line. And then the building itself, during a SVV [city council meeting], still under Louise Schröder, they stormed the building. . . . And later when the police was split, we worked under police watch, and it became more and more obvious that it might come to a division. I had a big typewriter—later, well you start thinking about what you're going to do—first of all I took materials, paper, pencils . . . because you just knew something was in the air. I had a sick colleague, who'd left her jacket, and then I wrapped the typewriter in her jacket and laid it over my arm, as if it was a jacket, with a newspaper on top . . . and then they called after me, oh my god, I thought. Another colleague brought out a big briefcase and then we met at the train station and I put the typewriter in it and took it home. That was our only typewriter at first, after the split. . . .
    Later, 1 December 1948, they announced on the radio, certain people should report to such an address. Our people were to go to the Nürnbergerstraße. It wasn't a real [office]. The rooms were cold and we took newspaper and crumpled it up and played soccer to keep ourselves a bit warmer. From the Hotel am Zoo, there were a few typewriters, so we could pick one [more] up [there] and slowly things got going.[7]

On one level, Pelsdorf's account of the administrative division of Berlin suggests she was an active, if inadvertent, eyewitness to history. She did not have the luxury of choosing among employers, and did not consider herself politically active. Initially, she saw the position in the *Stadthaus* as an opportunity for steady income at a time of high unemployment. Yet even if she was too busy to participate in ideological debates, Pelsdorf was neither oblivious to political developments nor neutral in her opinions. Rather, observing that "something was in the air," she began smuggling office supplies into the West, an activity that could have easily led to her dismissal and arrest. Pelsdorf's vague allusion to a general sense of foreboding most likely covers conversations with colleagues or perhaps a pro-West supervisor, all of whom probably worried about job security in the tense months of the Blockade. As various branches of the municipal administration split throughout the fall and winter, Pelsdorf was both making a political statement and increasing the chances of her own future employment in the West by smuggling out typewriters, paper, and other necessities. Whatever her motivations, Pelsdorf's actions confirmed authorities' fears that bordercrossers did illegitimate things. Whatever her motivations, she had in fact stolen a typewriter—state property, in fact—and smuggled it across what was gradually becoming an international border.

Pelsdorf also constituted a problem for western authorities. By working in the East in 1948–1949, she joined the group of West Berliners deemed most likely to accept increased food rations offered by Soviet occupation officials. This second category of officially defined *Grenzgänger* was least significant in terms of numbers. Nonetheless, it became an important focus of political propaganda during the airlift, when, for the only time in postwar history, East Berliners had more food, coal, and other necessities than their western counterparts. Frau Klinkert, a native of Friedrichshain, explained this unique situation.

It was, as I said, *Frontstadt Berlin*, the phrase was common, which is why I mention it, we lived here as if on the front. . . . In 1948, West Berlin got this western money and we in the East had eastern currency and the western was more valuable. . . . A Berliner, he could travel back and forth in the S-Bahn—everywhere for twenty *Pfennigs*. [He could] reach the West Sector . . . and then in these exchange bureaus that were set up, [one] traded eastern money for western money; the rate was sometimes 1:3, 1:4, 1:5 or 1:7, that is, for seven eastern marks one west mark. The rate was better for [East] Berliners, since people in the Zone, to which Leipzig, Dresden, etc. belonged, they had to sit themselves in a train to reach Berlin, and when they got here, the rate had changed again. . . . And those in the Zone, they always accused us, "you Berliners have it good, but we in the Zone. . . ." And it was true, they had it worse of course.

Berliners always had an advantage somehow. First, all East Berliners had West Berlin relatives and West Berliners likewise relatives [in the East] . . . who traded with one another, food or clothes or whatever, you know? During the Blockade we had a bit more vegetables, the *Wessis*, they for all I know had candy, chocolate and such from the Raisin-bombers and came to us and gave a bit of something sweet, and we got them a cabbage. . . . Our relatives came from Kreuzberg, just simple seamstresses . . . they came and then we gave them coal, since the Raisinbombers didn't drop coal. Yes, the coal [situation] in West Berlin that winter was even worse than here. . . .

We traded everything, we traded parachute silk, parachutes from the war and when the war was over. . . [one] made blouses out of them. There was also parachute yarn/floss; it was all sewn together with this heavy thread and we took it apart and then knitted or crocheted or such. . . and traded all that with our relatives in Kreuzberg. . . relatives stuck together more then than now, perhaps because it was a time of want and then in general since all families had children; these single-households didn't exist like today, they're egotistical somehow, because they never have to share. . . . That's a trait that has been totally lost today, but it stems from hard times.[8]

Like many Berliners, Klinkert had regularly traversed sector boundaries before 1948, crossing the remnants of the *Oberbaumbrücke* to visit relatives in Kreuzberg. The Blockade turned these family gatherings into acts of political subversion or humanitarianism, depending on one's perspective. On the one hand, East German authorities didn't want their citizens mitigating the physical hardship caused by the Blockade; by depriving West Berliners of basic necessities, the SED hoped to break down their political loyalty to the western allies. On the other hand, images of East Berliners sharing with their needy western neighbors would demonstrate the success and charity of socialist Germans.

Klinkert herself highlighted the humanitarian nature of her efforts to smuggle coal and food to her western relatives. In her opinion, West Berliners could not possibly have survived the winter (1948–1949) without help from friends and relatives in the East. She also offered a commentary on American culture and values, implying that occupation forces valued luxury items—such as chocolate—more than fundamental necessities (coal). In a way, her memories confirmed the contemporary observations of communist officials, who repeatedly argued that the airlift was inadequate and that the western allies were inhumanely exploiting West Berliners for political purposes.

Klinkert's account is also a more general commentary on free-market capitalism and the American way of life. While acknowledging a certain lack of luxury items, she pointed out that socialism did provide her family's basic needs. West Berliners, in contrast, were unable to make ends meet during the Blockade, and in Klinkert's eyes, the United States seemed to be flaunting its wealth by importing chocolate. Such incongruencies have been made even more obvious to Klinkert and other East Berliners in the years since unification; she, like most other easterners, lamented the higher rents and food prices that have accompanied economic freedom.

A third category of bordercrossers included Berliners who lived and received coupons in the East, but worked—or studied, in the case of Herr Binkert—in the West. Binkert, born in 1927, completed secondary school shortly after the war, and was in the midst of an administrative training program when the Blockade began.[9]

I went on to the *Abitur*; we were all a bit shaky . . . [but] we were just glad to have the *Abitur* at all. . . . What to pursue as a profession? I was seriously considering three options. . . . My father was a *Kriminalbeamter*, but then I would've had to wear a uniform for years, and I'd had enough of wearing uniforms. . . . Teacher; I come from a family of teachers, but I didn't know if I had the patience so with children and all. So I started at *Bezirksamt Prenzlauer Berg* . . . and we did get certain advantages. . . . So we learned there, worked more really, the training was shortened to two years because we had the *Abitur*. . . . There were about eighty of us trainees, that was a lot. The specialists were all gone, most of the [new] applicants were women. That was nice for us [boys], so few of us and so many female colleagues, you know. But otherwise, the conditions were, it was very cold. . . . I started there because they said there were good chances for advancement, with an *Abitur*. And that's why my friend and I ended up there. . . . We would've stayed there, my colleague and I, if it hadn't come to these conflicts in 1948, Berlin Blockade and so forth. And we realized, now things didn't look so good for us. Chances for promotions and the like, and on Unter den Linden [later the Humboldt University] they gave preferential admission to the sons of workers and farmers. I applied to Unter den Linden, was rejected and then I applied to the Free University. . . . I think they took something like two hundred from about eight thousand applicants.   So of course I was glad when I got the acceptance. . . .

It was no problem going from Prenzlauer Berg to Dahlem. With the subway there were no problems. But I know at the Free University much was improvised. The lecture rooms were poorly lit; we sat there listening to lectures by candlelight. There weren't enough books and the professors were in part flown in for us from West Germany. . . . The FDJ, I actually joined, because the FDJ was founded as a nonpartisan organization, and I thought, "That's how you can be active without joining a political party." I wanted to be politically independent. But then as things developed . . . I didn't drop out immediately; the F.U. didn't exist yet and I thought, "you might need a *Rückendeckung* [cover] for the university," but in my mind, I'd already quit.[10]

Binkert had been vocally critical of the communist party, yet seemed prepared to work for an administration dominated by the SED. He described himself as very interested in politics, frequently engaging friends in long, heated debates, and rejected a number of other career options for a job that allowed him—so he thought—to remain politically independent.   Binkert saw working in the Bezirksamt not only as stable employment, but also as a way to become a more informed citizen. Contrary to stereotypes of this cohort, Binkert considered himself a political idealist. He and his friends, for example, accepted the early paroles of the FDJ at face value. Binkert in fact joined that FDJ because he yearned for a forum in which he could voice opinions without committing to a predetermined ideology.

Binkert never explained exactly why "things no longer looked so good" for him after 1948. Nonetheless, growing tensions between East and West made it harder to maintain a neutral stance at FDJ gatherings. Looking back through a half-century of Cold War division, Binkert drew a clear line between his class background and his rejection from the university on Unter den Linden. Noting that he was admitted to the nascent Free University in the American sector, Binkert reveals his belief that, by 1948, a bourgeois background severely limited educational opportunities in the Soviet sector.

Recognizing that the Free University had offered him a second chance, Binkert undertook a daily commute (about an hour each way) between his home in Prenzlauer Berg and the university in Dahlem, where he clearly enjoyed an academic atmosphere that encouraged debate and discussion. Matriculating at the Free University, however, constituted an ideological statement, and Binkert could not escape the political ramifications of his decisions. In a separate interview, Binkert's friends explained that he eventually sought political asylum in West Berlin.

Frau D: '51 was the incident with Helmut [Binkert], just before our wedding. You came by and said you couldn't come tomorrow or the next day because you had to lug suitcases. I'd just met him shortly before.

Herr D: Yes, he'd said to me that things were getting too hot for him. His father had come from the POW camp and gone straight to Bonn. And Helmut had had trouble with the State Security. And since I worked [and traveled a lot] for the DEFA, I could say his luggage was mine. I knew his things more or less. He was already out, already over in West Berlin, and I went back to his old flat, picked up the luggage, and went out the back way. Already as I left, I saw people standing around [watching the place]. It was very last minute. His mother went back to the flat [later], and they were guarding the doors. She heard the men: "So the light's gone out up there, now we know he's coming down." And they arrested another young man, held an interrogation, a rough interrogation, until he finally confessed that *he* was Helmut. Who had gotten out at the last minute. . . .

A year later, I had a cousin. He wanted to join his in-laws in Hamburg. Had married a girl from Hamburg, straight out of a POW camp. He went over with his wife, and I with the baby carriage, packed full, pushed it over to West Berlin . . . he got away too.[11]

Herr Dinkel, a lifelong resident of Prenzlauer Berg, suggested that Binkert faced discrimination in East Berlin for several reasons. First, Binkert could not deny his family's bourgeois heritage. Second, Binkert's father had fled to West Germany immediately upon his release from Allied captivity. Finally, Dinkel described his friend's tendency to speak his mind rather too clearly; in the tense atmosphere of Blockade-era Berlin, it was understandable that Binkert had attracted the scrutiny of political officials.

Of course, Dinkel himself had also criticized political developments before, during, and after the war. It was he, not Binkert, who had been arrested by Nazi-era officials, who considered his loose tongue a bad influence on other youth. After the war, the friends had organized their buddies into an informal political research group, investigating and comparing the agendas and actions of various political parties. As a couple, the Dinkels clearly knew about Binkert's sudden departure, and sympathized with others who left the nascent GDR under similar circumstances. They themselves, however, remained in Prenzlauer Berg; by the time we spoke, they had had more than thirty years to reflect on this decision.

Frau D: A bit later, my father had to go too, he was under suspicion. . . . Later, '55–'56, we wanted to leave too, but were afraid with the baby.

Herr D: And her father really wasn't in favor of it.

Frau D: Yes, we wanted to go to him first, so, as a starting point. But he wasn't so excited about that. . . . But then finally we'd decided, 1960, '61, and they'd . . . I had a fur, a beautiful thing, my first fur, I still have the jacket . . . I'd already packed it up. I wanted to take that along at any rate, I had worked so hard for it. . . . And we had a piece of land that my father had left me. [Once he was in] the West, he stipulated that I should get it. We wanted to sell it first, so we'd have a bit of money. But then came the Wall; [we were] too late.

Herr D: It was difficult earlier, to cross over with a family. I didn't know if I could get a job, since things weren't so good in the film industry over there at the time, [it was] going downhill. I tried to ask around in the West, where it was possible, but I never found the right people, who could've helped me further. And I always thought about it, the position I had here I might never have had over there. I thought about that a lot. I wanted to stay in [my] profession in any case. And today looking back, I have to say it was right. In that sense it was right. I've been with DEFA forty-two years, more than a hundred films.

Having previously described himself as outspoken, idealistic and politically minded, Herr Dinkel's reasons for staying in Prenzlauer Berg were immediate and practical. He had a decent job and a young family. Looking back, however,

Dinkel still could, and did, identify himself as a bordercrosser; throughout his career with the DEFA, he frequently visited western states.

Political convictions or economic opportunity could also create permanent bordercrossers in the other direction, from West to East. Herr Birkmann had grown up in Zehlendorf, but transferred his residency status to the Soviet sector at the age of nineteen. Like Binkert, Birkmann described himself as a well-informed youth who made life-changing decisions based on ideological beliefs, personal experience, and sensible pragmatism. He found a voice for his political convictions at an FDJ-sponsored summer camp in 1947.

The camp director came after the meal and asked who was still hungry. No one dared say anything, but they [we went] in the kitchen and there was so much loaded on the plates that [we] were sick. . . . It was an FDJ camp, I wasn't a member. An emigrant explained to us the basics of democracy, a German, I'd say, who'd come back and the main point was that 51% of the population had to agree. . . . That was my first contact [to the FDJ]. And they recruited for membership. There was at that time an FDJ demand for the four basic rights of youth: the right to work, education, political activity and *Freude und Frohsein*. And winning those somehow was the goal and to do that one naturally needed a unified youth organization. After the experience in the Nazi *Reich*, everyone was very skeptical about a unified youth organization. But this question of the basic rights seemed logical to me. . . . And then I became a member, but had no organization in Zehlendorf to join with. They couldn't find me because of the bad handwriting [on the registry—KAR] and it wasn't until late '47 or '48, I read that there was to be a film shown in the school and there I met some who were members of the FDJ in Zehlendorf, who had organized. It was mostly the children of emigrants. . . . There was one group in central Zehlendorf and another up near us in the youth center by *Bahnhof Krümme Lanke*, and I was there 'til '49, then I moved here. I was there again to visit, but the whole leadership, they had already moved here into the eastern sector, 1948–49, so that their children were gone too.

Through Kahn's son I had the opportunity—it was during the unemployment crisis in the west—to get a job in the *Deutschen Wirtschaftsinstitut*. I was finished with my education, had gotten a driver's license, and the son said the institute was getting new vehicles. I went and applied, but there was the condition that I had to move to East Berlin. So I looked for a flat and found [one], and started working on 1 December 1949 and moved here at the same time. . . . I made a trade, there was a family with two children, they wanted to immigrate to the USA and the man took care of everything, he was a chimney mason. There had to be a *Kopftausch* [between the districts] and he organized everything. The fact is, I didn't go back over there. They did actually migrate over to the USA, and one of the children came here as an occupation soldier. . . .

[Earlier], we had no energy [to travel to the Soviet sector], we were so weakened. Once my aunt's daughter-in-law came from West Germany, saw how we lived there. I skipped school once . . . and we went *Hamsterfahren*. She went with me to some farmer and stood there and I was so ashamed, and then in the evening we came back. And I swore to myself, *never again*. We didn't have anything to trade. No! Never again! No! It was bad. That's why I said, "no more war." That's when I became a *Friedensfreund* (lit. Friend of Peace). [12]

Just as Binkert's quest for personal freedom seemed to confirm western stereotypes of East German oppression, so did Birkmann's narrative corroborate the SED's depictions of American occupation forces. It's not difficult to imagine Birkmann telling FDJlers about his difficult life in Zehlendorf. Even fifty years later, he contrasted the selfish, extravagant habits of U.S. occupation forces with his own struggles to support an aging grandmother. Recalling bouts of malnutrition and scurvy, Birkmann saw in the FDJ an organization that matched rhetoric with practical assistance during the Hunger Years.

Nonetheless, Birkmann, like so many of his peers, highlighted his self-sufficiency and explained that good food was not enough to win him over to socialism. Rather, he said, the FDJ's message simply made sense. Out of necessity, forward-looking young people should—and would—unify their efforts to improve society. International peace could only be achieved through international coopertation. Birkmann also felt he could trust FDJ members, who unlike the GIs he saw in Zehlendorf, acted on their political convictions and worked to bring about social change.

In December 1949, Birkmann traded his apartment in Zehlendorf for one in Lichtenberg (Soviet sector) only seven months after the Blockade was lifted. This move, like Binkert's, most likely had political as well as practical ramifications. On the one hand, SED officials encouraged such transfers by offering supplemental food to registered East Berliners. On the other hand, pro-western propaganda, as well as public opinion in West Berlin, criticized these *Umsiedler* as for their shortsighted self-interest. Looking back, Birkmann distanced his actions from the heated political and ideological climate of the time. He saw himself as a thoughtful, rational individual, and described the SED's approach as the only logical option.

The Dinkels also recalled spending considerable time debating Berlin's political evolution in the 1940s. However, while both Binkert and Birkmann felt directly impacted by political decisions, this couple described a more insulated relationship to the political environment. They recalled ideological discussions, and even helping relatives—his cousin and her father—flee to the West, but neither seemed to recognize the risks they themselves took by associating with such problematic bordercrossers. Over time, they seemed to have become quite philosophical about both their own missed opportunity and East German authorities.

The Dinkels' story also suggests why *potential* bordercrossers—even those critical of the SED state—remained in the GDR. They had certainly considered leaving Berlin and, aware of the evolving political situation, were gradually getting their affairs in order. However, the day-to-day demands of a growing family and career took priority. Busy (re)constructing their own personal material normalcy in the 1950s, the Dinkels simply never got around to emigrating until it was too late. Some ten years after unification, they seemed ambivalent about their "decision" to stay in the GDR. They displayed neither nostalgia for the East nor regret for missed opportunities in the West. Rather, the Dinkels described their GDR lives in terms of rewarding careers, a stable family life, and a few luxuries, such as a double flat and frequent travel privileges—indicators of the normalcy the young couple pursued in the 1950s.

The Dinkels' contemporary complacency is understandable; they'd learned to accept the parameters of life in the GDR and had enjoyed fulfilling, successful adult lives. In that first postwar decade, however, Berlin's officials could not count on such acceptance, and identified young *Grenzgänger* —both actual and potential—as particularly problematic, since both East and West needed them for physical and economic reconstruction.

The 1951 *Weltfestspiele* (WFS) further politicized the issue of youth crossing borders. This international festival was to facilitate the young GDR's integration into the international socialist community, by showcasing East Berlin as the capital of a German state that cared for the working masses. Festival guests enjoyed a plethora of cultural, athletic, and intellectual offerings at newly built theaters, arenas, and stadiums throughout East Berlin, and were warned against venturing into the "dangerous" western sectors of the city. Nonetheless, many delegates, particularly those from elsewhere in the GDR, included an excursion to the West in their intineraries; Charlottenburg, with its cultural and shopping opportunities was the most popular destination, welcoming some 14,000 festival delegates on a single day.[13]

Although such casual, curious one-time visitors constituted the majority of WFS bordercrossers, the festival drew particular attention to two other groups. WFS organizers and FDJ officials celebrated activists who crossed the borders en masse for political marches and demonstrations. On 15 August, for example, the FDJ Central Committee reported that some 20,250 youthful activists had crossed into western Berlin where some faced threats or actual attacks by armed police officers. According to the report, about 850 "peace loving youths were injured and another 150 arrested by the brutal *Stumm-polizei.*" Noting that the injured were "rescued" by the population of Wedding, the anonymous writer considered the march a success, as it proved the use of "violence and deception" by the West Berlin authorities.[14]

West Berlin officials had expected such demonstrations and media attacks, and had prepared for the WFS by creating a special *Jugendbüro*, charged with welcoming well-meaning *Grenzgänger*, providing asylum if needed, and countering negative propaganda. In this case, *Jugendbüro* officials countered the report of police brutality by suggesting that the FDJ had employed trained activists to confront western officials and incite a riot. "There is a camp of some 3,000 people along the *Müggelsee*, who have been retained from the third wave of [festival] visitors for an undetermined period. From this group came a portion of the provocateurs on 15 August."[15]

Although officials and local press in both East and West focused on such quasi-violent confrontations, the WFS also drew asylum seekers into the spotlight. For persecuted or disgruntled youths throughout the GDR, the festival provided an opportunity to try their luck in a western, capitalist society. On 9 August, for example, some 400 young Germans—of the more than 30,000 visitors to West Berlin's welcome centers—requested asylum.[16] Even these small numbers of would-be refugees troubled municipal authorities. Eastern officials saw them and the stories of political or economic oppression they told as delegitimizing an East German state that was trying hard to publicly assert its youth-friendly policies and attitudes. In West Berlin, officials worried about finding homes and jobs for the young asylum seekers, whose actions, albeit politically gratifying, only added to East-West tensions.

Although the WFS constituted an unusual situation, young *Grenzgänger* challenged postwar officials until (even after, in some cases) August 1961, when the GDR built the Berlin Wall. Like depraved girls and criminal youths, bordercrossers recognized the opportunities and risks of living in postwar Berlin. They reveal how, in the heated atmosphere of the early Cold War, individuals' actions could be and were manipulated for propaganda purposes. In their own minds, however, Berlin's *Grenzgänger* (much like those other problematic groups) were simply utilizing political realities to pursue personal needs and goals.

NOTES

1. Erika Hoerning, *Zwischen den Fronten. Berliner Grenzgänger und Grenzhändler 1948–1961* (Cologne: Böhlau Verlag, 1992), 51–52.
2. If you want to move someplace—Say from East into the West, Then you've got to swipe ten stamps And knock someone o'er the head. 'Cause no one 'll freely trade their home. And 'though a little madness is fine, This kind of crazy, this kind of nonsense I'll never understand.

Sylvia Conradt and Kirsten Heckmann-Janz, *Berlin halb und halb. Von Frontstädtlern, Grenzgänger und Mauerspechten* (Frankfurt am Main: Leuchterhand, 1990), 36.
3. In response to the better-known Soviet blockade, which lasted from 28 June 1948 to 12 May 1949, western occupation officials declared a counterblockade on 5–6 February 1949. Hoerning, 35.
4. Jörn Schütrumpf, "Zu einigen Aspekten des Grenzgängerproblems im Berliner Raum von 1948/49 bis 1961," in *Jahrbuch für Geschichte. Studien zur Geschichte der Deutschen Demokratischen Republik* 18 (1984): 333–58.   At the same time, more than 100,000 West Berliners were employed in the East.
5. Hoerning, 37–38, 49; Schütrumpf, 339.
6. Citing the *Berliner Morgenpost* of 29 January 1953, Schütrumpf notes that the term *Grenzgänger* entered into public parlance in the early 1950s.
7. Pelsdorf, 5.
8. Klinkert, 19–20.
9. Hoerning, 104.
10. Binkert, tape 1.
11. Frau and Herr Dinkel, joint interview, tape 2.
12. Birkmann, 3–4, 6.
13. "Bericht des Berliner Jugendbüros," 16 August 1951, LAB BRep 013 Acc 1160 72. The number of daily visitors increased throughout the festival, particularly in Charlottenburg, Kreuzberg, and Neukölln.   Records are at best only estimates, since many of these temporary bordercrossers did not wear uniforms and tried to blend in with local residents.   See the daily reports of the *Jugendbüro* (LAB BRep 013 Acc 1160 72).
14. "Bericht über die Friedensdemonstration an der Sektorengrenze und in West Berlin," 15.8.51, SAPMO NY 4036/727 405–10; Zentralrat der FDJ, Abt. Propaganda, "Fakten zur Friedensdemonstration am 15.8.51 in West Berlin und zum Wiederschentreffen der Teilnehmer am 16–17.8.52 in Halle," BBF FDJ 182, 1–8.
15. "Bericht des Jugendbüros," 17 August 1951, LAB BRep 013, 1160, 72.
16. "Bericht des Jugendbüros," 9 August 1951, LAB BRep 013, 1160, 72.

5

Difficult Passages

I never was a "teenager." But otherwise, I had a happy childhood and, thanks to my upbringing, a good youth, and after the war, well, actually I've had a fine life up until now, and hope it lasts a while longer. Really. With all the highs and lows, and hardship; of course we had difficult times, but you can't lose yourself in them. "Think positive," I always say. And, "without the past, the future is unthinkable," isn't it? But I can't afford to wallow in the past; I have to look forward, and just dismiss some things, names of certain people. . . . I have the gift of being able to lay things aside, not that I deny them or anything, but just set them aside, and if I ever need to, take them out again. But otherwise I don't, I go forward. . . . I rejoice over every new roof in the GDR or painted house or new garden fence. I don't need it for myself, but I'm glad.[1]

Coping with hardship without being consumed by it. Laying certain memories aside so as to move forward and shape an independent, satisfying life. Implicit comparisons with American youth. Offered over cookies and coffee as a summation of hours of conversation, several phone calls, and years of private rumination, Kanter's conclusions touch on many themes of this exploration of her cohort's experience of multiple mutually informing youthful transitions—the individual transition of maturation, the collective transition of a cohort, and the imposed transition of social and political structures. All encompassed leaving something familiar behind while lacking a clear sense of direction; all entailed carrying the baggage of the past into the void of an undefined future, and all have continued to inform individual and collective identities.

In examining how Kanter's cohort experienced these passages, I have asked how individual young Berliners created their own security.   Rather than dismissing a cohort as lost or skeptical, I have tried to show both the evolving spatial and mental parameters in which its members lived and how they found agency and rebuilt—over time—collective identities.   While acknowledging and incorporating social and political forces that have shaped cohort members' daily lives, priorities, and goals, I have focused on individuals' perspectives.   I have questioned the range of possible reactions and initiatives to these imposed parameters, and tried to explain what archival documents, structural studies, or pure memoirs cannot—what it meant to be young in the postwar period, and what it now means to have been young during that transformation of German society.

In this chapter, I step back from personal experience to explore in more general terms this cohort's youthful passage from a known past into what was then an uncertain future.   The first section explores parallels between the cohort's transition to adulthood and the German nation's transition from a single authoritarian state to two opposing successor states.   The second section reviews interviewees' experiences through a more sociological lens, examining their collective social passage from childhood to adulthood.   Finally, this chapter puts questions of cohort experience and memory into a more theoretical context, asking how cohort members' accounts relate to historians' concerns about oral sources and the nature of youth as both a personal passage and a social construct.

NATIONAL AND PERSONAL PASSAGES

Throughout this project, the individual experiences of a very small number of Germans have been intertwined with accounts of broader political developments affecting Berlin and the German nation.   This approach is rooted in the idea that Berliners born between 1926 and 1933 both experienced these developments and incorporated them into life narratives in ways that unite them as a unique cohort. Cohort members' personal passages from dependent childhood in the *Hauptstadt* of the Third Reich to autonomous adults in East and West coincided with a national passage from subservience to an authoritarian leader to the creation—and international recognition—of two, relatively autonomous successor states.

On both levels, establishing the nature of this passage is an elusive goal. Accounts of Germany's national passage typically reflect the values and cultures of chroniclers on either side of the Cold War divide and reveal an understandable focus on explaining or excusing the Nazi era.   Alternately, the early postwar years are often depicted as the prelude to what would become a half-century of division imposed upon the nation from external forces, that is, a relatively sudden but passive passage, in which Germans were abruptly sorted into East and West.   In either case, distinct historiographies portray not one, but two simultaneous transitions, so that it becomes difficult to even speak of a national passage out of Nazism.

Similar difficulties appear when reviewing personal passages of this cohort of youth. They too may have difficulty explaining their roots in the Third Reich, and have incorporated imposed national narratives and evolving societal expectations into their recollections of the past.   They challenge archival-based histories of both National Socialist and interregnum periods and offer their own equally biased memories as evidence of what life was really like.[2] Nonetheless, and even when both national and personal accounts are recognized as constructed narratives that serve specific, sometimes contrary goals, several related observations can be made.   First, and not surprisingly, cohort members' narratives, while blurring the political turning points that structure traditional master narrative accounts of this period, nonetheless parallel them in terms of content and presentation. Second, and despite these parallels, personal accounts typically omit political developments. Third, when overlaid upon each other, the two historical narratives present a picture of a particularly intense and significant passage through youth for this cohort.

One example of the compositional similarities between personal and national narratives is found in their frequent oversimplification of German society in the second half of the 1930s. Cohort members' overwhelmingly positive memories of the prewar years seem unstained by the knowledge they have since acquired about the Third Reich's treatment of Jews and other minorities. Too young to have noticed, let alone understood, much of the world beyond their immediate families, most interviewees ignored broader sociopolitical parameters altogether, and had little trouble integrating the first half of World War II into happy childhood memories. During its first years, "Hitler's War" was characterized by success, and with few exceptions, cohort members described being relatively unaffected.[3]

It could be argued, as did some observers of German youth after 1945, that cohort members' oversimplification of life and the shift from peacetime to mobilized society proved they were so successfully brainwashed by Nazi propaganda that they fail to distinguish between war and peace. In sociological terms, however, they had learned through experience what behaviors were appropriate in Nazi society, and those standards remained virtually unchanged in the first half of the war.[4] Abstract political ideas became interesting and relevant to this cohort only in the void following Nazi capitulation, but not necessarily because they had been brainwashed. Rather, they had matured and were seeking new realms beyond home and family; Birkmann, Binkert, and Dinkel believed, at least initially, that they might even be able to influence political developments.

Both personal and national narratives also describe a brief period of suspended animation in mid–1945. Western histories of postwar Berlin in particular emphasize the six-week monopoly enjoyed by Soviet officials, during which, stories of rape aside, the SMAD single-handedly imposed regulations and created a local administration comprised largely of hand-picked activists and returning émigrés, whose responsibilities consisted largely of announcing and executing Soviet decisions. Opportunities for local administrators and intellectuals who lacked leftist sympathies were few and far between, and once appointed, German officials had little voice in decisions. Even after the arrival of western forces in Berlin, total capitulation as well as wrangling among occupation officials slowed decisions and made it difficult for German voices to be heard.[5]

East German narratives describe this period in more active terms, highlighting spontaneous political activism at the local level as preparing for the "birth of a new Germany." However, it would soon become clear that this new society would not be one of Germans' own making (a unique German path to socialism), but rather constructed on the example of the Soviet Union. Furthermore, in Berlin at least, public efforts seemed to consist largely of verbal appeals to a population that had already begun identifying German communists with Soviet goals.[6] Even if one took local activism at face value, there existed, at this period in time, neither a nation nor two partial nation states, only four zones (and sectors) of occupation regulated by four (or more) sets of values and plans.

Referring to a similar suspension of agency, cohort members describe this Nirvana-like experience in very different terms. Even though their lives were regulated by imposed curfews and regulations, they offer few indications of having been frustrated by political forces beyond their control, in part because they had lived under such restrictions even before defeat. Rather, they seem to have relished what they saw as an escape from responsibility and the impositions of previous roles. They were no longer *verschickte Kinder*, Hitler Youth, antiaircraft gunners, or RAD volunteers; instead, they were just "young." Freed from the behavioral roles of Nazism, they could dance again. No one called them to *Dienst*; they could sleep undisturbed by air raid sirens or simply sit in the sun along the Wannsee. Unlike western political narratives, which suggest the detrimental effects of this brief period, or even eastern accounts wishing that more had been accomplished, this cohort reveled in the suspension of reality in summer 1945. Far more important than the material inconveniences was the fact that restrictive behavioral norms had been lifted.

Both national and personal passages of the mid-1940s are also marked by a relatively quick rejection of the past combined with at best a vague awareness of prospects for the future. Tensions had long existed among the Allied powers, and it was unclear where each side's breaking point lay. Reflecting the uncertainty of the future, political rhetoric consisted largely of backward-looking "anti" statements; reconstituted parties and their leaders necessarily declared themselves antiwar, antifascist and antimilitary, but were often vague about Germany's future.[7]

Similarly, although cohort members quickly learned it was wise to discard Hitler Youth emblems and other memorabilia, they had little idea of what to expect of the future. In sociological terms, the past had been ripped out from under them; consequently, they lacked a solid framework on which to construct future goals and identities.[8] Herr Birkmann, for example, had predicted that all males would be shot, and in fact wandered the streets of Zehlendorf looking for an appropriate execution site. Anything less than this was inconceivable to him at the time; he was stunned to discover that he could resume his apprenticeship by repairing Soviet, then American and British vehicles.[9]

By the early 1950s, the postwar passage of nation and cohort was essentially complete; a sense of a "new normalcy" was being cultivated on both political and personal levels. The two successor states were quickly being integrated into their respective blocks, and their future roles seemed clear. The GDR was to prove itself the "showplace of socialism," overcoming the past by asserting solidarity with the international workers' movement, and essentially pinning the blame for the past on economic exploitation and capitalist imperialism. The FRG, on the other hand, would mark the border of democracy, protecting the West from communism, which, in its totalitarian nature, was more or less equitable with Nazism.   Although the future was not so clear for individual cohort members, they too had established routines and a rudimentary political identity by the early 1950s.[10]

Despite these similarities, personal and national narratives of passage from Nazi authoritarianism to divided normalcy rarely acknowledged one another.   On the one hand, this project may overemphasize such exclusivity, since potential interviewees knew about my interest in personal experience.   On the other hand, the nature and content of the dual passages themselves likely also encouraged interviewees to distance themselves and their experiences from national and political developments, particularly during the Nazi period. Cohort members, as noted earlier, were very young, and have few memories of that time to begin with.   In addition, because the Nazi era constitutes the most difficult period in modern German history it is far easier for them to skim over political developments than to invite further queries as to their family's acceptance or complicity.

National and personal narratives of passage came closest to touching in the Hunger Years.   In part, this is likely because first, the German state lacked agency; political actors could do little more than describe problems and being empowered only to implement occupation officials' decisions.[11]   Second, archival records of the period are frequently incomplete, so that even national narratives must rely more heavily on the memoirs and personal recollections of actors, who felt the immediate effects of hardship.   Third, cohort members themselves frequently demonstrate greater interest in political developments during this period; they were formulating opinions about the occupiers and events like the currency reform and blockade directly impacted them.

By the 1950s, however, when the German successor states had been established in opposing eastern and western blocks, and when it became clear that Germany would, for the foreseeable future, have not one but two, diametrically opposed paths, national and personal narratives again diverged. Most cohort members focused on creating their own havens of normalcy and, having had virtually no voice in the establishment of either system, felt only the vaguest sense of loyalty to the one in which they for the most part happened to find themselves.[12]   Although the cohort increasingly accepted the existence of two German states as time passed, and seemed to adapt—at least in their public and professional lives—to new behavioral norms, both the FRG and the GDR worked to cultivate a sense of national legitimacy among its members.   The West German government relied on subsidized economic growth, clear measures to avoid repeating Weimar-era errors, and the integration of Berlin into federal structures to establish its legitimacy among residents.[13]   Meanwhile, the SED state, in which the potential for economic prosperity had been largely stripped by the Soviet Union, pursued cohort members' loyalty through ambitious work initiatives such as the NAW, continuing education opportunities, mobilization campaigns like the World Festival Games, and ultimately through force in June 1953.[14]

The interrelationship between accounts of national and personal passages is particularly relevant because it dramatically intensified this cohort's experience of youth as a stage of sociological and psychological development in which "past and future contend for mastery over the adult mind."[15]   Like other generations before and since, this cohort juggled confusion, curiosity, a desire to belong, a need to be unique, and a search for meaning; it did so, however, within particularly unstable social, political, and economic parameters.[16]

Of course, since one function of youth as a stage of individual development is the separation from parents and childhood, one could argue that coming of age in the postwar years made the passage from childhood to adulthood easier on this cohort. Ties to past roles were simply cut; mementos were destroyed in air raids, lost during evacuations, or sold on the black markets. Nostalgic recollections of adventures in the *Jungvolk* or HJ were, as Kanter implied, simply "laid aside"; sociopolitical parameters rendered such memories unacceptable, and they could serve no useful purpose in a society that needed to move forward as quickly as possible.

Given the circumstances, this cohort may also have had an easier time distancing itself from parental identities and values. Demographically, interviewees' parents could have voted for Hitler, and at the very least, they were members of the generation responsible for the postwar mess in which young people found themselves. More concretely, cohort members' parents seemed largely preoccupied by material concerns; interviewees' vague answers to direct questions suggest their fathers and mothers were frequently absent, if not physically, then mentally. Furthermore, social and economic conditions made it difficult to be overprotective or assert moral authority; in short, many families *relied* on youths' illegal or black market activities.[17]

However, despite these indications that sociopolitical parameters may have eased this cohort's passage, "the purpose of adolescence is not to *obliterate* [my emphasis] the past, but to immortalize what is valuable and to say farewell to those items of the past that stand in the way of a full realization of adult . . . potentials." Unlike a generation that comes of age in a relatively stable society, and rediscovers that community from a new, adult perspective, this cohort could never return to the society it left behind.[18] In other words, while conditions of postwar society facilitated a destructive dialectic, that is, a distancing from and dissolution of past roles, they also denied the cohort a crucial element of constructive dialectic, namely, a legitimate continuity with the community that had informed its childhood. Some of youths' favorite songs contained inadmissible lyrics. The camping trips many had enjoyed were initially criticized as paramilitary training. The older boys and girls whom cohort members had admired and emulated were now identified as untrustworthy. Even their volunteer efforts, through which they had helped neighbors or the unemployed, were delegitimized because they had served a condemned regime. In essence, the very structures that had informed their lives had been declared, by total strangers, detrimental to their development. Among the few lessons they could carry with them as they passed from childhood to adulthood were those of self-reliance and caution.

In addition, this cohort had few trustworthy guides to help it either deconstruct its past or engage potential future roles. It could not follow in the steps of a slightly older cohort and seemed to feel betrayed by many of the wise elders of its childhood, for example, pastors and parents. Some did find mentors—in a track coach or school director, for example—but both KPD and youth committee records suggest that substitute *Vertrauensfiguren* often had trouble understanding the mindset and needs of youths, and repeated assertions of "I did it myself" only underscore this perceived lack of suitable mentors.

Furthermore, the definition of youth itself, by nature somewhat ambiguous in virtually any cultural setting, seemed particularly unclear in the postwar years.[19] No one, not the occupiers, not German officials, nor even cohort members themselves, seemed to understand how to categorize this age group, which had actively participated in war effort yet was judged emotionally immature by psychologists. Interviewees saw symptoms of this confusion in their daily lives. On the one hand, they read flyers, posters, and newsletters telling them how important they were to the reconstruction of society, and were courted by political activists from across the spectrum.

On the other hand, they felt neither the practical benefits of childhood nor the legal privileges of adulthood. Evidence of this impractical in-between status appeared in the first weeks of occupation. For example, although interviewees frequently describe Russian soldiers as especially *kinderlieb*, only the youngest—or the youngest-looking—reaped the benefits of this friendliness. Similarly, the cohort saw Western soldiers handing out candy to younger children, but considered themselves ineligible for either informal or structured relief programs.

Too old to reap significant material benefits from either informal or structured charity, cohort members were frequently too young to make substantive contributions to developing postwar society. By the time politically interested cohort members such as Dinkel and Binkert had weighed their options and begun articulating their own visions for the future, the window of opportunity for personal expression had already begun to close under the weight of East-West tensions. The two interviewees recalled being frustrated as they saw the increasing futility of pursuing any truly new political or social ideas; once again, forces beyond their control clearly manipulated their future. While this cohort may not be unique in recognizing the limitations of sociopolitical parameters, its members, who arguably had struggled to become politically aware in the first place, found its hands tied at an age characterized by vivid dreams and plans.

Cohort members had a similarly difficult time integrating into an adult workforce. Although the number of would-be workers was lower than in the early 1940s, employment and training opportunities were rare, since Berlin's productive capacity had been stripped by both war and the SMAD. Furthermore, because only a minority had served time in prisoner of war camps, the males (and by definition the females) of this cohort rarely received preferential admission to diploma-completion programs or higher education.

Finally, this cohort had, until after the Berlin Blockade, only the vaguest notions about the future. In other words, individuals had no idea what they and their society were supposed to be evolving into. They could not know what roles they ought to pursue, what society expected of them, or what they in turn could expect from other members of society. What would it mean to be an autonomous adult in a postwar half-nation?

We had no idea what would become of Germany, what would become of Berlin. We were stuck in the middle of the Eastern Zone, nothing was certain. . . . [That's why] one had no secure viewpoints. We did have in our group a very enthusiastic young socialist, [such people] *existed*, of course . . . but it wasn't for us.[20]

LIFE PASSAGES

Although the length and nature of youth as a period of transition between childhood and adulthood is culturally specific, many societies have constructed similar kinds of turning points, ceremonies and activities through which youths establish their maturity and adults articulate an acceptance of a new cohort of equals. For individuals and their communities, these transitory experiences mark multiple intersections—between dependency and autonomy, naïveté and experience, young and old, past and future—and serve both social and psychological functions. Since the turn of the century, when Arnold von Gennep published *Rites de Passage*, sociologists and anthropologists have approached the issue of youth transitions by studying initiation rituals in ancient and tribal cultures, noting how specific activities and tests follow a pattern of separation, initiation, and return. Rites of passage seem to give structure to the passage of youth, drawing individuals physically and psychologically away from parental dependence and childish roles, demanding that they assert courage and independence, explaining new roles and expectations and then welcoming them back as new, full-fledged members of the community.[21]

Identifying rites of passage in modern, industrialized society has perplexed many scholars, leading some to suggest that youth has been in a perpetual state of crisis throughout most of the twentieth century. Observers of youth cohorts over the past hundred years blame an increasing emphasis on individuality, immediacy, and rapid socioeconomic change for undermining the sense of continuity and tradition on which traditional rites of passage depend. Consequently, some have shifted their focus away from identifiable rites that mark a break between childhood and adulthood. Emphasizing the interconnectedness of life stages, they instead explain the transition of youth as a period of gradual change characterized by certain themes. In this view, the passage of youth concludes once an individual has "developed a coping style consistent with the demands of their social world."[22] This social competency model shares with the *rite de passage* concept the idea that youthful passages serve both specific cohorts and broader society. They help individuals adapt to new roles and transmit societal values from one generation to the next. At the same time, the nature of the passage itself is informed by social structures and the opportunities for human agency they offer. Periods of crisis impede social continuity and, as sociologists such as Margaret Mead and Joseph Campbell have suggested, typically render these passages more difficult.[23]

National Socialism sought to influence youths' transitional passages by imbuing them with ideologically specific values including loyalty to the *Führer*, a sense of *Gemeinschaft*, and obedience. The KLV camps, for example, functioned much like ancient rituals of separation and maturation. Cohort members' recollections of the KLV camps demonstrate how the physical isolation and hardship—as well as the program's underlying social function—paralleled traditional rites of passage.

I was in the KLV camps off and on from about 1939, first the entire class and then [later] classes reconstituted classes. [Was it lonely?] No, not really. Rather it was a society of children . . . with conflicts like in adult life only even more intense. The strongest is the boss. . . . We were occupied all the time, from breakfast, from waking up to the bell to doing homework, organized by *Jungvolk* leaders . . . mostly really young people, they seemed old to me, I suppose about seventeen. They planned our free time, games, political lectures, the whole day. . . . Saying, "I don't feel like it," that was impossible. [If you said that] you'd be punished. For example, you'd have to [come down] in athletic clothes. Then, x minutes later in uniform and then x minutes later in some other outfit. Or physical exercise: [you'd] run, throw yourself into the dirt and then get up again, and run up and down . . . until you were filthy from head to toe, and then they'd announce a room inspection in half an hour. Everyone clean, everything brushed. . . . As a result, of course, some couldn't take it; they literally had emotional breakdowns. We had lots of bed-wetters . . . and some had to leave. It wasn't just the external pressure—school and HJ leaders—it was the living together.[24]

Equipped with little more than frequently reluctant parental blessings, Winkert and his peers were removed from a familiar environment and transplanted—for a relatively long period of time—into a community of peers led by a few elders, whose responsibility it was to teach practical skills and National Socialist values. The KLV experience also tested evacuees' maturity. Promoted as a protective evacuation program, it was intended to change participants and prepare them as a cohort for new roles in Nazi society.

If the KLV program was conceived as a potential wartime *rite de passage*, it failed to incorporate a sociologically significant part of the experience, the celebrated reintegration of participants into the community. The state closed camps with little fanfare, in some cases even failing to notify parents of their children's imminent return. Furthermore, evacuees were often unable to re-enter their former environment, for instance, if the neighborhood had been destroyed by air raids, if fathers or siblings had been conscripted, or if bombed-out strangers had taken rooms in the home. Most significantly, parents, who generally play a crucial role in ascribing social significance to initiation rituals, denied the KLV experience as a rite of passage. They rarely understood the nature of camp life and were frequently unable to welcome their now-initiated children as equals. In other words, they had given up their children not to facilitate their socialization in Nazi society, but simply to protect them from air raids, and were unprepared for the more mature youngsters who returned.

Descriptions of postwar familial relationships suggest cohort members who were drafted for labor or military service encountered similar problems; conscripted youths understood the experience as a rite of passage, although older relatives did not. Herr Dinkel described the frustration of being treated as a child when he—a veteran of the *Wehrmacht*—felt like an adult.

I didn't want to take orders, but people kept ordering me around. I didn't like it and that's why I had trouble [getting through] my apprenticeship, and with my father. I wasn't a little boy any more, but he wanted to continue his [method of] upbringing.[25]

While the KLV camps exemplify how a culturally specific practice might be constructed and immediately experienced as a rite of passage, most such rituals are comprised of both living acts and symbolic meanings. These rites, because they are tied to particular cultural values, often dissolve in periods of sociopolitical upheaval, particularly when they are forcibly imposed, as was the KLV. What remains, then, are a set of more gradual life passages, through which young people develop social competency as individuals and members of society.[26] These social passages typically occur over a period of months or years, and can be difficult to untangle, as they are shaped by multiple, often enduring cultural parameters—attitudes about money, gender, and authority, for example. Even these more gradual, fluid passages, however, are informed by specific societal structures and conditions. While long-standing western values persisted through the early postwar years, the deprivation and instability that characterized this period also took its toll. For a time, at least, the ways in which youths developed social competencies became more open-ended.

For instance, cohort members' passage to economic competency was often protracted during the Hunger Years; the high youth unemployment rate, which persisted into the early 1950s, prevented most from becoming financially self-sufficient. Economic necessity compelled many young people to take a series of temporary jobs, thus delaying their pursuit of occupational training and a better-paying, long-term job or career. These same conditions, however, could also hasten the passage, as youths found themselves suddenly needed as breadwinners. Even in these situations, however, wage-earning young people frequently had little control over their income. If they lived with their parents—as all but one of my interviewees did—the older adults usually managed the household, allocating funds as needed for food, clothing, and so forth.

For similar reasons, the passage to familial maturity, through which the parental household becomes subordinate to new family units of the next generation, was also drawn out during the late 1940s and early 1950s. Although interviewees rarely volunteered detailed information about their fathers or mothers, some offered a glimpse of how parent-child relationships changed as they matured and established their own families. Marriage is traditionally seen as the culmination of this passage, indicating maturity and independence as well as acceptance of moral norms of society.[27] In the early postwar years, it was also a particularly difficult process. First, given the hard times, young people were often discouraged from formalizing relationships through marriage, resulting in attenuated engagements.

On the one hand, this waiting period allowed partners to save ration coupons and exploit personal contacts to procure the festive clothing and refreshments they associated with nuptial celebrations.[28] On the other hand, it also increased the couple's risk of having what was delicately called a *Sechsmonatskind*. Conceiving a child out of wedlock suggested to older adults that the youths were unprepared to accept moral norms. Fear of the social implications of an illegitimate child, together with economic concerns, led some parents to closely chaperone unmarried couples, which not surprisingly undermined the youths' sense of independence and maturity.[29]

The passage to recognized maturity in the familial realm was further drawn out because even after marrying, young people remained dependent on their parents. The combination of high unemployment and a persistent housing shortage meant that newlyweds seldom had their own homes. Frau Barthe, for example, recalled sleeping with her husband and infant son in the hallway of her in-laws' flat.

They didn't have much room, when you walked in, you were right in the kitchen; there was no corridor. And then a little walk-through room, and then my in-laws' bedroom. That was all. [We lived] in the little hall room, we had a double couch, but we couldn't open it up, because they had to get through. And our son had a little bassinet, we put it sideways. And they'd always say—not to me, but to my husband, "This washing all the time, it steams [up the flat]." The diapers, I had to boil them in the kitchen. "It's too steamy, it can't go on," [they said] and "At the very least, if she has to wash, do it out in the stairway." I said, "I can't do that. With the draft from downstairs, I'll make myself sick." Always this nagging back and forth. I didn't dare say anything.

Then my mother-in-law got cancer . . . [and] died. It sounds terrible, but I was glad. I was going to pieces psychologically. [Later,] my father-in-law had a lady friend in Karlshorst, and was always over there, and one day my husband said, "Say, couldn't we trade? You, you hardly sleep here, maybe we could have the bigger room?"

"No, out of the question!" and he glared at me. "If it had been up to me, you'd have never moved here anyway." I had to just put up with it.[30]

Given the crowded quarters and mutual resentment, it is not surprising that the young couple found it difficult to assert their independence as a new family unit. Sufficient space, however, was not always a solution. As observed in Chapter 3, the parents of this cohort had often been physically and emotionally drained by the war. Frau Pestopf described how her attempts to establish a sense of normalcy in her own household were undermined when her parents and siblings expected her to resolve their fights, which were sometimes violent.[31]

Socioeconomic conditions also affected this cohort's spiritual passage to maturity. Although the majority of interviewees had attended church as children, most note that religion lost its previous significance by the mid-1940s. This could suggest that the HJ's strategy of planning activities on Sunday mornings was successful. Most interviewees, however, cited an inability to reconcile tenets of Christianity with recent experiences as the reason they abandoned organized religion.

I'm not against the people, but rather the leadership. On both sides the clergy blessed the soldiers and sent them into battle—like on M*A*S*H, but there at least the pastor stays out of it pretty much. And the slogan of the church was Peace on Earth! . . . And then, in the American sector, you, a member of the church, starve, while the *Amis* . . . lived really well. CARE packages, what nonsense! Once or twice I got a liter of soup in the Argentinische Straße youth club . . . and that's why I left the church.[32]

Sentiments like Birkmann's were only reinforced when cohort members met local clergy who, while encouraging them to attend worship, were seemingly unable to reconcile the existence of a loving and perfect God with the exposed horrors of the war and the Holocaust. Youths frequently felt the church had failed them, and they rejected it as hypocritical, or at the very least, overly naïve. This is even true of many who were confirmed in the church in the early postwar years. They attended the preparatory classes and submitted to the rite, but only to placate elderly relatives, for whom it apparently meant so much. Consequently, confirmation signified not their entrance into a mature religious community, but rather the end of their association with the church; such individuals note that they did not encourage their own children to pursue confirmation.

This broken-off relationship with traditional religious institutions may be a contributing factor in the emphasis on self-sufficiency and pragmatism observed in the narratives of cohort members in East and West. For younger East Berliners, the transition to a spiritual competency divorced from religion was facilitated, even encouraged, by the new socialist state. By the early 1950s, the SED and FDJ had begun promoting the revival of the *Jugendweihe*, a coming-of-age ceremony that had been practiced by workers' movements before and during the Weimar era. Tolerant rhetoric aside, the promotion of the *Jugendweihe* as a secular alternative to confirmation was clear from the outset. SED officials purposefully adapted the earlier passage to fit their needs, imbuing it with messages about peaceful solidarity and a strong antireligious significance.[33] In place of pastor-led Bible studies and theological discussions, *Jugendweihe* mentors cultivated youths' understanding of dialectic materialism, the lives of Marx and Engels, and the history of the international workers' movement.[34] The celebration itself emulated the formality and dress of the religious ceremony. Frau Klinkert recalled having begun the confirmation process, but dropping out to join classmates preparing for the *Jugendweihe*.

The *Jugendweihe* was intended for children who were atheists, who didn't belong to any church, and later under socialism almost all children participated. . . . There were four in our class who registered for the *Jugendweihe*. . . . Half starved, ten kilos underweight, and the big question was what could we wear? The *Jugendweihe* was a fine [occasion]. . . . And textiles were rationed . . . we had an aunt, who had some flag-red fabric, [had it re-dyed] and it was alright. We were glad we each had a dress, and then came the next drama: [finding] shoes . . . gloves and the bouquet and a veil. . . . We used a crocheted tablecloth, got roses and borrowed gloves and that was our *Jugendweihe* . . . in the *Metropol-Theater* . . . a very beautiful, large hall, there was a speech and then we were called up and well, congratulated. . . . Of course they didn't talk about God, but rather told us socio-political, progressive, realistic stories. About society and how people behave.[35]

One of the first participants in the GDR's *Jugendweihe* program, Klinkert demonstrates how this new marker of maturity attracted young people. Taking advantage of an existent dissatisfaction with the church, the SED offered more "realistic" answers to maturing youths' questions about the nature of the world and their place in it.[36]

In retrospect, the *Jugendweihe* also served another function as it, like the KLV of the Nazi era, quickly evolved from a voluntary program to one that was nearly compulsory, at least in practice. The dissolution of the KLV is frequently associated with the collapse of societal structures; as noted previously, children were often evacuated from the camps abruptly and with no idea where they were going, how they would get there, or who would care for them. Leaving the camps, in fact, initiated the *wir* to *ich* transition that prepared them for the chaos of the Hunger Years. The *Jugendweihe*, nearly a decade later, signified the return of structure. It persisted throughout the GDR's existence and even after its demise, uniting not only a single cohort but also—as had confirmation in earlier times—successive generations through a common set of practices and meanings.

Despite the importance afforded these passages to maturity, interviewees seldom offered unprompted accounts of their evolving social competency. Instead, looking back on their youth, most emphasize how they developed individual competency—self-awareness, responsibility, and confidence—in spite of these hurdles. A focus on self and personal agency during youth is not unique to this period or cohort. On the contrary, this "quietistic emphasis on personal experience and exploration" is widely understood as characteristic of youth, at least in the twentieth century.[37] However, cohort members' recollections do stand out in several ways. First, as noted previously, many interviewees root this focus on individual competency in a personal turning point that occurred in the last months of World War II. Unlike their postwar passages, which often seem to have been complicated or protracted by immediate parameters of life, interviewees suggest a sudden break from the *wir* of the Nazi era to a postwar *ich*. This new self was apparently unfazed by unaccompanied journeys through the war-torn Reich and able to "to get what we needed, according to our interests."[38]

Second, this emphasis on the *ich* seems to structure interviewees' accounts of their adult lives; in other words, they do not associate it strictly with their youth. Cohort members repeatedly used variations on the phrase *Ich hab's ganz allein gemacht* (I did it all by myself) to answer questions about how they made decisions and where they sought emotional support. This emphasis pervaded the narratives of interviewees from both East Berlin, where housing and basic necessities were subsidized by the SED state, and West Berlin, which received substantial social and economic support from the FRG.   Furthermore, this cohort's adult experience was shaped by the Cold War era, during which Berliners often seemed to be pawns in the hands of the superpowers. Interviewees' focus on personal agency despite structural parameters may well reflect all of these factors.

The confidence interviewees describe as they recount their youthful accomplishments, social savvy, and decision-making skills did not transfer to the political realm. They "filtered news for ourselves," and seemed confident in their ability to discern sincere promises from empty rhetoric, but rarely seemed eager to join political organizations.[39] Nor did they volunteer explanations of either causes or implications of crises such as the 1948–49 Blockade or 1953 workers' strike. Although Herr Birkmann recalls being glad that he and his fellow Germans were finally recognized by the international community during the World Festival Games, it remains unclear how or when this cohort negotiated a passage to civic competency.

THE PASSAGE OF TIME

Just as the transformation of Germany from authoritarian dictatorship to divided Cold War states corresponded with this cohort's maturation through youth, so too has the process of reunification largely coincided with its passage into retirement. Once again, interviewees' personal and collective roles are changing just as the societies that have co-constructed these roles and given meaning to them are in flux. The costs of unification have led cohort members to question their economic security; some are simply unable to maintain their standard of living, while others are extending careers or assuming unanticipated roles (as childcare providers, financiers, or landlords) in the lives of their children. More generally, although not surprisingly, as cohort members age, many demonstrate more interest in reflecting on the past. Distel and Mostel, for example, have spent long hours reading and compiling personal archives about the GYI program. Rennebach has researched his recent family history, questioning living relatives and using thousands of note cards to record factual details and interesting episodes that shaped his and his family's past. The Völkers have compiled scrapbooks for each of their children that preserve their experiences and identity as Berliners, Catholics, and historical actors.

Such efforts, however, strike me as more than simply hobbies developed to fill retirement years, as the individuals with whom I spoke typically had very active lives, fitting interviews in between social engagements, volunteer activities, and familial obligations. Nor do cohort members seem primarily motivated to reconsider their past lives by the curiosity of children or grandchildren; the Völkers, in fact, specifically noted their children's lack of interest in their attempts to compile a family history. Rather, interviewees seem acutely aware of having lived through a unique—and now closed—period of Berlin's and Germany's history. Looking back at the Nazi and interregnum past through forty years of division, this cohort engages, at times quite explicitly, broader questions of identity construction, social relations, and historical scholarship.

One such question is how cohort members acknowledge the legacy of division as they talk about the past. Although the physical markers of Berlin's division are rapidly being swept away by the virtual—although not absolute—disappearance of the Wall, by massive construction projects around *Potsdamer Platz*, and by equally nasty traffic jams along both western and eastern thoroughfares, a mental chasm remains, particularly for this cohort, which has learned to associate division with normalcy. New, inconvenient, and undesired when imposed in the early 1950s, the labels *easterner* and *westerner* have become ingrained elements of cohort members' adult identities.[40] Unification has not eliminated these terms, but rather highlighted their experiential and attitudinal, as opposed to geographical, substance.

West Berliners have a much easier legacy with which to cope. Through the passage of time, they have become known as stalwart defenders of democracy. Westerners have become "the best Americans," observed one cohort member; speaking to an American researcher, they rarely criticize historical developments—or the United States' role in them—of the past half-century.[41] Even the 1961 construction of the Wall, which broke personal ties and restricted freedom of movement, and which many easterners suggest the United States could have easily prevented, is described in positive terms by retrospective West Berliners.

One was always a bit scared, Cold War and so on, what would become of Berlin. . . . There was always this East-West tension, [then after] the Wall, we felt practically more secure . . . because we knew, well, that's that and now they're over there and we're here and with the Wall there they won't just swallow us up. . . . People complained horribly about the Wall, but at least things were cleared up.[42]

Looking back, the Wall—and the forty years of division it represents—has made West Berliners inadvertent heroes, simply for carrying on their daily lives in their hometown.   Once frustrated at being simultaneously too old and too young, their age now seems a blessing. They were too young to be blamed for creating division, and are too old to be charged with undoing its legacy, but have been credited for having endured it for most of their lives. Unification came as a surprise, and has created some difficulties for western cohort members, but has not substantially challenged such identities.

No one ever really believed in reunification; it was very unexpected, all within six months . . . we believed well, now everything would be very nice . . . and they'd sort themselves out over there; we'd help of course, but there might be this Eastern economic wonder. . . . But now we see these problems, it turned out a bit differently. . . . It's a shame that East and West couldn't come together in a more humane way.[43]

For East Berliners, the legacy of division is, of course, more problematic. Interviewees had considered their lives successful in the GDR and, like their peers in the West, feel no responsibility for Germany's division. They learned to master new societal norms, and have built careers and raised families in a divided normalcy.   They too have carried on in a divided city.   Unlike West Berliners, however, easterners now face a second occupation by foreign politicians, institutions, and values.

Forty-two years. In one street, one district, and I'll probably live here until I die. . . . You saw our block from the street, for the last five years they [the city] have promised to renovate our block, and in the fourth year they start, and it's still not finished. . . . They're fixing things up to our satisfaction, but [the cost!]—from a rent of 47,80 GDR it's gone to 831,00 DM, and yes, you heard correctly. All for the renovation; if you didn't have the money you had to move. *That* was the result of the *Wende*. Of course it wasn't great in GDR times . . . everyone had to fix things up a bit themselves, but now whoever doesn't have the money. . . . That's what came along with capitalism, it's not so simple.[44]

Once again, both past and future have been complicated for these East Berliners by forces seemingly beyond their control; their self-cultivated sense of normalcy has been undermined by unification.   Although they welcome long-absent accoutrements of western normalcy such as automobiles and telephones, they are tied by experience to a system in which they understood their own roles. Furthermore, even as they enjoy the material advantages of the West, they are now just as likely to be confronted with the associated problems—high rents, for example. Finally, they find themselves needing to simultaneously defend and distance themselves from the delegitimized SED. Not unlike their parents decades ago, they need to explain their passive acceptance of (or active participation in) a now-defunct political system, a task which may challenge the themes of independence and self-reliance in their narratives.[45]

   With such diverse legacies laid over common experiences of childhood and similar, "*Ich hab's allein gemacht*" adult identities, could this cohort be expected to recover an experience based Berliner identity like that they shared in the early 1940s? On the one hand, a few have renewed relationships with people and places long absent from their daily experience. Sisters Barthe and Pastler drink coffee together each week and have joined a local history club, through which they are getting to know each other's cities. Binkert has revived his old friendship with Dinkel, and has engaged former colleagues from the *Bezirksamt Prenzlauer Berg* in discussions comparing past and present. On the other hand, initiatives such as the *Zeitzeugenbörse* have had difficulty recruiting older volunteers for workshops and oral history projects intended to bring together easterners and westerners, and few interviewees cite any need to revisit the past by crossing the now-invisible sector borders. Furthermore, easterners and westerners may be united in their desire to avoid another global war, but they remain divided as they consider the consequences of the last one. Zelle, an East Berliner, evaluated the causes of armed conflict with the resignation of one disappointed by society's inability to learn from the past.

I fear that the moment that we . . . pass away, there will be another war, a large scale war . . . nothing's changed . . . as long as conditions don't change, so that economic conditions in this world are altered, we won't make any progress. It's always the same, whether it's in Bosnia, in the former Yugoslavia, Iran/Iraq—this last action against Sadam Hussein, it's idiotic and only about money. . . . I'm glad that the Greens took a stand on this at their convention but I have to warn them, they're pursuing an illusion that can never be realized. At least not without other changes first.[46]

Bistop, however, epitomized the more ambiguous response of many West Berliners, for whom vivid memories of wartime violence and destruction have been at least somewhat mitigated by the Federal Republic's postwar development.

I was sixteen at the end of the war, in May '45; I'd been drafted into the *Volkssturm* at fifteen . . . and had to defend Berlin with a grenade launcher. . . . We [were cut off from] friends in East Prussia, and . . . sometimes I thought, "Hitler, this whole nonsense with *Volk ohne Raum*; if they'd only fertilized better there would've been enough *Raum* to feed eighty million!" ...a piece of *Heimat-Gefühl* is gone . . . but otherwise I must say, without the war I'd have never [met] the 18th Second Airborne Division and learned English; would've perhaps never listened to British radio and so on. . . . If the war had ended somehow in 1940 . . . or the Nazis had somehow vanished in the 20 July coup, the nation would've been in a bad way. . . . It was lucky [how things turned out] . . . and when I think about my East/West experiences . . . I have to say, we've become a bit friendlier and more relaxed than in East Germany . . . not that the Germans will win an Oscar for friendliness and politeness any time soon, but the [Anglo-American] influence *has* done a lot.[47]

Although Bistop acknowledged that war may be unjustified and that World War II devastated both societies and individuals, West Berliners rarely echoed the strong antiwar sentiments asserted by the SED state in the 1950s and identified by eastern cohort members as one of the persistent problems of western society. In fact, for Bistop, the passage of time has proven that this particular war was fortuitous in its consequences. Unification—and personal experience before and since—has proven what he long suspected. In the big picture, total war made possible necessary changes in German society. Looking back, the 1989 *Wende* has allowed westerners to begin reincorporating political developments into personal narratives because the one now legitimizes the other. Unification proved more than ever that Berliners chose wisely when they began pursuing ties to the West.

The passage of time also allowed cohort members to compare themselves with other generations. Having constructed their own sense of normalcy, they compared their values with those of younger cohorts that lack the formative experience of World War II and the Hunger Years.

I always said to my children, I wish you everything in the world except war . . . and I always [did my best], although things were really bad sometimes, I thought, "They should have it better, and they shouldn't notice how difficult I found it. . . ." And then my daughters, they spoiled their children so much; at Christmas I always thought, "They'll be so spoiled later on; is that all necessary?" but I never trusted myself to say they were overdoing things. . . . They had to limit themselves when they were young and perhaps they wanted to give their kids something better.[48]

Gently critiquing their children's values and actions, interviewees also pointed out how my own youthfulness has imposed structure upon their experiences and memories. Only a post-68er, several cohort members suggested, could blithely ask questions about youths' leisure habits, as if all were entitled to personal space and hours of unstructured free time. At the same time, interviewees criticized their parents' generation for similarly lacking an awareness of sociopolitical parameters and dangers.

I must say, *we* never let ourselves be so influenced by things, so that we took one [viewpoint] as gospel; rather, we were always critical in our evaluations... otherwise the *Wende* 1990 wouldn't have been possible. . . . My mother, she never saw things as critically as I. . . . She took what she got and tried to deal with it. *We* saw things critically, had a totally different perspective.[49]

Still vague, and even protective of his mother's relationship to the Nazi regime, Zelle finally, after half a century, found opportunity to articulate what made his cohort so different. Learning at an early age to question official rhetoric and maintain a critical distance served him well, first in the 1940s, then in the GDR, and now in a reunited German state.

Such intergenerational comparisons also allowed interviewees to confront stereotypes about their own cohort and to challenge the labels of "lost" or "skeptical." Asked to comment on such generalities at the end of often lengthy, detailed, and sometimes emotional narratives that emphasized their initiative and self-sufficiency, they rarely accepted broad generalizations, but through introspection, did engage some broader issues that inform modern historical scholarship and studies of the German past.

First and most obviously, they breached the issue of memory's malleability. Knowing I was most interested in postwar experiences did not stop interviewees from offering sometimes lengthy stories about growing up in the Reich. These accounts highlighted the niches in which children exist, while also asserting a distance from the shadow of the Holocaust. Given the intense debates about German complicity and complacency, interviewees have likely clung to, and perhaps enhanced, these images of childhood innocence to assert distance from Nazism.

That said, the successor states' conflicting interpretations of Germany's Nazi and postwar history seemed to be of little interest to cohort members, who admittedly have had little occasion to formally study the recent past.[50] Rather than acknowledging how societal pressures reshape history, interviewees engaged the mutually informing relationship between memory and the passage of time on a personal level, recognizing their own susceptibility to recoloring the past and romanticizing their youth.

Youth, regardless how difficult, is the best time of life. It's perhaps more difficult stricter, if like me one's at the front, but you repress that quickly afterwards, forget it . . . one thing is clear, i.e. the first years after the war, you can't get rid of that; I still dream about [my work with] DEFA. Everything you lived so intensely, you can't forget that. You can't prove it, or [even really] understand it if you weren't there.[51]

On the other hand, most inherently trusted their memories. They readily admitted having forgotten some things or perhaps making light of others, but generally believed in their ability to recall accurately what they do remember, particularly about this period of their lives.[52] Dinkel's comment about clearly recalling intense experiences is supported by researchers in the field of social psychology, who have identified a "memory bulge" of increased content and accuracy for events that occurred when subjects were roughly twelve to twenty-five years old.[53] While such studies also support free narrative interview models and offer tools to evaluate the reliability of recollections, they have difficulty addressing how either historical context individuals or the passage of time contributes to memory formation.[54] Cooperative efforts between historians and psychologists might help overcome such hurdles. Historians, for example, could offer case studies to offset the artificiality of short-term laboratory settings. Social psychologists, in exchange, might help historians distinguish between "wild fabrication" and "sober report" as they study oral sources, and understand how individuals and groups negotiate between realities of the past and necessities of the present. Such collaboration could help historians more fully understand both content and structure of remembered accounts and explain contradictions between oral and archival sources.[55]

Cohort members also engaged questions of progress in history and, most explicitly, the "crisis of modernity" that has long troubled western society. As noted above, this cohort demonstrated no particular interest in the modernization question as it relates to Hitler, asking, "Was Nazism modern?" Rather, they articulated broader questions, such as the propensity of rapid social change to produce hypocrites.

There was this girl [in our class, Gisela], she was *Mädelführerin* or something in the BDM, and she always told us all the things she'd done. And she said to me, "What do you do in the BDM?"

"Oh, I'm not in the organization."

"What, you're not in it?!"
"No, why should I be?"

"As a German girl, You should be ashamed!"

And the joke is, when it became East and West here after the war, a friend [of mine], Uschi, she had a wonderful voice . . . and often when the FDJ had programs . . . she'd sing, operettas and such. And she invited us to come once. And there I met Gisela B. who'd told me I should be ashamed [there she stood] with a *blue* shirt on. . . . I said, "Hello Gisela," and she got such a red face. "Hello, oh sorry, I don't have time," and zip, she was gone . . . just changed colors [from brown to blue]; I'd never have believed it if you'd told me she'd end up with the communists. She said herself that she'd kill herself if Hitler was dead . . . and then FDJ leader!?!⁵⁶

Having twice experienced how people around them have responded to political transition and new tensions, cohort members seemed sympathetic to individuals' need to construct niches in which to nurture stability and protect identity. Unlike those who identify such niches as characteristic of private life in the GDR or of authoritarian societies, interviewees suggested niche construction may be an element of modern society in general. Bistop (a West Berliner) presented this idea most directly, as he sought to generalize about his youth.

I never found it so awful that I couldn't muddle through somehow. . . . You have to find holes, in [any] system that exerts pressure. I think it was Thornton Wilder who said that. Individuals develop the positive within themselves only out of necessity . . . you have to wall yourself off. . . . And the wider the circles [in which you move], the more you have to put on masks and disguise yourself.⁵⁷

Cohort members' coping strategies suggest that one response to the crisis of modernization, that is, to the increasingly rapid pace of daily life and societal change, the disintegration of traditional social rites, and the blurring of private and public spheres, is the construction of private niches. Such sanctuaries are both physical and mental, consisting of both personal living space and independent identities, and offer the opportunity for a sense of normalcy that can persist through social turmoil and transitions. Interviewees' accounts of the postwar years highlighted efforts to create these niches or "micro-environments"; they often described distancing themselves from imposed institutional structures and questioning public rhetoric. This same strategy may protect individuals from the increasingly rapid transformation of external environments and simultaneous apparent blurring of behavioral norms that characterize the contemporary world.⁵⁸

Finally, interviewees addressed what it means to "be young." On the one hand, their definitions were caught up in concerns about modernization, as nostalgia for the past merges with critical commentaries about the present. Observing how today's young Berliners flock to shopping centers, movie theaters, and concerts or expect parents to underwrite vacation trips, cohort members observed that "my way wasn't so wrong." Others expressed dismay at contemporary youths' seemingly high expectations of the social welfare state, wondering whatever happened to the value of personal initiative and self-reliance. At the same time, most cohort members, even those who were raped or conceived children out of wedlock, asserted a sense of sexual naïveté, through comments such as "going off in couples was taboo," or "I didn't know anything; I was just a child." Such comments not only defied archival reports depicting the cohort's overt or latent immorality, but also distinguish this cohort—at least in their own minds—from later generations and contemporary youths in particular.

On the other hand, interviewees also questioned the "essence" of youth—that which links experiences of young people across temporal and geographic boundaries. They were curious about others' interpretations of their cohort's past and thoughtfully engaged questions about having "lost" their youth. All but a few denied the relevancy of such statements. Bistop, for example, acknowledged that life was difficult at times, but concluded, "I can't say that through want and hunger, I lost my youth to the Nazi period *or* the postwar period; I did all those things that belong to youth."[59]

What "belongs to youth," they seemed to have concluded, is less a matter of external conditions than mindset. Cohort members cultivated a frame of mind that has enabled them to feel self-reliant (distancing themselves from parents and making their own decisions), to have fun (chatting in the sunshine or dancing), and to create, at least retrospectively, their own collective stability. This cohort's youth experience does more than put a human face on the confusion and hardship of the Hunger Years. It also sheds light on the assertions of independence and search for meaning that, despite imposed parameters, impart social significance on this particular lifestage and unite cohort members with prior and future generations.[60]

This cohort was exploited under Hitler, then lost the support of stable social structures and witnessed dramatic transformation of their home town. Nonetheless, cohort members have constructed for themselves a youth complete with leisure activities, assertions of independence, and rites of passage, that is, a surprisingly normal transition from childhood dependency to adult autonomy. More important, in part because history and society have made it so difficult to explain the 1930s and 1940s as "normal," this cohort devoted its youth to the pursuit of personal normalcy, to "just being young." Postwar Berlin's sociopolitical parameters and subsequent development necessarily shaped the very nature of that constructed normalcy. Cohort members' enthusiastic memories of "that very rich period" were rooted in collective images of youth, lessons of their own past, and year of living normal lives despite Berlin's abnormal division.

NOTES

1. Kanter, 23–24.
2. Most specifically, several interviewees criticized Karl-Heinz Füssl's 1994 study of relationships between German youth and Allied occupation forces, questioning both sources and interpretations of the GYA program.
3. Although not unique to this cohort, the sense of continuity is more apparent because their lives were so far removed from the political sphere. A slightly older cohort would have been more conscious of events like *Kristallnacht*, as well as domestic or international reactions to National Socialist policies and military actions. On the depoliticization of memories of the Nazi period, see: Ulrich Herbert, "Good Times, Bad Times: Memories of the Third Reich," in Richard Bessel, ed., *Life in the Third Reich* (Oxford: Oxford University Press, 1987); Alexander von Plato,

"The Hitler Youth Generation and Its Role in the Two Post-war German States," in Mark Roseman, ed., *Generations in Conflict* (New York: Cambridge University Press, 1995).

4. Botcheva, 113. Arno Klönne has argued that the most significant effect of the HJ was not that it imposed Nazi ideology per se, but rather that it discouraged critical political thinking and experimentation. Klönne also argues that the HJ eliminated the opportunity for adolescence (i.e., denying individuals the gradual transformation of youth). See: Arno Klönne, *Jugend im Dritten Reich—die Hitler Jugend und ihre Gegner. Dokumente und Analysen.* (Düsseldorf: Elgen Diderichs Verlag, 1982).

5. The reparations question, for example, led to much inter-Allied wrangling and a split from the previous decision to treat Germany as a single economic unit.

6. Christoph Kleßmann, *Die doppelte Staatsgründung* (Bonn: Bundeszentrale für politische Bildung, 1986), 299–301; Henry Krisch, *The German Democratic Republic: The Search for Identity* (Boulder: Westview Press, 1985).

7. This backward-looking rhetoric was also due to the fact that many activists hoped to revive parties of the Weimar era.

8. Vivian C. Seltzer, *The Psychological Worlds of the Adolescent: Public and Private* (New York: John Wiley and Sons, 1989), 18.

9. Birkmann, 1–2.

10. Mary Fulbrook, *German National Identity after the Holocaust* (Cambridge: Polity Press, 1999), 108–10, 156–57. See also: Konrad H. Jarausch, ed. *Zwischen Parteilichkeit und Professionalität: Bilanz der Geschichtswissenschaft der DDR.* (Berlin: Akademie Verlag, 1991); Georg G. Iggers, *New Directions in European Historiography* (Middletown, CT: Wesleyan University Press, 1984); ibid., ed., *Marxist Historiography in Transformation: East German Social History in the 1980s* (New York: Berg, 1991).

11. The Allies' hands-on control of policy and administration contrasted intentionally with the terms imposed on Germany in 1918.

12. Kleßmann, 298.

13. For example, reflecting back on the problems of Weimar, the 1948–1949 parliamentary council reduced the power of the federal president, established the so-called five percent hurdle, and permitted only constructive no confidence votes (before voting out a cabinet, the opposition had to demonstrate the capacity to bring in a new one that was capable of governing). See: V.R. Berghahn, *Modern Germany: Society, Economy, and Politics in the Twentieth Century* (New York: Cambridge University Press, 1987); David P. Conradt, *The German Polity* (New York: Longman, 1989).

14. Krisch (1985); Childs (1988). Krisch points out that the GDR was not based on popular legitimacy, but rather on the specific goals of the SED. Childs sees the GDR of the 1980s as having established economic legitimacy after fluctuations throughout the postwar period and using economic concessions to counter political severity.

15. Louise J. Kaplan, *Adolescence—the Farewell to Childhood* (New York: Simon and Schuster, 1984), 14.

16. Grof, "Rites of Passage: A Necessary Step toward Wholeness," in Louis Carus Mahdi, Nacny Geyer Christopher and Michael Meade, eds., *Crossroads: The Quest for Contemporary Rites of Passage* (Chicago: Open Court, 1996), 4–5. For comparison, see: Luba Botcheva, "The Gains and Losses of Bulgarian Youths during the Transition from Socialism to Democracy: A Longitudinal Study," in Jari-Erik Nurmi, ed., *Adolescents, Cultures and Conflicts—Growing Up in Contemporary Europe* (New York: Garland Publishing, 1998).

17. Again, Kanter constitutes the chief exception to this generalization, asserting her parents' guidance throughout her childhood and youth.

18. Joseph Campbell quoted in Grof, 5–6; Louise J. Kaplan, *Adolescence—the Farewell to Childhood* (New York: Simon and Schuster, 1984), 19.

19. Claire Wallace and Sijka Kovatcheva, *Youth in Society: The Construction and Deconstruction of Youth in East and West Europe* (New York: St. Martin's Press, 1998), 3.

20. Völker, 8.

21. Arnold van Gennep, *The Rites of Passage* (London: Routledge and Kegan Paul, 1977). Also: Grof; Joseph Kett, *Rites of Passage: Adolescence in America 1790 to the Present* (New York: Basic Books, Inc., 1977).

22. Gerald R. Adams and Thomas Gullotta, *Adolescent Life Experiences* (Pacific Grove, CA: Brooks/Cole Publishing Company, 1989), 7. See also: S.N. Eisenstadt, "Archetypal Patterns of Youth," in Erik Erikson, ed., *Youth: Change and Challenge* (New York: Basic Books, 1963), 24. Evaluating social competency is also a response to postmodern arguments questioning the existence of a stable adult self and, consequently, a single transition in identity. Stephen Baron, Sheila Riddell, and Alastair Wilson, "The Secret of Eternal Youth: Identity, Risk and Learning Difficulties," in *British Journal of Sociology of Education* 20:4 (December 1999), 483–99.

23. Grof, ibid. Also Michael Meade, "Introduction" In Mahdi, Christopher, and Meade (1996), xxi–xxv; Johanna Wyn and Peter Dwyer, "New Directions in Research on Youth in Transition," in *Journal of Youth Studies* 2:1 (February 1999), 5–21.

24. Winkert, 1–2. Although the Third Reich took the connection between youth transition and nationalism to an extreme, recent research suggests that, at least in Europe, the passage of youth has been closely linked to ideas about the nation throughout the last century. Jean Charles Lagree, "Youth in Europe: Cultural Patterns of Transition," in *Berkeley Journal of Sociology* 41 (1996–1997) 67–101; Gill Hubbard, "The Usefulness of Indepth Life History Interviews for Exploring the Role of Social Structure and Human Agency in Youth Transitions," in *Sociological Research Online* 4:4 (http://www.socresonline.org.uk/4/4/hubbard.html), 6 August 2003.

25. Dinkel, 14.

26. Martin Bloom, "The Psychosocial Constructs of Social Competency," in Thomas P. Gullotta, Gerald R. Adams, and Raymond Montemayor, eds., *Developing Social Competency in Adolescence* (London: Sage Publications, 1990), 11; Gary Peterson and Geoffry K. Leigh, "The Family and Social Competence in Adolescence," in ibid., 98.

27. This is particularly true for women.

28. Rippe, 16; Tinker, 12–14.

29. Barthe, 19–20, quoted at length in Interlude I. See also: Bruno Bettelheim, "The Problem of Generations," in Erikson (1963), 64–92.

30. Barthe, 9.

31. Pestopf, 1–2. Also: Peterson and Leigh, 124–125; Eisenstadt, 30–31.

32. Birkmann, 15. Also: Kanter, 17–18.

33. Freiburg and Mahrad (1982), 160–61; Robert Goeckel, *The Lutheran Church and the East German State* (Ithaca: Cornell University Press, 1990); Gregory Wegner, "In the Shadow of the Third Reich: The Jugendstunde and the Legitimation of Anti-fascist Heroes for East German Youth," *German Studies Review* 19:1 (1996), 127–146.

34. Although this ceremony had roots in the Weimar Republic and in workers' movements of earlier eras, it had never been adopted by the Soviet Union and was not

particularly associated with socialism. Relatively few of this cohort personally took part in the *Jugendweihe*, but by the end of the 1950s, nearly 95 percent of East German youths participated, and cohort members do seem to recognize it as a social rite of passage. By 1954, the regime had been attacking the *Junge Gemeinde* movement, which it recognized as offering a last alternative to the FDJ, for more than five years. *DDR Handbuch* (1979), 449.

35. Klinkert, 9–10. Also: Zelle, 16.

36. The post-1989 persistence of the *Jugendweihe* as a coming of age ritual testifies to the significance it has come to have in socialist society; Wegner suggests it symbolizes a resistance to the century-long church monopoly over rites of passage. Wegner, ibid.

37. Kaspar D. Naegele, "Youth and Society: Some Observations," in Erikson (1963), 54.

38. Zelle, 11.

39. Birkmann, 8-9.

40. Such labels, of course, impose broad generalities on populations comprised of many unique groups and individuals. Even when speaking only of East Berliners and West Berliners, they risk reducing infinite variations of experiences to collective stereotype. However, the East/West identity is one of the ways Berliners (and most adult Germans) identify themselves. See Fulbrook (1999), 150–53.

41. Zelle, 21.

42. Rippe, 7-8.

43. Rippe, 8.

44. Klinkert, 26.

45. Gisela Helwig suggests that the rights of women are one realm in which easterners assert the GDR's progressivism and explain their loyalty. See: Gisela Helwig and Hildegard M. Nickel, eds., *Frauen in Deutschland 1945–1992* (Berlin: Akademie Verlag, 1993).

46. Zelle, 26–27. At the time of my last visit, the *Zeitzeugenbörse*, established to bring together researchers and elderly Berliners willing to share their experiences, had only a very few West Berliners in its database. One staff member had begun a workshop series intended to stimulate conversation between former teachers from East and West, but reported that the recruited West Berliners rarely came to the meetings.

47. Bistop, 24–25.

48. Pastler, 35. Frau Pastler lost her husband just after the birth of her second child, and shortly thereafter was treated for cancer.

49. Zelle, 21.

50. While a good number of interviewees attended school after 1945, the immediate past (i.e., the Nazi era) was not part of Berlin's school curriculum until at least 1948. Instructional and cultural magazines from the period, such as *Horizont* in the West and *Junge Generation* in the East, contain biographical and even historical essays, but focus on recovering or reinterpreting the nineteenth century. See Wegner (1990).

51. Dinkel, 14. Maurice Halbwachs, *On Collective Memory*, trans. Lewis A. Coser (Chicago: University of Chicago Press, 1992), 49; Karl Mannheim, cited in Howard Schuman and Jacqueline Scott, "Generations and Collective Memories," *American Sociological Review* 54 (June 1989), 359; Gugleilmo Bellelli and Mirella Amatulli, "Nostalgia, Immigration and Collective Memory," in James W. Pennebaker, Dario Paez, and Bernard Rime, eds., *Collective Memory of Political Events: Social Psychological Perspectives* (Mahwah, NJ: Lawrence Erlbaum Associates, 1997), Ch. 10.

52. Halbwachs suggests that most societies view the remembering and interpreting of the past as one of the elderly's primary social functions. Halbwachs, 48–50; Edward R. Hirt, Hugh E. McDonald and Keith D. Markman "Expectancy Effects in Reconstructive Memory: When the Past Is Just What We Expected," in Steven Jay Lynn and Kevin M. McConkey, eds., *Truth in Memory* (New York: Guilford Press, 1998), 62.

53. L.R. Berney and D.B. Blane, "Collecting Retrospective Data: Accuracy of Recall after 50 Years Judged Against Historical Records," *Social Science Medicine* 45:10 (1997), 1519–25; Martin Conway, "The Inventory of Experience: Memory and Identity," in Pennebaker et al., eds., Ch. 2; Pennebaker and Becky L. Banasik, "On the Creation and Maintenance of Collective Memories History as Social Psychology," in ibid., Ch. 1; Howard Schuman, Robert Belli, and Katherine Bischoping, "The Generational Basis of Historical Knowledge," in ibid., Ch. 3.

54. Edward R. Hirt, Hugh E. McDonald, and Keith D. Markman, "Expectancy Effects in Reconstructive Memory. When the Past is Just What We Expected," in Steven Jay Lynn and Kevin M. McConkey, eds., *Truth in Memory* (New York: Guilford Press, 1998), 62–89; Norbert Schwarz, Hans-J. Hippler, and Elisabeth Noelle-Neumann, "Retrospective Reports: The Impact of Response Formats," in Norbert Schwarz and Seymour Sudman, eds., *Autobiographical Memory and the Validity of Retrospective Reports* (New York: Springer Verlag, 1994), Ch. 12.

55. Examples of promising moves in this more integrative approach: Lupicinio Iniguez, Jose Valencia and Felix Vazquez, "The Construction of Remembering and Forgetfulness: Memories and Histories of the Spanish Civil War," in Pennebaker, Ch. 12.

56. Barthe, 12.

57. Bistop, 24.

58. Botcheva, 112–114. Botcheva defines four developmental environments: macro (broad society), exo (institutions, regulations, etc.), meso (direct community), and micro (relationships and roles) and is interested in how the most intimate (one's micro-environment) reflects changes in the others.

59. Bistop, 24.

60. Grof, 4–5, Kaplan, 19.

Selected Bibliography

ARCHIVES AND COLLETIONS

Archiv für Berliner Schulgeschichte, Freie Universität Berlin. Tracy Strong Collection. I/238, 17/65, I/136.

Berliner Geschichtswerkstatt. Uncatalogued collection, recorded interviews.

Bezirksarchiv Kreuzberg. Uncatalogued collection, exhibit materials.

Bezirksarchiv Neukölln. 1277, 1967, 1974, 1977, wall newspaper collection.

Bundesarchiv Potsdam. DC-4.

Deutsches Institut für Internationale Pädagogische Forschung—Bibliothek für Bildungsgeschichtliche Forschung und Forschungsstelle Berlin. FDJ collection.

Deutsches Rundfunk Archiv—Standort Berlin Historisches Archiv. B202-00-01, B 202-00-06, B204-02-01, B203-02-06, B204-02-06.

Diakonisches Werk Archiv. EKD, Berlin, ADW, Hb-B 62.

Heimatgeschichtliche Sammlung Lichtenberg. Uncatalogued collection.

Heimatmuseum Charlottenburg. Uncatalogued exhibit materials, interview transcriptions, recorded oral accounts.

Heimatmuseum Friedrichshain. Uncatalogued exhibit materials.

Hoover Institute Archives. TS National Socialism Y67.

Kreuzberg Museum für Stadtentwicklung und Sozialgeschichte. Uncatalogued exhibit materials.

Landesarchiv Berlin. Rep 1 Acc 889, Rep 15 Acc 1431, Rep 118, Rep 120, Rep 135/1, Rep 206 Acc 3070, Rep 207 Acc 3075, B-Rep 13 Acc 1046, B-Rep 13 Acc 1160, B-Rep 13 Acc 1327, C-Rep 900, C-Rep 900 IV L-2/10/397, STA Rep 101, STA Rep 135/1, I/3/9/096, I/3/2/064, I/3/9/111, I/20/040.

Prenzlauer Berg Museum für Heimatgeschichte und Stadtkultur. Uncataloged exhibit materials.

SAPMO Bibliothek FDJ 182, 3333, 3404, 3646.

Stiftung Archiv der Parteien und Massenorganisationen der DDR im Bundesarchiv (SAPMO). DY 24/115, DY 24/802, DY 24/1334, DY 30/IV 2/16, DY 34/23219, DY 34/20255, DY 4090/515, NY 4036/727, NY 4090/515, NY 4090/516.

ORIGINAL INTERVIEWS

Note: Per my agreement with interviewees, all but two have been rendered anonymous
through the use of pseudonyms. I also quoted from the preinterview surveys,
which are in my possession; such references are indicated in the relevant notes.

Barthe, 24 April 1998
Binkert, 11 and 19 December 1997
Birkmann, 4 and 8 December 1997
Bistop, 23 March 1998
Burkhardt, 21 January 1998
Dinkel, 2 and 6 February 1998
Distel, 12 March, 5 and 12 May 1998
Gottwald 19 March 1998
Heinemann, 10 February 1998
Hirsch, 30 December 1997
Kanter, 2 April 1998
Kestler, 3 April 1998
King, 17 December 1997
Klinkert, 24 January 1998
Kösel, 6 March 1998
Middler, 13 January 1998
Miller, 24 March 1998
Mostel, 16 March 1998
Pastler, 5 March 1998
Pelsdorf, 9 March 1998
Pestopf, 15 May 1998
Quade, 19 February 1998
Rennebach, 27 February and 30 April 1998
Rippe, 7 May 1998
Schäfer, 26 March 1998
Schneider, 2 March 1998
Stumpf, 19 January 1998
Tinker, 25 March 1998
Völker (as a couple), 23 January 1998
Winkert, 17 February 1998
Zelle, 10 March 1998

PERSONAL ACCOUNTS, DIARIES, AND NOVELS

Andreas-Friedrich, Ruth. *Battleground Berlin, Diaries 1945–1948* . New York: Paragon
House, 1990.
Beilmann, Christel. *Eine katholische Jugend in Gottes und dem Dritten Reich. Briefe,
Berichte, Gedrucktes 1930–1945. Kommentare 1988/89*. Wuppertal: Peter Hammer
Verlag, 1989.
Boveri, Margaret. *Tage des Überlebens*. Munich: R. Piper, 1977.
Brückner, Peter. *Das Abseits als sicherer Ort. Kindheit und Jugend zwischen 1933 und
1945*. Berlin: Wagenbach, 1994.
Clay, Lucius. *Decision in Germany*. Garden City, NY: Doubleday, 1950.
de Bruyn, Günter. *Zwischenbilanz. Eine Jugend in Berlin*. Frankfurt: Fischer
Taschenbuch Verlag, 1997.

Dolata, Werner. *Chronik einer Jugend. Katholische Jugend im Bistum Berlin 1936–49*. Hildesheim: Bernwar Verlag GmbH, 1988.

Erman, Hans. *Bei Kempinski. Aus der Chronik einer Weltstadt*. Munich: List Verlag, 1965.

Geuelmann, Rolf. *Wie aus Feinde Freunde wurden*. Berlin: Bezirksamt Steglitz, 1993.

Heck, Alfons. *A Child of Hitler—Germany in the Days When God Wore a Swastika*. Frederick, CO: Renaissance House, 1985.

Herman-Friede, Eugen. *Für Freudensprünge keine Zeit. Erinnerungen an Illegalität und Aufbegehren 1942–1948*. Berlin: Metropol Verlag, 1991.

Hermand, Jost. *Als Pimpf in Polen. Erweiterte KLV 1940–45*. Frankfurt am Main: Fischer Taschenbuch Verlag, 1993.

Höcker, Karla. *Die letzten und die ersten Tage. Berliner Aufzeichnungen 1945*. Berlin: Verlag Bruno Hessling, 1966.

Holmsten, Georg. *Berliner Miniaturen. Großstadtmelodie*. Berlin: Deutsche Buchvertriebs- und Verlagsgesellschaft, 1946.

Honecker, Erich. *From My Life*. New York: Pergamon Books, 1981.

Krollpfeiffer, Hannelore. *Damals in Berlin*. Munich: Knaur, 1997.

Kubitza, Liselotte. "Die Luftbrücke." 1997 [photocopy].

Kunstamt Kreuzberg and Kreuzberg Museum, eds. *Kürbisse im Böcklerpark. MuseumbesucherInnen erzählen von Kriegsende und Neubeginn*. Berlin: Gerike, 1995.

Kupffer, Heinrich. *Swingtime. Chronik einer Jugend in Deutschland 1937–1951*. Berlin: Verlag Frieling & Partner GmbH, 1987.

Maschenmann, Melitta. *Fazit. Mein Weg in die Hitlerjugend*. Munich: Deutscher Taschenbuch Verlag, 1980.

Riess, Curt. *Berlin Berlin 1945–1953*. Berlin-Grunewald: Non Stop-Bücherei, 1953.

Ronke, Christa. "Eine Jugend in Kriegs- und Nachkriegszeit." Undated manuscript (photocopy).

Schemmann, Christine. *Wie man kleine Nazis Machte*. Berlin: Frieling, 1996.

Schirmer, Ruth. *Berlin dritter Akt*. Tübingen: Rainer Wunderlich Verlag, 1965.

Schneider, Peter. *Der Mauerspringer: Erzählung*. Hamburg: Leuchterhand, 1984.

Schumann, Walter. *Being Present: Growing Up in Hitler's Germany*. Kent, OH: Kent State University Press, 1991.

Shelton, Regina Maria. *To Lose a War: Memories of a German Girl*. Carbondale: Southern Illinois University Press, 1980.

Sprechen nach dem Schweigen. Kreuzberger Lebensberichte aus den Jahren 1933–1945. Berlin: Nachbarschaftsheim Urbanstraße, 1991.

Studnitz, Hans-Georg von. *While Berlin Burns: The Diary of Hans-Georg von Studnitz 1943–1945*. Englewood Cliffs, NJ: Prentice-Hall, 1965.

von der Grün, Max. *Wie war das eigentlich? Kindheit und Jugend im Dritten Reich*. Darmstadt: Luchterhand, 1983.

Wildberger, Erich. *Ring über Ostkreuz*. Hamburg: Rowohlt Verlag, 1953.

OTHER SOURCES

Adams, Gerald R., and Thomas Gullotta. *Adolescent Life Experiences*. Pacific Grove, CA: Brooks/Cole Publishing Company, 1989.

Alter, Peter. "Das Nationalbewußtsein der Deutschen: Entwicklungslinien und Anfragen." In *Geschichtsbewußtsein der Deutschen. Materialien zur Spurensuche einer Nation*, ed. Werner Weidenfeld, 97–110. Cologne: Verlag Wissenschaft und Politik, 1987.

Badstübner, Rolf, and Wilfried Loth, eds. *Wilhelm Pieck. Aufzeichnungen zur Deutschlandpolitik 1945-1953.* Berlin: Akademie Verlag, 1994.

Bark, Dennis. *Die Berlin-Frage 1949–1955.* Berlin: Walter de Gruyter, 1972.

Baumeister, Roy, and Stephen Hastings. "Distortions of Collective Memory: How Groups Flatter and Deceive Themselves." In *Collective Memory of Political Events: Social Psychological Perspectives,* ed. James W. Pennebaker, Dario Paez and Bernard Rime, Ch. 13. Mahwah, NJ: Lawrence Erlbaum Associates, 1997.

Bellelli, Guglielmo, and Mirella Amatulli. "Nostalgia, Immigration and Collective Memory." In *Collective Memory of Political Events: Social Psychological Perspectives,* ed. James W. Pennebaker, Dario Paez and Bernard Rime, Ch. 10. Mahwah, NJ: Lawrence Erlbaum Associates, 1997.

Benz, Ute, and Wolfgang Benz. *Sozialisation und Traumatisierung. Kinder in der Zeit des Nationalsozialismus.* Frankfurt am Main: Fischer Taschenbuch Verlag, 1992.

Berghahn, V.R. *Modern Germany: Society, Economy, and Politics in the Twentieth Century.* New York: Cambridge University Press, 1987.

Berlin Geschichtswerkstatt. *Vom Lagerfeuer zur Musikbox. Jugendkulturen 1900 bis 1960.* Berlin: Geschichtswerkstatt, e.V., 1985.

Berlin in Zahlen. Berlin: Das Neue Berlin, 1947.

Berney, L.R., and D.B. Blane. "Collecting Retrospective Data: Accuracy of Recall after 50 Years Judged against Historical Records." *Social Science Medicine* 45 (1997): 1519–25.

Bezirksamt Charlottenburg, ed. *Kinderlandverschickung 1940–1945. Texte zur Ausstellung.* Berlin: Bezirksamt Charlottenburg, 1997.

Bezirksvorstand und Fraktion der PDS Friedrichshain. *Ausgangspunkt Chaos. Vom Neubeginn rund um den Schlesischen Bahnhof, Mai und Juni 1945—der Tobias Nachlaß.* Berlin: paper point kassner, undated.

Bias-Engel, Sigrid. *Zwischen Wandervogel und Wissenschaft: zur Geschichte von Jugendbewegung und Studentenschaft 1896–1920.* Cologne: Verlag Wissenschaft und Politik, 1988.

Boll, Friedhelm. *Auf der Suche nach Demokratie. Britische und deutsche Jugendinitiativen in Niedersachsen nach 1945.* Bonn: Dietz Verlag, 1995.

Borkowski, Dieter. *Wer weiss ob wir uns wiedersehen.* Frankfurt: Fischer Verlag, 1980.

Botcheva, Luba. "The Gains and Losses of Bulgarian Youths during the Transition from Socialism to Democracy: A longitudinal Study." In *Adolescents, Cultures and Conflicts—Growing Up in Contemporary Europe,* ed. Jari-Erik Nurmi, Ch. 5. New York: Garland Publishing, 1998.

Brandenburg, Hans-Christian. *Die Geschichte der HJ – Wege und Irrwege einer Generation.* 2nd edition. Cologne: Verlag Wissenschaft und Politik, 1982.

Braungart, Richard G. "Historical Generations and Youth Movements: A Theoretical Perspective." *Research in Social Movements* 6 (1984): 95–142.

Breuilly, John. *The State of Germany.* London: Longman, 1992.

Breyvogel, Wilfried, ed. *Piraten, Swings und Junge Garde. Jugendwiderstand im Nationalsozialismus.* Bonn: Dietz Verlag, 1991.

Bridenthal, Renate, Atina Grossmann, and Marion Kaplan, eds. *When Biology Became Destiny: Women in Weimar and Nazi Germany.* New York: Monthly Review Press, 1984.

Brücher, Bodo. *Die sozialistische Jugendbewegung Deutschlands. Politisch-pädigogischer Konzept und Realität sozialistischer Jugend und Erziehungsarbeit in den Nachkriegsjahren.* Werther i. W.: Paegelit Verlag, 1995.

Bude, Heinz. *Deutsche Karrieren: Lebenskonstruktionen sozialer Aufstieger aus der Flakhelfer-Generation.* Frankfurt: Suhrkamp Verlag, 1987.

Bundesministerium für Gesamtdeutsche Fragen. *SBZ von 1945 bis 1954*. Bonn: Deutscher Bundes-Verlag, 1956.

Burkert, Hans-Norbert, Klaus Mataßek and Doris Obschernitzki. *Zerstört Besiegt Befreit. Der Kampf um Berlin bis zur Kapitulation 1945*. Stätten der Geschichte Berlins Band 7. Berlin: Hentrich, 1985.

Büro für Gesamtberliner Fragen. *Berlin Sowjetsektor. Die politische, rechtliche, wirtschaftliche, soziale und kulturelle Entwicklung in acht Berliner Bezirken*. Berlin: Colloquium Verlag, 1965.

Childs, David. *The GDR: Moscow's German Ally*. Boston: Unwin Hyman, 1988.

Conradt, Sylvia and Kirsten Heckmann-Janz, *Berlin halb und halb. Von Frontstädtlern, Grenzgänger und Mauerspechten*. Frankfurt am Main: Leuchterhand, 1990.

DuBois-Reymond, Manuela. " 'I Don't Want to Commit Myself Yet': Young People's Life Concepts." *Journal of Youth Studies* 1, no. 1 (February 1998): 63–79.

Dunaway, David K., and Willa K. Baum, eds. *Oral History: An Interdisciplinary Anthology*. Nashville: American Association for State and Local History, 1984.

Elkins, T.H. *Berlin: The Spatial Structure of a Divided City*. New York: Methuen, 1988.

Epstein, Catherine. "The Production of 'Official Memory' in East Germany: Old Communists and the Dilemma of Memoir Writing." *Central European History* 32, no. 2 (1999): 181–201.

Fischer-Rosenthal, Wolfram, and Peter Alheit, eds. *Biographien in Deutschland: soziologische Rekonstruktionen gelebter Gesellschaftsgeschichte*. Opladen: Westdeutscher Verlag, 1995.

Flemming, Thomas. "Besatzer und Besetzte." In *Die wirren Jahre Deutschland 1945–1948*, ed. Jürgen Engert, 10–49. Berlin: Argon, 1996.

Forschungsinstitut der Deutschen Gesellschaft für Auswärtige Politik, e.V. *Dokumenten zur Berlin-Frage 1944–1962*. Munich: R. Oldenbourg Verlag, 1962.

Franciso, Ronald A., and Richard L. Merritt, eds. *Berlin Between Two Worlds*. Boulder: Westview Press, 1985.

Fulbrook, Mary. *The Divided Nation*. New York: Oxford University Press, 1992.

———. *German National Identity after the Holocaust*. Cambridge: Polity Press, 1999.

Füssl, Karl-Heinz. *Die Umerziehung der Deutschen, Jugend und Schule unter den Siegermächten des Zweiten Weltkriegs 1945–1955*. Paderborn: Ferdinand Schoeningh, 1994.

Gennep, Arnold von. *The Rites of Passage*. London: Routledge and Kegan Paul, 1977.

Gesamtdeutsches Institut, Bundesanstalt für gesamtdeutsche Aufgaben, ed. *Geteilte Hoffnung. Deutschland nach dem Kriege 1945–1949*. Lübeck: Wullenwever Druck, 1990.

Gimbel, John. *The American Occupation of Germany: Politics and the Military 1945–49*. Stanford: Stanford University Press, 1968.

Girbig, Werner. *Im Anflug auf die Reichshauptstadt. Die Dokumentation der Bombenangriffe auf Berlin, stellvertretend für alle deutsche. Städte*. Stuttgart: Motorbuch Verlag, 1970.

Gotschlich, Helga, ed. *Links und links und Schritt gehalten. Die FDJ: Konzepte, Abläufe, Grenzen*. Berlin: Metropol Verlag, 1994.

Gotschlich, Helga, and Edeltraud Schulze, eds. *Deutsche Teilung—deutsche Wiedervereinigung. Jugend und Jugendpolitik im Umbruch der Systeme*. Berlin: Metropol Verlag, 1996.

———, Katharina Lange and Edeltraud Schulze, eds. *Aber nicht im Gleichschritt: zur Entstehung der Freien Deutschen Jugend*. Berlin: Metropol Verlag, 1997.

Grathwol, Robert P., and Donita M. Moorhus. *Berlin and the American Military—a Cold War Chronicle*. Ed. Gareth L. Sleen. New York: New York University Press, 1999.

180   Selected Bibliography

Gravenhorst, Lerke, and Carmen Tatschmurat, eds. *Töchter-Fragen, NS Frauen Geschichte*. Freiburg: Kore, Verlag Traute Hensch, 1990.

Gröschel, Roland, and Michael Schmidt. *Trümmerkids und Gruppenstunde*. Berlin: Elefanten Press, 1990.

———. *Gruppenleben und politischer Aufbruch*. Berlin: Elefanten Verlag, 1993.

Grosinski, Klaus, and Mattias Schreyer. *Aus der Schule geplaudert. Schule und Schulalltag in Berlin in zweieinhalb Jahrhunderten* Berlin: Moritzdruck, 1994.

Grotum, Thomas. *Die Halbstarken. Zur Geschichte einer Jugendkultur der 50er Jahre*. New York: Campus Verlag, 1994.

Gullotta, Thomas P., Gerald R. Adams, and Raymond Montemayor, eds. *Developing Social Competency in Adolescence*. Newbury Park, CA: Sage Publications, 1990.

Hain, Simone. "Zwischen sowjetischer Europapolitik und linkem Nationalismus. Ein Versuch, sich der Stalinallee zu nähern." In *Berlin—Hauptstadt der DDR 1949–1989. Utopie und Realität*, ed. Bernd Wilczek, 33–51. Baden-Baden: Elster Verlag, 1995.

Hanauske, Dieter. *Sitzungsprotokolle des Magistrat der Stadt Berlin 1945–46*, Part I, 1945. Berlin: Berlin Verlag, 1995.

Heidelmeyer, Wofgang, and Günther Hindrichs, eds. *Documents on Berlin 1943–63*. Munich: Oldenbourg Verlag, 1963.

Heimann, Siegfried. *Die Falken in Berlin. Erziehungsgemeinschaft oder Kampforganisation? Die Jahre 1945–1950*. Berlin: Verlag für Ausbildung und Studium in der Elefanten Press, 1990.

Heinemann, Manfred, ed. *Erziehung und Schulung im Dritten Reich*. 2 vols. Stuttgart: Klett-Cotta, 1980.

Helwig, Gisela, and Hildegard M. Nickel, eds. *Frauen in Deutschland 1945–1992*. Bonn: Bundeszentrale für politische Bildung, 1993.

Henige, David. *Oral Historiography*. New York: Longman, 1982.

Herbert, Ulrich. "Good Times, Bad Times: Memories of the Third Reich." In *Life in the Third Reich*, ed. Richard Bessel, 97–110. Oxford: Oxford University Press, 1987.

Hermand, Jost. "All Power to the Women: Nazi Concepts of Matriarchy," *Journal of Contemporary History* 19, no. 4 (1984): 649–667.

Herrmann, Ulrich. "Das Konzept der 'Generation.' Ein Forschungs- und Erklärungsansatz für die Erziehungs- und Bildungssoziologie und die historische Sozialisationsforschung." Chap. in *Jugendpolitik in der Nachkriegszeit Zeitzeugen, Forschungsberichte, Dokumente*. Weinheim: Juventa, 1993.

Herzfeld, Hans. *Berlin in der Weltpolitik 1945–70*. New York: Walter de Gruyter, 1973.

Hilberg, Raul. *The Destruction of the European Jews*. New York: Holmes and Meier, 1983.

Hilzheimer, Achim. *Von der Frankfurter zur Stalinallee. Geschichte einer Straße*. Berlin: Heimatmuseum Friedrichshain, 1997.

Hirschfeld, Gerhard, ed. *The Policies of Genocide: Jews and Soviet Prisoners of War in Nazi Germany*. London: Allen and Unwin, 1986.

Hirt, Edward R., Hugh E. McDonald, and Keith D. Markman. "Expectancy Effects in Reconstructive Memory: When the Past is Just What We Expected." In *Truth in Memory*, ed. Steven Jay Lynn and Kevin M. McConkey, 62–89. New York: Guilford Press, 1998.

Hoecker, Beate. and Renate Meyer-Braun. *Bremerinnen bewältigen die Nachkriegszeit*. Bremen: Steintor, 1988.

Hoerning, Erika. "Memories of the Berlin Wall." *International Journal of Oral History* 8, no. 2 (1987): 95–111.

———. *Zwischen den Fronten. Berliner Grenzgänger und Grenzhändler 1948–1961*. Cologne: Böhlau Verlag, 1992.

Hohn, Maria. "Frau im Haus und Girl im Spiegel: Discourse on Women in the Interregnum Period of 1945–1949 and the Question of German Identity." *Central European History* 26, no. 1 (1993): 57–90.

Holmsten, Georg. *Die Berlin Chronik: Daten, Personen, Dokumente.* Düsseldorf: Droste Verlag, 1984.

Horn, Hannelore. "Berlin—Brücke zwischen Ost und West." Chapter in *Berlin als Faktor nationaler und internationaler Politik.* Berlin: Colloquium Verlag, 1988.

Hornstein, Walter. *Jugend in ihrer Zeit.* Hamburg: Marion von Schröder Verlag, 1966.

Hubbard, Gill. "The Usefulness of Indepth Life History Interviews for Exploring the Role of Social Structure and Human Agency in Youth Transitions." *Sociological Research Online* 4, no. 4 (February 2000), http://www.socresonline.org.uk.

Huber, Karl-Heinz. *Jugend unterm Hakenkreuz.* Berlin: Ullstein Verlag, 1982.

Hurwitz, Harold. *Die Eintracht der Siegermächte und die Orientierungsnot der Deutschen 1945 bis 1946.* Demokratie und Antikommunismus in Berlin nach 1945, vol. 3. Cologne: Verlag Wissenschaft und Politik, 1984.

Jahnke, Karl Heinz, and Michael Buddrus. *Deutsche Jugend 1933–1945. Eine Dokumentation.* Hamburg: VSA Verlag, 1989.

Jaide, Walter. *Generationen eines Jahrhunderts. Wechsel der Jugendgenerationen im Jahrhunderttrend. Zur Geschichte der Jugend in Deutschland 1871 bis 1985.* Opladen: Leske & Budrich, 1988.

Jansari, Ashok, and Alan J. Parkin. "Things That Go Bump in Your Life: Explaining the Reminiscence Bump in Autobiographical Memory." *Psychology and Aging* 11 no. 31 (1996): 85–91.

Jarausch, Konrad H., ed. *Zwischen Parteilichkeit und Professionalität: Bilanz der Geschichtswissenschaft der DDR.* Berlin: Akademie Verlag, 1991.

———, and Mattias Middel, eds. *Nach dem Erdbeben: (Re-)Konstruction ostdeutscher Geschichte und Geschichtswissenschaft.* Leipzig: Leipziger Universitätsverlag, 1994.

———, ed. *Dictatorship as Experience.* New York: Berghahn Books, 1999.

Jordan, Erwin, and Dieter Sengling. *Jugendhilfe. Einführung in Geschichte und Handlungsfelder, Organisationsformen und gesellschaftliche Problemlagen.* Munich: Juventa, 1988.

Kantorowicz, Alfred. *Suchende Jugend. Briefwechsel mit jungen Leuten.* Berlin: Alfred Kantorowicz Verlag, 1949.

Kaplan, Louise J. *Adolescence—the Farewell to Childhood.* New York: Simon and Schuster, 1984.

Keiderling, Gerhard. *Die Berliner Krise 1948/49 Zur imperialistischen Strategie des kalten Krieges gegen den Sozialismus und der Spaltung Deutschlands.* Berlin: Akademie Verlag, 1982.

———. *Berlin 1945 bis 1980. Geschichte der Hauptstadt der DDR.* Berlin: Dietz Verlag, 1987.

———. *"Rosinenbomber" über Berlin: Währungsreform, Blockade, Luftbrücke, Teilung.* Berlin: Dietz Verlag, 1998.

Keim, Wolfgang. *Erziehung unter der Nazi-Diktatur.* Darmstadt: Wissenschaftliche Buchgesellschaft, 1995.

Kenkmann, Alfons. *Wilde Jugend. Lebenswelt großstädtischer Jugendlicher zwischen Weltwirtschaftskrise, Nationalsozialismus und Währungsreform.* Essen: Klartext Verlag, 1996.

Kleßmann, Christoph. *Die doppelte Staatsgründung.* Bonn: Bundeszentrale für politische Bildung, 1986.

Klönne, Arno, ed. *Jugend im Dritten Reich—die Hitler Jugend und ihre Gegner. Dokumente und Analysen.* Düsseldorf: Elgen Diderichs Verlag, 1982.

————. "Kulturkampf: Bemerkungen zur Schul- und Jugendpolitik der Besatzungsmächte in Deutschland nach 1945." *Jahrbuch für zeitgeschichtliche Jugendforschung 1994/95*. Berlin: Metropol Verlag, 1995.

Krisch, Henry. *German Politics under Soviet Occupation.* New York: Columbia University Press, 1974.

Krüger, Heinz Hermann. "Geschichte und Perspektive der Jugendforschung - historische Entwicklungslinien und Bezugspunkte für eine theoretische und methodische Neuorientierung." Chap. in *Handbuch der Jugendforschung.* Opladen: Leske & Budrich, 1993.

————, ed., *"Die Elvis-Tolle, die hatte ich mir unauffällig wachsen lassen." Lebensgeschichte und jugendliche Alltagskulture in den fünfziger Jahren.* Opladen: Leske & Budrich, 1985.

Kulturamt Friedrichshain. *Ausgangspunkt Chaos. Neubeginn in Friedrichshain.* Berlin: Druckerei Banetzki, 1995.

Langer, Hermann. "Zur faschistischen Manipulierung der deutschen Jugend während des zweiten Weltkrieges." *Jahrbuch für Geschichte* 26 (1982): 335–365.

Langguth, Gerd, ed. *Berlin vom Brennpunkt der Teilung zur Brücke der Einheit.* Cologne: Verlag Wissenschaft und Politik, 1990.

Larass, Klaus. *Der Zug der Kinder. Kinderlandverschickung.* Munich: Meyster Verlag GmbH, 1983.

Lindemann, Rolf, and Werner Schultz. *Die Falken in Berlin. Geschichte und Erinnerung. Jugendopposition in den 50er Jahren.* Berlin: Verlag für Ausbildung und Studium in der Elefanten Press, 1987.

Maase, Kaspar. *Bravo Amerika: Erkundigungen zur Jugendkultur der Bundesrepublik in den fünfziger Jahren.* Hamburg: Junius, 1992.

————. "Lässige Boys und schicke Girls. 'Amerikanisierung' und Biographien Jugendlicher in den 1950er Jahren." In *Biographien in Deutschland. Soziologischer Rekonstruktionen gelebter Gesellschaftsgeschichte*, ed. Wolfram Fischer-Rosenthal and Peter Alheit, 137–52. Opladen: Westdeutscher Verlag, 1995.

Mahdi, Louis Carus, Nancy Geyer Christopher, and Michael Meade, eds. *Crossroads: The Quest for Contemporary Rites of Passage.* Chicago: Open Court, 1996.

Mählert, Ulrich and Stephan Gerd-Rüdiger. *Blaue Hemden Rote Fahnen. Die Geschichte der Freien Deutschen Jugend.* Opladen: Leske &Budrich, 1996.

Meyer, Sybille, and Schutze, Eva. *Wie wir das alles geschafft haben. Alleinstehende Frauen berichten über ihr Leben nach 1945.* Munich: Verlag C.H. Beck, 1984.

Meyer-Braun, Renate. "Frauen ohne Männer." In *Bremerinnen bewältigen die Nachkriegszeit*, ed. Beate Hoecker and Renate Meyer-Braun, 166–74. Bremen: Steintor, 1988.

Middlebrook, Martin. *The Berlin Raids: R.A.F. Bomber Command Winter, 1943–44.* New York: Viking, 1988.

Mittag, Detlef. *Kriegskinder, 10 Überlebensgeschichten.* Berlin: Internationale Liga für Menschenrechte, 1995.

Neisser, Ulric and Robyn Fivush, eds. *The Remembering Self.* Emory Symposia in Cognition 6. New York: Cambridge University Press, 1994.

Nicolaisen, Hans-Dietrich. *Die Flakhelfer. Luftwaffen- und Marinenhelfer im zweiten Weltkrieg.* Berlin: Ullstein, 1981.

————. *Gruppenfeuer und Salventakt.* Büsum: Selbstverlag Nicolaisen, 1993.

Niethammer, Lutz, Alexander von Plato and Dorothee Wierling. *Die volkseigene Erfahrung. Eine Archäologie des Lebens in der Industrieprovinz der DDR.* Berlin: Rowohlt, 1991.

Niethammer, Lutz, ed. *Die Jahre weiss man nicht, wo man die heute hinsetzen soll. Faschismuserfahrungen im Ruhrgebiet*. Bonn: Dietz Verlag, 1983.

Parson, Walter. "Zur Rolle der FDJ während der sozialistischen Revolution in der DDR." *Wissenschaftliche Zeitschrift der Universität Rostock. Gesellschafts- und Sprachwissenschaftliche Reihe* 24, no. 2 (1975): 145–55.

Pennebaker, James W., Dario Paez and Bernard Rime, eds. *Collective Memory of Political Events: Social Psychological Perspectives*. Mahwah, NJ: Lawrence Erlbaum Associates, 1997.

Petzold, Joachim. *Ideale und Idole im Schatten Hitlers und Stalins. Dresdener Oberschüler auf dem Wege aus dem Dritten Reich in die DDR*. Potsdam: Verlag für Berlin-Brandenburg, 1997.

Peukert, Detlev. *Inside Nazi Germany—Conformity, Opposition, and Racism in Everyday Life*. New Haven: Yale University Press, 1987.

Plato, Alexander von, and Almut Leh. *"Ein unglaublicher Frühling" Erfahrene Geschichte im Nachkriegsdeutschland 1945-1948* . Bonn: Bundeszentrale für politische Bildung, 1997.

Poiger, Uta. "Rock 'n' Roll, Female Sexuality and the Cold War Battle over German Identities." *The Journal of Modern History* 68 (1996): 577–616.

Prell, Uwe, and Lothar Wilker. *Berlin Blockade und Luftbrücke 1948/49. Analyse und Dokumentation*. Berlin: Arno Spitz Verlag, 1987.

Preuss-Lausitz, Ulf, et al. *Kriegskinder, Konsumkinder, Krisenkinder. Zur Sozialisationsgeschichte seit dem Zweiten Weltkrieg*. Weinheim: Beltz, 1983.

Raabe, Felix. "Brücke zwischen Ost und West." In *Die Kraft wuchs im Verborgenen. Katholische Jugend zwischen Elbe und Oder 1945–1990*, ed. Bernd Börger and Michael Kröselberg, 101–19. Düsseldorf: Verlag Haus Altenberg, 1993.

Ranke, Winfried. *Kultur, Pajoks und Care-Pakete: eine Berliner Chronik*. Berlin: Nishen, 1990.

Rathfelder, Schubert, and Jacob Henry Wild. *GYA. Das Jugendarbeitsprogram der amerikanischen Armee im Nachkriegsdeutschland*. Leinfelden: Burkhard Fehrlen, 1987.

Read, Anthony, and David Fischer. *The Fall of Berlin*. New York: W.W. Norton, 1993.

Reisser, Frank-Ulrich. *Mit Kohldampf auf den Trümmerberg. Die Nachkriegszeit in Berlin-Neukölln*. Berlin: Bezirksamt Neukölln von Berlin, 1990.

Ribbe, Wolfgang, and Jürgen Schmädeke. *Kleine Berlin-Geschichte*. Berlin: Stapp Verlag, 1994.

Richie, Alexandra. *Faust's Metropolis: A History of Berlin*. New York: Carrol and Graf, 1998.

Riess, Curt. *Berlin Berlin 1945–1953*. Berlin-Grunewald: Non Stop-Bücherei, 1953.

———. *Alle Straßen führen nach Berlin*. Hamburg: Hoffmann and Campe, 1968.

Roberts, Ulla. *Starke Mütter- ferne Väter. Töchter reflektieren ihre Kindheit im Nationalsozialismus und in der Nachkriegszeit*. Frankfurt: Fischer Taschenbuch Verlag, 1994.

Rosenthal, Gabriele. "May 6, 1945: The Biographical Meaning of an Historical Event." *International Journal of Oral History* 10, no. 3 (1989): 183–93.

———. *Erlebte und Erzählte Lebensgeschichte: Gestalt und Struktur biographischer Selbstbeschreibungen*. New York: Campus Verlag, 1995.

Ruhl, Klaus-Jörg, ed. *Unsere verlorene Jahre. Frauen in Kriegs und Nachkriegszeit 1939–1949 in Berichten, Dokumenten und Bildern*. Darmstadt: Leuchterhand, 1985.

Rupieper, Hermann-Josef. "Bringing Democracy to the Frauleins. Frauen als Zielgruppe der amerikanischen Demokratisierungspolitik in Deutschland 1945–1952." *Geschichte und Gesellschaft* 17 (1991): 61–91.

Rupp, Leila. "Mother of the Volk: The Image of Women in Nazi Society." *Signs* 3 (1977): 362–79.

Schelsky, Helmut. *Die Skeptische Generation—eine Soziologie der deutschen Jugend.* Düsseldorf: E. Diederich, 1963.

Schenkel, Johanna. "Lust und Leid und Liberty." In *Die Wirren Jahre Deutschland 1945–1948* , ed. Jürgen Engert, 60–62. Berlin: Argon, 1996.

Schörken, Rolf. *Luftwaffenhelfer und Drittes Reich. Die Entstehung eines politischen Bewußtseins.* Stuttgart: Klett-Cotta, 1984.

———. *Jugend 1945: Politisches Denken und Lebensgeschichte.* Opladen: Leske & Budrich, 1990.

Schuman, Howard, and Jacqueline Scott, "Generations and Collective Memories." *American Sociological Review* 54 (June 1989): 359–81.

Schütrumpf, Jörn. "Grenzgänger—Pendler zwischen Ost und West im Berlin der 50er Jahre," *Journal Geschichte* 1988, no. 1: 19–27.

———. "Zur einigen Aspekten des Grenzgängerproblems im Berliner Raum von 1948/49 bis 1961." In *Jahrbuch für Geschichte. Studien zur Geschichte der Deutschen Demokratischen Republik* 18 (1984): 333–58.

Senat von Berlin. *Berlin. Behauptung von Freiheit und Selbstverwaltung 1946 bis 1948.* Schriftenreihe zur Berliner Zeitgeschichte, vol. 2. Berlin: Spitzing Verlag, 1959.

———. *Berlin. Kampf um Freiheit und Selbstverwaltung 1945 bis 1946.* Schriftenreihe zur Berliner Zeitgeschichte, vol. 1. Berlin: Spitzing Verlag, 1961.

———. *Berlin. Ringen um Einheit und Wiederaufbau 1948 bis 1951.* Schriftenreihe zur Berliner Zeitgeschichte, vol. 3. Berlin: Spitzing Verlag, 1962.

———. *Berlin. Quellen und Dokumente 1945 bis 1951.* Berlin: Spitzing Verlag, 1964.

Smit, Erik, Evthalia Staikos, and Dirk Thormann. *3 Februar 1945. Die Zerstörung Kreuzbergs aus der Luft.* Berlin: Verlag Gericke, 1995.

Steinbach, Peter. "Zwischen Bomben und Gestapo—Berlin als Reichshauptstadt und Hauptstadt des deutschen Widerstandes." In *Berlin als Faktor nationaler und internationaler Politik,* Hannelore Horn, ed., 23–44. Berlin: Colloquium Verlag, 1988.

Strawson, John. *The Battle for Berlin.* London: Batsford, Ltd., 1974.

Thurnwald, Hilda. *Gegenwartsprobleme Berliner Familien.* Berlin: Weidmann, 1948.

Tobin, Elizabeth H., and Jennifer Gibson. "The Meanings of Labor: East German Women's Work in the Transition from Nazism to Communism." *Central European History* 28, no. 3 (1997): 301–42.

Tusa, Ann. *The Last Division. A History of Berlin 1945–1989.* New York: Addison-Wesley, 1997.

von zur Mühlen, Bengt, ed. *Der Todeskampf der Reichshauptstadt.* Berlin: Chronos, 1994.

Wagner, Beate. *Jugendliche Lebenswelten nach 1945. Soziologische Jugendarbeit zwischen Selbstdeutung und Re-education.* Opladen: Leske & Budrich, 1995.

Weinberg, Gerhard L. *A World at Arms:. A Global History of World War II.* New York: Cambridge University Press, 1994.

Weiß, P. "Fragen an Ella Kay." In *60 Jähre Gesetz für Jugendwohlfahrt 1922-1982.* Berlin: Jugendamt Berlin, 1982.

Weisz, Christoph, ed. *OMGUS Handbuch. Die amerikanische Militärregierung in Deutschland 1945–49.* Munich: R. Oldenbourg Verlag, 1994.

Welsh, Helga A., Andreas Pickel, and Dorothy Rosenberg. "East and West German Identities: United and Divided." In *After Unity: Reconfiguring German Identities*, ed. Konrad H. Jarausch, Ch. 3. Providence, NJ: Berghahn, 1997.

Wetzel, David, ed. *From the Berlin Museum to the Berlin Wall: Essays on the Cultural and Political History of Modern Germany.* Westport, CT: Praeger, 1996.

Wetzlaugk, Udo. *Berlin und die deutsche Frage.* Cologne: Verlag Wissenschaft und Politik, 1985.

————. *Die Allierten in Berlin.* Berlin: Arno Spitz Verlag, 1988.

————. *Berliner Blockade und Luftbrücke 1948/49.* Berlin: Landeszentrale für politische Bildungsarbeit, 1998.

Wierling, Dorothee. "A German Generation of Reconstruction: the Children of the Weimar Republic in the GDR." In *Memory and Totalitarianism: International Yearbook of Oral History and Life Stories* 1 (New York: Oxford University Press, 1992): 71–88.

————. "The Hitler Youth Generation in the GDR: Insecurities, Ambitions and Dilemmas." In *Dictatorship as Experience*, ed. Konrad Jarausch, 307–24. New York: Berghahn Books, 1999.

————, and Franz Josef Brüggemeier. "Oral History Kurseinheit 3: Auswertung und Interpretation" (unpublished course material). Fernuniversität Hagen, 1986.

Wilczek, Bernd, ed. *Berlin–Hauptstadt der DDR 1949–1989. Utopie und Realität.* Baden-Baden: Elster Verlag, 1995.

Willemar, Wilhelm, ed. *The German Defense of Berlin.* Foreign Military Studies Series. Historical Division Headquarters (Germany): U.S. Army Europe, 1954.

Zinnecker, Jürgen. *Jugendkultur 1940 bis 1985.* Opladen: Leske & Budrich, 1987.

Index

About the Author

KIMBERLY A. REDDING is Assistant Professor of History at Carroll College. She earned her Ph.D. in History at the University of North Carolina, Chapel Hill, in 2001, with emphases on Modern Germany and Social History.